CRISIS IN URBAN SCHOOLS:

A Book of Readings for the Beginning Urban Teacher

Edited by
Thomas E. Glass
Indiana University

MSS Information Corporation
655 Madison Avenue, New York, N.Y. 10021

This is a custom-made book of readings prepared for the courses taught by the editor, as well as for related courses and for college and university libraries. For information about our program, please write to:

MSS INFORMATION CORPORATION
655 Madison Avenue
New York, New York 10021

MSS wishes to express its appreciation to the authors of the articles in this collection for their cooperation in making their work available in this format.

Library of Congress Cataloging in Publication Data

Glass, Thomas E   comp.
    Crisis in urban schools.

    1. Education, Urban--United States--Addresses,
essays, lectures.   I.   Title.
LC5131.G54   370.19'348'0973   73-4330
ISBN 0-8422-5095-6
ISBN 0-8422-0298-6 (pbk)

CONTENTS

INTRODUCTION

This book has been compiled in hopes of assisting beginning teachers and student teachers facing the inner-city school for the first time. A great deal of the current literature in the field of education in recent years has covered various aspects of education for culturally different children living in inner-city environments; however, little methodology has been advanced for the beginning teacher. Most beginning teachers, irregardless of their ethnic origin, are overwhelmed in their first experience in the inner-city school. They are frustrated by the bureaucracy and the apparent hopelessness of accomplishing their assigned task of administering an educational program. The children in their rooms are not children with a singular problem which prevents them from learning, but instead are multiple problem children and the environments in which these children live are said not to be condusive to learning in the school. Also, the problems in the inner-city school oftentimes appear to be so large and so numerous that many young teachers resign themselves to failure and either leave or just ride along with the status quo.

Certainly, the problems facing teachers in the inner-city schools of this country are many and oftentimes complex; however, are they unanswerable? This question is the most serious one facing educators in this country today. If we as educators cannot design a system of instruction for culturally different children, which will provide them with an equal educational opportunity, how can we say that our work is truly a profession? The legitimacy of the educational enterprise in this country is in serious doubt as long as millions of children are not provided an equal educational opportunity.

Perhaps the key or even answer to the problem of the education of culturally different children in our inner-city schools, especially, is the better training and preparation of teachers. The common consensus of most educators in urban areas today is that teachers emerging from teacher training institutions are inadequately prepared to deal with and positively influence the schools in which they are asked to teach. Common complaints heard from urban administrators are that new teachers are not prepared to use the curriculum materials in use in urban and inner-city schools and that they are not culturally aware. This means that educational courses taken within the confines of the ivory tower colleges are not relevant to the real world of the inner-city school. This is understandable to almost any educator who has ever suffered through the methods classes and the basic foundation courses of almost any college or

school of education. Unfortunately, most teaching expertise seems to be learned by the teacher while on the
job, not in the pre-service type of situation.

Even though many colleges and universities are
beginning to see that they are not presently meeting
the needs of the educational profession, especially in
preparing teachers to teach culturally different and
inner-city children, only tokenism is being shown toward
solving the problem. Some of this reluctance toward
serious commitment of the teacher training institutions
to inner-city and multi-cultural education is the result
of predominantly white-middle-class college professors
with little or no knowledge of culturally different
children. They simply do not know how to go about the
task. Also, it must be remembered that higher education
in America has been the maintainer of the status quo in
the society, never a significant catalyst for social
change. Thus, change within the higher education institution appears at times to be more difficult and more
impossible a task than serious and substantive reform of
inner-city schools. Even though institutions need
changing and revitalizing, people within those institutions are in more serious need of renewing. It is obvious that great changes are occurring in almost every

sector of the society, and that change itself is about the only constant factor in the modern day world. However, it is easy to see how institutions of teacher education and schools in urban areas battle to preserve the past even though little logic exists for the retention of outmoded and irrelevant practices. One such practice is that of student-teaching which in most teacher education institutions is left to the first or second semester of the senior year. This is tragically illogical as students are trapped into completion of a teaching certificate whether they want to teach or not. Once senior status is obtained so many hours have been spent in attaining educational course requirements that a point of no return has been reached as far as a degree goes. With the current oversupply of teachers in many areas and specialities it would seem that teacher education institutions would make serious moves toward more careful identification and training of future teachers. What is needed at present is not quantity but quality. However, it is easy to see that teacher education institutions are still mentally operating under the stigma of a decade that demanded teachers to meet a teacher shortage. Also, teacher education institutions have grown fat personnel-wise and radical movement toward programs of early competency identification and field experience really are not in line with individual research efforts. However, the most serious problem existing in the teacher training institutions is the lack of expertise on the part of faculties in designing successful strategies of education for _all_ of the children in this country. Instead of serious design, fancy pieces of curriculum and various packages are produced at terrible dollar costs for those sectors of the educational world able to pay for them. A well-known fact is that urban schools are the most poverty stricken and can ill afford these expensive educational packages incessantly offered by the ivory tower academicians.

What is desperately needed by urban school systems with culturally different children to serve is quality trained teachers. In the large cities of this country urban school administrators have been extremely vocal of late toward urban universities to move their teacher education programs more in line with the needs of urban schools. Federal agencies, such as the Office of Education have also been contributors of substantial sums to universities to design programs of teacher education for culturally different children. However, the size of these efforts has done little to solve the whole problem of teacher preparation for inner-city schools and schools containing the culturally different child. Tokenism is so apparent when the number of beginning urban teachers and experienced urban teachers returning to the teacher training institution are compared with the number of vacancies in special educational programs designed to prepare teachers for inner-city schools.

Migrants from the rural areas of this country pour daily into the urban areas, often exchanging rural poverty for urban poverty. The lure of jobs and prosperity bring them to the city where they usually find slums and unemployment. Their children enter urban school systems which are continually faced with declining revenues as property evaluations decrease. The slums grow larger as the white exodus to the suburbs continues.

The inner-city school is especially a dysfunctional one in that the curriculum and training of the teachers is always middle-class orientated, since the urban school systems are unable to afford the expertise to design their own curriculum and train their teachers in programs which would be relevant to their needs. In fact, many times urban school systems have a difficult time in determining exactly what their needs are. Too often, much emphasis is placed on the elevation of standard achievement test scores rather than teaching the children and their families how to cope with the patterns of living in the urban environment. However, all parties in the urban community agree that better-prepared teachers is a definite need. This is particularly true of the community as they see only one way out of the urban poverty syndrome for their children and that is through a quality education. Community people really do not understand educational packaging products but they do understand sympathetic teachers working hard to help their children. Better prepared teachers are also certainly needed in the rural areas of the country containing Mexican-American, American Indian and Appalachian whites' children.

It is often said in the mass media that the educational institution is facing a "Crisis in Education"; however, this might be more appropriately called the second crisis of a large proportion. The first crisis in education in this country has been around a long time. The present crisis has only been born of the recent civil rights movement and the Black ethnogenesis process which has occurred in the past ten years.

Before the present crisis developed in the mass media there were many millions of white, brown and

Indian children not receiving an equal education for various reasons. One main reason was that after the turn of the century the present concept of the secondary school came into being. That is, prime influence in curriculum began to move toward college preparation. This has continued up to this day. Thus, the design of the curriculum and intent of instruction moved away from the preparation of working class citizens toward a more middle-class intellectual elite. As this new system of education emerged the training of teachers also changed from the one room, self-contained school-house toward more urban and specialized classroom types. Culturally different and poor children were rarely seen in the high school and college classrooms. Simply speaking, the production of middle-class white teachers began in earnest.

The problem for educators today is how to change the trend of middle-class educational doctrine. What is needed without doubt is a system which is in tune with many cultures and which at the same time makes all children competitive in the modern day society. Much is said about equality of opportunity for all Americans but the real question is how is it going to be achieved. Surely, equal educational opportunity is one way toward this goal, even though equal education might not insure equality in the general society.

It is the hope of the editor that a few new ideas and ways in which to deal with the education of the culturally different child living in the inner cities of the United States will be imparted to new educators about to undertake the task of teaching. The overall purpose of this book is not to present new doctrines or programs for education in the inner city but merely to present the thoughts of various educators concerning general problems. One of the persistent criticisms of teachers new to slum schools or schools containing culturally different children is unawareness of problems in the classroom. The articles in this book attempt to deal with some of these situations and conditions and suggest some thoughts toward reform and alternatives. Hopefully the reader, by reading these articles, will get a glimpse of the problems found in inner-city schools and, if already working in such a school, gain a few new, additional insights. However, what is important is that the reader be led toward a creative and critical view of urban education and multi-cultural education, making his own decisions and developing his own strategies of change.

Change and what type of change and how it is to be arrived at is the crucial problem facing educators today.

New teachers with new ideas and socio-cultural understanding will undoubtedly bring about much of the educational change of the future. Hopefully this book
of readings will be a small part of this rebirth of
American education which is truly public education for
all of the people of this country.

CHAPTER I: THE PEOPLE OF THE CITY

"Is There a Folk in the City?" Urban communities after the advent of World War II saw a population growth almost unparalleled in history. The country moved toward mass industrialization and in the process needed masses of workers on the assembly lines, in the furnaces, and for the trades. Workers, both male and female, were needed to fill the employment demands of American industry and the rural poor streamed into the cities. The promise of jobs drew them away from impoverished small communities and rural areas that had been the homes of their families for many generations. These urban migrants were for the most part ill educated to function in a highly technical urban world and they too often traded the poverty of the South for the poverty of the North in urban slums. Often they faced far worse conditions in urban slums than in their former rural homes. Blacks, especially, were the ethnic group streaming into the industrial cities of the North such as Chicago, Detroit, and New York. They took up many of the roles previously held by earlier immigrants such as the Poles, Jews, and Italians who themselves had taken over the slums from Irish and other West European immigrants. Now today, we are seeing the influx of a new group of immigrants to the city, the Puerto Ricans who are taking over the

slums once lived in by Blacks in New York City. The
city moves on, slums continue to exist and probably no
amount of urban renewal will ever destroy them altogether.
In thinking about the various ethnic groups of peoples
that have filtered through the urban school systems
during this century only one real definitive statement
can be made. That is, none of these migrant and immigrant groups were provided with an educational system
that took into account their cultures, heritages, and
special problems in the total society. Instead, the
great hoax of the melting pot theory was applied to them
which expected them within a generation or so to melt
in with the rest of America. This program of design
did work fairly well as long as there were plenty of
unskilled jobs available and before the color of the
migrants changed from white to black and from black to
brown. Also, the educational qualifications for the
majority of jobs available in the economy changed from
an eighth grade education to a high school degree.
Thus, the urban migrant of today is faced with the
battle of race, employment, housing, medical care, and
education for his children.

When an urban migrant arrives in the city it is
usually with an absolute minimum amount of money and no

job. He moves into the cheapest available housing which is usually in the heart of the inner city. Next, he begins the search for a job, any job, until he can get a few dollars ahead and can search for a job which he really wants. Thus, he takes the first job available, whatever it might be, and begins the process of putting aside enough money to move to a more desirable area of the city. Often, these rural migrants do not even bother to register their children in school as they think they will be in the ghetto only until better living accomodations can be found. Usually, they register their children in the nearest school which is often quite aged, staffed with inexperienced teachers and possesses an educational program designed for middle-class children living in the suburbs.

The struggle of the children in the school begins the first day when they find out how different their world is from the one in which the teacher lives. In the case of many children, they find that the teacher speaks standard English which is almost a foreign language to them. They also discover their dialect vocabulary is not acceptable in many instances, as is the case with their home life and social values. In short, many times they discover for the first time that they are inferior Americans.

Urban schools and their teachers do not usually take into account cultural differences. Instead, the school staff usually stands behind the idea that all children in the school are to be treated the same and the same expectations will be impressed on each child. The efforts toward the standardizing of the culturally different child is apparent in almost every urban school. Rare is the school that makes it a policy to respect individual differences and try to make positive educational gains using the cultural background of the child. Most schools that do take cultural differences into account are usually those urban schools where the community has a strong voice in the policies of the school.

The tremendous culture shock suffered by the urban migrant has been given little study by ethnologists, sociologists, and especially educators. Studies describing the types of values, mores, and customs brought to the city by the urban migrant and retained over the years of urban habitation are rarely studied. However, they are present in every classroom and sometimes create crisis in those classrooms.

The articles in this chapter try to give the reader a little insight into the traumatic effect of movement from rural areas to urban areas and the new

demands to be met by urban living. The families change
in various ways which in turn change the lives of children. Composition of nuclear and extended families is
an area which, unfortunately, is neglected by educators
desiring to create curriculum and programs.

RICHARD M. DORSON

Is There a Folk in the City?

NORTH UIST LIES AMONG THE OUTER HEBRIDES in the Atlantic coastal sea, a Scottish outpost on the western edge of Europe. When the plane from Inverness swoops down toward the airport at Benbecula, the isle looks like a lonely crater of the moon, pockmarked with hollows and lifeless lakes, striated with mountainous ridges, coated with vapor. A nearer view is no more encouraging. There are no hotels, no villages, nothing but solitary crofters' stone cottages scattered at long intervals over the empty moors. A driving rain and wind blow across the moors, stinging the face and dampening the clothes. Trousers do not keep a press long in the Hebrides. Roads are primitive, and cars when they meet must jockey to find a "passing place," a widened shoulder of the road located at intervals, because the roads are all one way, whichever way you are going. Gaelic is the tongue everyone speaks from birth, and English is the second language.

This is the country and here are the folk known to folklorists. No richer tradition in the western world has been uncovered than the Gaelic treasure found in the Hebrides. John Francis Campbell of Islay gathered his classic four-volume *Popular Tales of the West of Scotland* (Edinburgh, 1860–1862) from the Hebrides and Highlands. Alexander Carmichael amassed five volumes of folk blessings, hymns, charms, and incantations from the same area in his *Carmina Gadelica* (Edinburgh and London, 1928–1953). At the present time John Lorne Campbell, laird of the Isle of Canna, continues to mine the isles, with book-length collections from single narrators on Barra and South Uist, while his wife, Margaret Fay Shaw, has brought forth a substantial sheaf of folksongs from South Uist. Even the hoard of Campbell of Islay and his collectors is still being tapped in the twentieth century, with two posthumous volumes of folktales and the impressive cache of local historical traditions titled *The Dewar Manuscripts* (Glasgow, 1964).

North Uist and the Hebrides are the case I offer as a classic illustration of the terrain of the folklorist and the concept of the folk. I was there the end of August 1967, accompanying a collector from the School of Scottish Studies in the University of Edinburgh, John MacInnes, himself island born and raised. Although the Hebrides have been so amply collected, and although only some two thousand

JOURNAL OF AMERICAN FOLKLORE, 1970, Vol. 83, No. 328, pp. 186-216.

souls remain on North Uist, John says there are layers upon layers of tradition still to be peeled, a lifetime of work. The people of North Uist are all one; their names begin with Mac, they appear all at some point to be interrelated; they have inhabited this isle for ten clear centuries. In common they speak Gaelic, farm the land, cut peat, and tend the sheep; and they visit each other in sociable *ceilidh*s in which they recall marvelous events of yore occurring on the isle. The name of almost every locality and landmark involves a tradition. Only in faith are they divided between Catholics and Protestants.

If the remote countryside, symbolized by North Uist, has provided the questing ground of the folklorist, what business has he in the city? One ready answer is that the folklorist deals with people, and the people have left the country and flocked to the cities. While North Uist has dwindled to a couple of thousand crofters, Gary in northwest Indiana has risen from empty sand dunes in 1906 to become a metropolis of 200,000, peopled by over fifty nationalities. To Gary and its neighbor East Chicago, one-third its size, I went in February 1968, to live under field conditions. Knowing no one, I sought to form contacts and interview representatives of the dominant ethnic groups. Gary received nation-wide publicity when it elected a Negro mayor, Richard G. Hatcher, on November 7, 1967, an election reflecting the rise in the city's colored population to over 50 percent. The other major groups in Gary are the Serbian, Croatian, Greek, and "Latin," a term that includes Mexicans and Puerto Ricans. Throughout Lake County as a whole the Poles predominate. East Chicago has proportionally a smaller Negro and a larger Latin element, with its mayor, John B. Nicosia, representing an earlier, now established Italian colony. When speaking of East Chicago the commentator must include Indiana Harbor, a community within the city; before they were combined, East Chicago and Indiana Harbor were known as the twin cities. They are still physically separated by a forest of giant oil drums and installations lined along Route 20. Close connections bind the two—or three— cities, for they are all part of the steel kingdom that has sucked into its fiery vortex the manpower of many peoples. Inland and Youngstown in East Chicago and U.S. Steel and Bethlehem in Gary are the regal plants that must be fed twenty-four hours a day, seven days a week, with iron ore and coal and tended by men and women. The need for laborers in the mills is never sated. First it was met by East Europeans from every Balkan country, then by southern Negroes, then by Mexicans and Puerto Ricans brought up in truckloads and planeloads concurrently with southern whites, who streamed north from Kentucky and southern Illinois, Virginia and Tennessee, Alabama and Louisiana. "Eighty-five percent of them around here is from the South," one Kentuckian observed airily.

Such a complex of ethnic and regional groups is bound to attract the folklorist, especially when the groups involved derive from the peasant-farmer and laboring classes. Linda Dégh and her husband Andrew Vaszonyi first penetrated Indiana Harbor in the winter of 1964–1965 and again in the summer of 1967, speaking with the sizable body of emigrants from their native Hungary. They had soon realized that one ethnic group led into another, and my mission was to explore in a preliminary way these other groups. Born and schooled in New York City, living in London for three stretches totaling two years, and in Tokyo for ten months, I had experienced the world's largest cities, but never as a collector of folklore. My folklore field trips had taken me to the country towns. My present purposes were threefold: to ascertain if the folklorist could ply his trade in the city; to contrast the vitality of the traditions among the various ethnic and racial groups; and to observe the effect of life in an urban, industrial center upon these imported cultures.

Obviously a stay of twenty-three days can only begin to probe these questions. But experiences in the field can be intense and concentrated, they may yield intimate revelations into lives, experiences, hatreds, fears, and cherished symbols that one may never encounter in years of routine living. By "the field" I mean an area in which the folklorist lives completely divorced from his own usual schedule, occupation, and residence—a period in which he devotes all of his waking moments to making contacts, interviewing, recording, listening to and observing the people with whom he is concerned. In this sense I lived in the field in Gary, staying downtown in the environs of the Negro ghetto, in the recently bankrupt Hotel Gary, an integrated, gloomy structure no longer patronized by middle-class travelers.

Gary lies in northwest Indiana hard by Lake Michigan, a city created overnight on flat dunes in 1906 to house steelworkers and now grown to over 200,000 souls who live off steel. The reputation of Gary matches the sullen glow of the ever-lit furnaces in the mills, for, thanks in good part to a *Time* article, Gary symbolizes the urban jungle, crime-ridden, race-wracked, and cultureless. One's first impression driving into Gary along the endless central avenue of Broadway bisecting the city confirms the worst—particularly if the day (February 2, 1968) is rainy and drear, the surrounding countryside brown and muddy, and the roadsides deep in water. Broadway is lined with one-story joints, bars, liquor stores and increasingly crummy shops as one gets further down town into the Negro ghetto. A movie marquee reads "Greek movies on Saturday, Spanish on Sunday." Polluted air envelops the city, dust and grime cover the buildings, litter fills the alleys. Gloom, ugliness, and apprehension set the tone of Gary. Armed guards stand on the ready in every bank, and the buses cease running in the early evening because of knifings of waiting passengers. Drivers lock their car doors and sweat out the red lights. "We were held up here last month on payday at noon by four Negro gunmen, when the guard stepped out for a coffee break," a welfare agency director told me my first day in Gary. "I'm hoping to move the office away from here [16th and Broadway] soon; we're right in the midst of the pimps, queers, dope pushers, and whores. Even while I've been talking to you someone has been observing the layout." And he nervously wiped his white brow and looked at the sea of black faces.

One of the quests of this trip was to see if and how a folklorist could operate in a strange city among a number of ethnic and racial groups. To make contacts I visited Negro Baptist churches on four successive Sundays; called on Harold Malone, father of a Negro student of mine in Bloomington; dropped in on the International Institute of Gary, where a Serbian, a Greek, and a young black woman all introduced me to people; made the acquaintance of William Passmore, head of the Job Corps office in East Chicago, who kindly offered me a wealth of leads; looked up likely informants from student folklore collections turned in to a folklore course at the Northwest Campus in Gary; hung around the dilapi-

24

dated Baltimore Hotel opposite the Inland Steel plant; followed suggestions from a trustee of Indiana University living in Gary, Robert Lucas. It was the old story of developing contacts through all likely means, chasing around town, calling people up to make appointments, trying to explain my mission. But I found persons in every group hospitable and friendly and often anxious to talk of their experiences and of life in the "Region," as this pocket of northwest Indiana is locally called. The following pages, some extracted from my field diary, attempt to convey a sense of the cultural pluralism in urban folklore.

The Negro

My few weeks in Gary and East Chicago did not uncover a master folk narrator, although one may well be there. In no group indeed did I encounter a narrator of this type, though I did meet excellent talkers. Let me consider Negro tradition under the heads of proverbs, tales, voodoo, and the folk church.

On two occasions I heard northern-born, educated Negroes—who had looked blankly at me when I asked about Old Marster and Brother Buzzard—employ patently Negro proverbs to crystallize an idea and drive home a thought in the course of a tense discussion. The first situation developed in the Job Corps office on Columbus Avenue in East Chicago, where I met Willie P., both of whose legs had been amputated while he was in his teens because of a spinal disease. His mother, Laura, 73, a snowy-haired fragile old lady born in Alabama, granddaughter of a slave, related to me with quavering voice and perfect command of dates the series of long hospital sieges and near-fatal operations that Willie had endured patiently and even cheerfully. The Déghs had put me in touch with Willie, who knew all the civic leaders in East Chicago and gave me every assistance. This morning Willie—boyish, studious-looking and gentle, who at times had double-dated with Mayor Hatcher—was giving a little moralizing talk to three Negro boys of fourteen and fifteen, dropouts and potential delinquents. The boys squirmed and twisted uneasily as Willie lectured them from his wheelchair behind his desk. Willie had lapsed into the soft, slurred tones that colored people frequently use with each other. He reiterated the need for them to stay in school, to train themselves for their future jobs, to learn discipline. "A hard head makes a hard bed," he said climactically.

No proverb could have been more appropriate. "Hard head" is a phrase current among southern Negroes, who use it in jocular ghost tales about revenants that return in answer to a relative's prayer but outstay their welcome; hence the comment, "Brother, that's how come you dead now, you so hard-headed." The teller explains parenthetically, "Head hard or head long means you go looking for trouble."[1] Willie summarized and capped his message with this pithy saw.

Another day I was in the Children's Public Library of East Chicago talking with Mrs. Edna W., college-educated, precise in speech, decorous in manner, a world away from Old Marster. She began speaking about the conditions of the Negro and the election of Mayor Hatcher, but in a note rarely reported. This was a note of mistrust of Negro aggressiveness, a fear of consequences stemming from Hatcher's election, distress at the stridency of Negro youths no longer respectful of their elders. "There are one-third of us who feel this way, but our

[1] See Richard M. Dorson, *American Negro Folktales* (New York, 1967), 328.

voice won't be heard. I won't be heard in Washington." She was telling me more than she had ever told anyone. Mrs. W. was opposed to open housing. Let the whites and the blacks each live by themselves; people are not comfortable in surroundings they are not used to. "I don't want to be a fly in the buttermilk," she said. And so, to dramatize her opposition to the open-housing ordinance, so strong an article of faith to Negro militants and white liberals, the librarian had recourse to a Negro proverb with apt color imagery.

The tales that seemed to me so much a touchstone of Negro folk tradition were slow in coming. At first I was the carrier and the teller. But in the course of two evenings (one in the home of the Reverend H. J., pastor of a store-front church, with an evangelist preacher and a deacon present, the other in the home of the Reverend B. G., pastor of a Baptist church, along with his deacon L. T., southerners all and steelworkers all) tales came to the surface, one triggering another. They were old favorites: "The Coon in the Box," "Dividing Soul," "Poll Parrot and Biscuits," "Why the Fox Has a Short Tail." But as I was going out the door, the Reverend H. J. thought of one entirely new to me, "The Train Going Uphill and Downhill," employing slow, drawn-out phrases for the uphill climb, and fast, chug-chug phrases for the descent.[2] Charles K. of the Gary Human Relations Commission told me a number of civil-rights stories with which he and his companions had whiled away the time during his six jail confinements for demonstrating. One was a television variant of the old Negro down South who hollers "Help!" on the radio when urged by southern governors to tell how well he is treated.[3] Another was a Negro variant of a Jewish joke about the would-be radio announcer with a dreadful stutter who claims he is the victim of bias. Civil-rights stories (the phrase is the informant's) are one segment of the southern Negro repertory which thrives and expands in northern cities.

One interview disclosed a displacement of tale tradition by book tradition, albeit not a learned book tradition. Todd R., 70, who had come from Alabama to Gary in 1922 and worked for forty years in the steel mills before retiring, remembered nostalgically the South and "country living" as the best in the world. But he told only one tale, "The Race" (Type 1074), in the shortest version I ever heard: "The rabbit and the turtle had a race; the rabbit stopped to pick berries and the turtle won." He stirred briefly to the legend of the snake and the child and said he had heard in Alabama that the girl died when her father killed her pet snake. Todd's real interest lay in reciting names, dates, and facts about Negro Americans, garnered from two battered and tattered booklets he showed me: Afro-American World Almanac, and A Tribute to Achievement issued by the Pfeiffer Brewing Company.

Voodoo or cunjer seemed at first as invisible as folktales. Harold M. took me calling on a family friend, Mrs. Katie S., a school matron born in Memphis, friendly, poised, and proper. The only element of tradition she displayed dealt with cuisine, "soul food," the Negro diet of turnip greens, chitterlings, corn bread, cabbage, sweet potatoes, which kept together bodies and souls of colored folk in the South. The cheaper cuts and leavings of the hog and cow—neckbone, pig feet, pot licker—were nutritious. Old Marster gave them to the slaves, and

---

[2] Compare "The Mean Boss," Ibid., 156–157.
[3] See "The Governor's Convention," Ibid., 319–320.

26

the slaves throve, while the white people fell prey to rare diseases. To my question whether she liked the food of other groups in Gary, Mrs. S. replied that she enjoyed *tacos* until she heard that the Mexicans were cutting up cats for the meat. When we left her house I asked Harold Malone about her husband. Andrew S. had been born in Coldwater, Mississippi, had come to Gary in 1943, and was now laid up in the hospital, claiming he had been voodooed by his son, who had given him canned corn that turned to worms.

Another voodoo case was headlined in the Chicago *Daily Defender*, the only American Negro daily, on February 20, the day I drove into its offices with Bill Passmore, who wrote a weekly column for them on East Chicago news. The city editor, Thomas Picou, a severe young intellectual, talked to me about his paper's philosophy of cohesion and adequate news coverage for the Negro. He did not have much to say about the banner headline of the day, "Possessed by 'Voodoo': Mother Charged in Triple Slaying," blazoned on the front page. The news story appeared on page three and is reproduced below.

MOTHER OF FOUR CHARGED IN 'VOODOO' SLAYING

Husband, Two Aunts
Killed at Reception

By Donald Mosby
(Daily Defender Staff Writer)

A 27-year-old mother of four, who thinks she is possessed by "a voodoo lizard," was charged yesterday with killing her husband and his two aunts at a suburban wedding reception.

Held without bond is Mrs. Ruby Luckett, 107 Riverview Ave., Lockport, whom, one wedding guest said, "looked as if she were in a daze," moments before she reputedly shot the trio Sunday night. Mrs. Luckett is accused of killing her husband, Peter, 29, a laborer, and his aunts, Mrs. Sadie Porter, 62, of 404 E. 72d St., and Mrs. Lisa Harper, 43, of 118 Oak Ave., of Lockport. Luckett died yesterday in St. Francis Hospital.

According to Dixmoor Ptl. John North, the shooting deaths grew out of an argument between Mrs. Luckett and her husband in the basement of 14337 S. Honore, Dixmoor, where a wedding reception for Luckett's sister was in progress. The home belongs to Sullivan Wright, brother of the groom.

North said Mrs. Luckett shot her husband during the height of an argument and repeated the attack upstairs when she saw Luckett's aunts—Mrs. Harper and Mrs. Porter—sitting on a couch.

Luckett was shot in the chest, Mrs. Harper, in the chest and Mrs. Porter in the head.

According to the suburban policeman, Mrs. Luckett feared her relatives were practicing some kind of "voodoo power" against her.

Mrs. Luckett was driven to Dixmoor police headquarters by some departing wedding guests, who were apparently unaware of what had happened inside the home.

According to police, Mrs. Luckett admitted shooting the trio, and handed over to police a .38 calibre revolver, believed to be the death weapon.

In court yesterday, she told a judge her relatives had put a lizard in her stomach as part of a voodoo spell and that she had to keep salt and water under her bed to satisfy the voodoo curse. Mrs. Luckett is scheduled to appear in Midlothian Court March 21.

The *Daily Defender* story called to the mind of one of my companions, Larry J., an account he had heard of a girl who voodooed the man of her desire. This man was paying her no heed, so on the advice of a girl friend she obtained two pairs of his pants and hung them up in her closet, and now the couple were living together.

For the core of Negro traditional expression, behavior, and belief we must turn to the church. Gary possesses over two hundred Negro churches. On successive Sundays I visited the First Baptist, the Calvary Baptist, and the St. John Primitive Baptist churches; these represented, in descending order, the scale of affluence, status, prestige, and denial of southern Negro culture. The First Baptist Church building was brand new, facing a pleasant park, cathedral-like in its dimensions, upper-class white in its service. Professional people attended this church—doctors, lawyers, teachers. The women vied with each other in the loftiness and dazzling colors of their hats. All was decorous and efficient; the congregation sang from hymnbooks, the minister preached with dignity, and only the faintest responses of "Amen" and "That's the truth" echoed his words. But with the Calvary Baptist Church—also in a new but much less pretentious building—the institutions of southern Negro folk religion came into view. Here was a highly personal, joking, exhorting, chanting pastor, F. Brannam Jackson, recalling the days when he was a little old barefoot boy on the bayou, and mosquitoes were so large they were called gallinippers, and when they stung you, you felt as if you had lockjaw. Here was a swaying, throbbing choir, singing without hymnbooks, reinforced by pianist and organist and the responsive congregation, spurred on by ecstatic soloists, who would interrupt their songs to cry "Shout out." In the front row sat a uniformed nurse, who sprang into action when a heavy woman a few rows back "got happy" and with some others fanned her vigorously back into normalcy.

A news item in the Gary *Post Tribune* had caught my eye, "Negro Plight is Theme," announcing the "annual Homecoming Day" at the Calvary Baptist Church in honor of Negro history week, with a full program of service, chicken dinner, panel speakers, and a slavery-time play, in honor of Negro History week. The three speakers were each in his own way highly articulate and impressive. Twenty-four-year-old Bill Joiner, first Negro manager of a branch of the Gary National Bank, was modest and quiet-spoken; Mrs. Nancy Brundige, an urban sociologist for the city of Chicago, was positive and direct; and Charles H. King, director of the Gary Human Relations Commission, was a performer of shattering eloquence. These were Negro intellectuals telling the Negro folk about business opportunities, historical achievements, and spiritual strengths of their race with a conviction and force deeply admired by the one white auditor. The whole day was indeed a testimonial to the facility of Negro oral expression in singing and speaking. As King said, Negroes were the greatest singers in the world because church singing was their one permitted mode of utterance. He rocked the audience with illustrations of phrases from spirituals taken in their innocuous literal sense by the slavemasters, but intended in quite specific and material ways by the singers (a matter often debated by white scholars). King made a number of effective points: that segregation began after, not during, slavery, for the slave could attend the same church as his master, even though he had to sit in the gallery (hence Lincoln's Emancipation Proclamation was the biggest lie in American history); that the church was the center of Negro fellowship and community

28

life, for it was the Negro's only social organization ("The Negro stays in church all day, while the white man comes for an hour and leaves; isn't that so, Professor?"); that the Baptist church was most available to the Negro, for it required no superstructure of outside authorities.

After these speeches and a comment I was called on to make, the chairs were rearranged, and an informal playlet presented, "De Lawd, the Negroes' Hope in a New Home." The scene was ostensibly laid on a slave plantation, and the appearance of members of the congregation in cotton dresses and sun bonnets, idly stroking a butter churn and a wash board, sent the spectators into spasms of laughter. Most of the action was confined to a chorus singing such spirituals as "Climbing Jacob's Ladder," "Deep River," and "There'll be a Great Day When We All Gather Home." At the conclusion the attractive young wife of the pastor made a statement on the zeal of the performers (one had canceled a trip to New Orleans in order to be present) and the historical relevance of the drama. "I would rather be the persecuted than the persecutors." Negro church songs were often hard to follow. I asked a Negro friend about this, and he said he himself could not be sure of the words, since the singers picked up words listening to each other.

The Primitive Baptist Church represented still another aspect of Negro worship, the extended family unit with aspirations for autonomy. A dozen adults and a dozen children were present the two Sundays I attended, and the obese woman who led the choir of five—and supplied one daughter to the choir and five to the Sunday school—was the pastor's sister-in-law. Yet the group met in a neat, fresh-painted room in their own small building, acquired four months before for five thousand dollars. Previously they had held services in a dingy store-front up the block. Elder George M. had carpentered and plastered the new church himself. He had worked in the steel mills for eleven years and made thirty-seven dollars a day instructing crane operators, although he could neither read nor write. When I expressed surprise he called his wife, "Tell this guy how I can't read." He had been born in Arkansas and educated at Muncie Central on a football scholarship, apparently doing well in classes in spite of his handicap. He received special instruction from a white teacher at Ball State University. He had possessed the gift of preaching since he was five, being ordained by the Lord.

Handsome, athletic, still young, he preached with fervor and intensity, dipping his knees, holding a handkerchief or book to his right cheek, intoning phrases in a rising cadence with closed eyes, sometimes opening out and shaking his palms. The Primitive Baptists believed in "making a joyful noise unto the Lord" and in footwashing, which they practiced one Sunday in the month. Elder M. gave me permission to record the service the following Sunday, and asked me to play it back in church. Listening intently, he remarked, "That sounds just like country singing." Any listener would marvel at how so small a group could fill the room with song, chant, and response in swelling harmony. The elder had served as minister for five years and commented about himself, "I'm the most unlearned pastor they had, and carried them the furthest." He obtained historical references from a book his wife read to him, which he showed me, *World's Great Men of Color, 3000 B.C. to 1946 A.D.* by J. A. Rogers, published at 37 Morningside Avenue in New York.

Negro folk religion or traditional worship, as characterized in these observations, is directly connected with civil rights and urban politics. This point was ingeniously made by Charles H. King when I recorded a talk with him in his basement office in the Gary Municipal Building. King was forty-two, dark and mottled in complexion, burly in physique. His mother had been born in Boston, his father in Atlanta, and he himself in Albany. A regular contributor to *Negro Digest* with perceptive articles on the Negro church, King had shown me an autobiographical chapter of an unpublished manuscript in which he described the attempt of his father, a preacher in Harrisburg, Pennsylvania, to have young Charles "get religion" through exposure to a visiting revivalist. Charles was not converted and was painfully embarrassed. He ended the chapter by saying he later experienced religion in his own way. When I asked him how, he related an experience that had befallen him when he was eighteen as a sailor in the United States Navy on shore leave. Two shore patrolmen, southern whites, ordered him, "Boy, straighten your cap," and when he reacted too slowly, poked him in the ribs and called him nigger. King slugged one, and they dragged him off to the guardhouse and lashed him two hundred times with a belt, the buckle leaving permanent scars on his back. At his trial, the ship's captain mocked him publicly, saying, "So they called you nigger. Well what did you expect them to call you?"

After that episode King felt a need for faith, but he developed his own concept of social relevance in his ministry, employing the techniques of the southern Baptist preacher while rejecting the escapism into heavenly hopes. King pointed out that Negro civil rights leaders—and he named a string, beginning with Martin Luther King—were all former ministers. He too belonged to this sequence, having pastored for three years at Clarksville, Tennessee, and for ten years at Evansville, Indiana. Negro civil rights agitators used the same devices on the platform they had employed on the altar—the incantatory repetition (Jees-us, Jees-us), the encouragement of shouting, the emotional singing—but now it was all channeled into the specific goals of earthly recognition for the Negro. King cleverly illustrated the mincing, polite singing of an all-white church at Miller whose choir had practiced a spiritual in his honor the day he came as guest preacher, and his own booming, leather-lunged rendition he demonstrated to them as a corrective. "When I was finished, there were at least eight people with wet eyes." Such expertly manipulated sounds induced in the Negro congregations the mass hypnotism or cataleptic trances popularly known as "getting happy," and now Negro social reformers and politicians were arousing their audiences with these traditional means. King himself decried unbridled emotionalism for either theological or extremist ends, and gave me an article he had just written, "The Specter of Black Power," describing a Black Power symposium he had attended, and sharply criticized, at Howard University.[4]

An extraordinary opportunity to see a concrete illustration of King's thesis came the evening of February 14, when I found myself in a crowded basement room where the Political Alliance Club of Northwest Indiana was meeting. This was an organization for minority groups, but the members were all Negro save for one or two Puerto Ricans. A tense, chunky white woman, obviously under con-

---

[4] *Sign: National Catholic Magazine* (February 1968), 13–17.

siderable strain, sat in the speaker's chair. This was Marion Tokarsky, now a celebrity for revealing the vote fraud attempted against Mayor Hatcher.[5] That very day she was on the front page of the Gary *Post Tribune*, in a garbled story saying the prosecutor was dropping charges against her—her punishment by the machine for her public revelations—in return for her turning state's evidence. The only white person present besides myself was a policeman, appointed by Hatcher as part of her twenty-four-hour protection. Mrs. Tokarsky spoke a rough and sloppy English, not the clumsy English of the immigrant but the street English of the little-schooled American. She delivered her recital of the attempted vote fraud, and her decision to break with the Democratic Party machine and support Hatcher, in the form of a divine revelation.

"I am no saint," she began, "just an instrument of the Lord," and she repeated this thought at intervals. Her tale was a melodrama which would make Hollywood thrillers seem plausible. She had been a staunch Democratic committeewoman for twelve years in Glen Park, the residential center of the anti-Negro east Europeans. The machine turned against Hatcher, not because he was a Negro but because he would not do their bidding. Last July they had given her a sample voting machine with instructions on how to split the ticket and vote against Hatcher. She smuggled a sample voting machine in her shopping bag to show Hatcher, who had a picture taken of it. Democrats and Republicans alike were working to defeat Hatcher; some 5,280 names were removed from the voting rolls. Marion Tokarsky went through a period of doubt and confusion, at one time questioning Hatcher's loyalty. "I prayed as I never prayed before." The federal government flew in, and assured her she would not be involved or have to go to court.

Then one day the subpoena came. She turned over the matter all day Saturday, and at twelve o'clock Mass the Sunday before election she prayed directly to God. She explained to her Baptist audience that as a Catholic she had always before prayed to Saint Anthony or the Blessed Virgin, who could get the ear of the Lord in her behalf. But now she prayed directly. " 'God, please just give me the courage to go to court tomorrow. If I find just a few words in this missal I'll have courage'. And it was as if He had come right down from heaven." She opened the missal, and right before her eyes, in the Book of Psalms, was the word she had requested: " 'In the midst of the Assembly he opened his mouth. . . . The mark of the just man tells wisdom and his tongue tells what is right.' And I thanked God. Now I asked God to show me that Hatcher would win. 'Cause I knew I was crucified if he didn't.''

Again the Lord answered her with an apt quotation.

And the next day when I went to court I didn't have to think, the words came right out of my mouth. And the defense lawyers asked me questions that I gave answers to, made them look like jackasses. So it was someone bigger than me doing it. They asked, "Mrs. Tokarsky, will you testify that a Democratic official asked you to do something illegal?" "Yes," I said, "if you'll name them one by one." "Why won't you name them, don't you know them?" "Yes," I answered, "but I don't know if you do." At that they reddened and asked two names, to which I said yes, and then they stopped. I called the mayor Sunday evening and said, "Dick, this is Marion. You know, you're going to win the election." And I read to

[5] *Time*, November 17, 1967, p. 26.

him out of the missal. He said to me, "Ever since the primary I knew I was going to win. But this is the most glorious thing that has happened to me."

There was a good deal more in this vein. Mrs. Tokarsky was fired from her job, arrested and jailed, her children spat on, her husband, who had just renovated his gas station, threatened. But the Lord sustained her throughout. "The day that I was arrested and they put me in jail, I didn't feel one ounce of sorrow or regret. I felt elated." This was on December 29, and on New Year's Eve, alone with her children, she asked God for another message and found it in Psalms 19:13, "O Lord, you heard His voice cry to you from the temple . . . devising a plot and they will fall into it themselves."

Throughout the narration, the listeners interjected the customary responses of Baptist congregations, especially when Mrs. Tokarsky underlined her points with such precepts as "'Faith can really move a mountain" and "God helps those who help themselves." At the end of her talk an elderly gentleman in the front row cried out, "That's the gospel. It should be heard all over the world." Defying all the rules, the representative of the Slavic groups in Glen Park had made common cause with the ghetto Negroes. Their medium of communication was the political revival meeting, and together they saw Mayor Hatcher as blessed by the Lord in the battle against the forces of evil. Marion Tokarsky was the prophet through whom God has spoken. In recompense for her sacrifice, the Negro community is heavily patronizing her husband's gas station.

Serbians

"The Serbians live on tradition and heritage," observed one of my new Serbian friends. More than any other ethnic group in Gary and East Chicago, the Serbians do indeed cherish and abide by their Old World inheritance, an inheritance vivid and sorrowful in their minds, from the battle of Kossovo in 1389, when they sank heroically in defeat before the Turks, down to the Chetnik battles against Nazi Croatians and Tito's Communists. This is not book history but live and remembered history, as Americans rarely remember and identify with their own. Several Gary Serbs explained that orally recited history kept alive the Serbian spirit during five centuries of Turkish oppression and darkness. When the Turks blinded the learned clergy, the priests sang from memory heroic recitations of the Serbs, accompanying themselves on the one-stringed fiddle, the *gusle*, which they improvised from a stick and a strand of horsehair after the Turks confiscated their musical instruments. All the Serbs I met were proud and sad. Eighty-year-old George R., still erect and twinkling, recited emotionally a *gusle* song he had learned over seventy years before in Serbia. Thirty-one-year-old Walter T. has been in the States only since 1956, with his wife Milly (Miholjka), whom he brought over in 1963 from his native village, making sure she wasn't "brainwashed." Red-haired Milane S., a fiery Montenegrin with an Ll.D., rushed at me when I came into her boss's office carrying a tape recorder and asked if I was a Communist spy; but I ended by taping her experience as a Chetnik fighter who escaped through Communist lines. Dragich B. ("Blaz"), an ex-waiter and former Chetnik, thrust his story upon me in the Chetnik-run Europa cafe. Rade R., the oak-chested leader of the mother church group in East Chicago, wept three times while recounting atrocities committed against his people in the second World War.

These and other Serbs showed the effects of a common tradition. They shuddered at the crimes of the hated Ustashis, who allegedly had butchered two million Serbs during the last war. Walter T. gave me a booklet, *The Crime of Genocide*, published by the Serbian National Defense Council of America (Chicago, 1951), that contained shocking pictures of mutilated women and children and a decapitated priest's head held by grinning Ustashis as well as an introductory anecdote about Ante Pavelich, the Croatian Ustashi leader, exhibiting on his desk a wicker basket filled with forty pounds of human eyes. Rade R. gave me a copy of the book *Genocide in Satellite Croatia, 1941–1945* (Chicago, n.d.) by Edmond Paris, translated from the French, and documenting these horrors. I recorded eye-witness atrocities related by Walter T. and his godfather; by Milos R., who had lost fifteen members of his family during the war ; and by Rade R. and his wife, Mira, born in Novi Sad. Rade, as a Belgrade policeman, had been called to pick up the bodies of eight children floating down the Sava river with the head of their mother nailed to a board, under a sign reading, "A present from the Ustashis." Mira had seen the Hungarian troops bomb the Danube ice and push Serbian and Jewish families into the water underneath. Overwhelming bitterness against the Croatians, the Nazis, and the Communists filled their talk. The Communists especially aroused their passion, and they saw signs of communism and communist propaganda everywhere in America—among the Negroes, the hippies, the clergy.

A great split rent the solidarity of American Serbs in 1963, over the so-called mother church issue. One wing rejected the authority of the mother church in Belgrade and its edict redistricting the American diocese, whose seat was in Libertyville, Illinois. They called the opposing faction communists, and were in turn labeled schismatics. The issue resulted in bitter litigation, still in progress, and divided the Gary and East Chicago Serbs into two churches in each city. Rade represented the mother church faction in East Chicago, and he minimized the differences between Serbs and Croats, saying both fought equally with the Chetniks and Partisans. He himself had been born in Croatian Bosnia but belonged to the Serbian church. He told of Ustashis so hungry they ordered the camp cooks to fry livers of young boys. Both factions presented their case vigorously to me, and the only sure conclusion one could draw was that the most cohesive of all the ethnic groups in Steeltown had fallen into civil war.

National and folk traditions blend in the lives of the Serbian steelworkers. *Gusle* singers perform in Gary at saint's day family parties and recite the old heroic lays. Draža Mihajlovich, the Chetnik leader whom the Serbs feel was betrayed by Roosevelt and Churchill at Yalta, is the most recent of the venerated heroes extending back to Marko Kraljevich and Miloš Obilich. The analogy between oppression under the Turks and under the Communists is often drawn. Historical plays presented in Saint Sava Church so excited emotions that members of the audience pelted the Turks, played by their own friends. George R. recited for me in Serbian the "Gusle Song" describing a renegade Serbian who joined the Turks. One day finding a *gusle,* he attempted to play it but could not, because "the *gusle* does not lie." He bent tearfully over the instrument, imploring

33

forgiveness, and a Turk whacked off his head. In the basement of Saint Sava Church I observed a program of Serbian songs, dances, and speeches with not a word of English used. After the stage program young and old joined hands in the traditional *cola* dance to the accompaniment of two thumping accordion players.

The most striking example of Serbian cultural nationalism in Gary is the story of Bishop Varnava Nastich. He was born in Gary on January 31, 1914, the son of an immigrant barber, and was baptized Voislav in the Saint Sava Serbian Orthodox Church. As a child he excelled at *gusle* performances, and clippings refer to him as a youthful prodigy in reciting Serbian folklore and old ballads, even being taken on tour to Serbian communities in other cities. He also served as altar boy in Saint Sava Church. At the age of nine, in 1923, he left Gary with his parents, brother, and sister for Yugoslavia. His father operated the popular "American Restaurant" on King Alexander Avenue in Sarajevo. Within three or four years after their return, Voislav had won the gold medal awarded by King Alexander to the best boy *guslar*. At eighteen he undertook theological studies and graduated from the theological faculty of the University of Belgrade in 1937. Three years later he took monastic vows in the monastery at Mileshevo and changed his name to Varnava. During the war years, 1941–1945, Varnava refused a bishopric in the so-called Croatian Orthodox Church of the Nazi puppet state under Ante Pavelich. In 1945 he was ordained a priest, and in August 1947 he was consecrated a bishop. Within a year he was arrested and brought to trial by Tito's government, actually for speaking against communism, ostensibly for collaborating with the Ustashi, an infamous charge. There followed eleven years of imprisonment, harassment, surveillance, brutality, and death by poisoning, according to half a dozen informants, including Saint Sava's priest, Father Peter Bankerovich, who with others tape-recorded for me a statement about Varnava. Father Peter recalled how a telegram announcing the death of Bishop Varnava was delivered in the midst of the high celebration in church on the fiftieth anniversary of the founding of Saint Sava, November 14, 1964. He gave me a copy of the 368-page commemoration book printed in Gary in both Serbian and English, and concluded his taped remarks by reading from the communication sent by Bishop Varnava from Monastery Beocin on September 3, 1964. One paragraph reads:

"I rejoice, because your Feast is my personal feast also, for I was among the first of your Altar-boys, and I was the first one after the formation of your Church congregation to whom was given the rank of 'Chtec'—Reader—under the arch of your Church. Under the blessed heaven of your Church Community, my first formation of my physical and graceful-spiritual life sprouted."[6]

A play was written and produced in Gary in January 1965 about Bishop Varnava, "Martyr to Communism," acted in the Saint Sava Church auditorium by children, to acquaint them with his heroic life and death. I read the typescript of the play in the home of its author, Daisy Wuletich, Gary-born, who had visited the Bishop in 1961 in Beocin Monastery with her mother, born in Montenegro.

[6] *St. Sava Serbian Orthodox Church Fiftieth Anniversary: Our Religious Heritage in America, 1914–1964; November 14–15, 1964.* (Gary, n.d.)

Daisy had drawn from personal letters of the Bishop, from an account of the trial in the booklet *Our Spiritual Hero*, and from her personal observations. The play itself was simple fare, a first act depicting the trial, in which the bishop defied the communist judges to the cheers of the crowd, and a second act set in the hospital showing him in familiar scenes before receiving a fatal injection. Thus he talks with his uncle about the car "pesho," a Peugeot given him by the Gary church so that he could travel around the country. He writes in a letter to his Gary friends, "I realize that at any time my car can turn into a Cross for me. This is its Cross-aspect and this Cross-aspect, too, is one and not the least of the reasons for my loving it so." The car became a symbol of his persecution, for it was exorbitantly taxed by the Communists. In the play this dialogue takes place:

Uncle: How sentimental you are about the car! You take better care of it than some people do of their own children.
Bishop: My little Pesho is important to me.
Marko: How fervently you speak of your car!
Bishop: I do speak of it fervently and I love it fervently! One reason being, of course, the American-red blood in me.

In another place in the play Bishop Varnava alludes to a visit he made to the shrine of Saint Basil (Vasilije) at Ostrog in Montenegro to pray for his sick mother. Daisy and her mother, Cveta, had also visited Ostrog, and Cveta, a sickly old woman, now told in Serbian, and Daisy translated, a miracle she had heard in Trebinje, the town where she was born in 1893.

A Turkish girl in Trebinje was all doubled up. No doctor could help her. So her parents finally took her to the shrine of Saint Basil in a basket up the mountain. They left the basket there all night. And when they came in the morning she was perfectly well and straight and walked down the mountain. The basket was placed at the foot of the coffin. The girl left a necklace of gold ducats in the chapel as her gift.

Then the people asked her what kind of a doctor is this Vlasha (a derogatory term used by the Turks against the Serbs). She answered, "No doctor, just a stiffened Vlasha." And that night when she went to bed, her body was deformed again. In the morning she found the ducats under her pillow.

She went back two or three times again but was never cured.

The Wuletichs showed me pictures of the monastery of St. Basil carved out of the mountainside, and Cveta graphically illustrated, with sudden animation and sweeping gestures along the wall, how the Nazis had bombed all around the shrine without ever effecting a direct hit. So the modern legend of Bishop Nastich has formed a link with the historic legend of Saint Basil. There is also a connection with Saint Sava, the patron saint of children, since the play was performed by children on January 31, the birthday of Bishop Nastich and the nearest Sunday in 1965 to January 27, the death day of Saint Sava.

Another evening found me in the home of Mrs. Emily B., a first cousin of the bishop, who had in her possession boxes full of letters, photographs, clippings and memorabilia of Varnava's career. Her father had come to Gary in 1906 from a town in Montenegro near that of Varnava's father and helped lay tracks for the streetcar. Her husband Djordje had fought with the Chetniks alongside Milane Spadijer. Emily, a sad, darkhaired woman of fifty-six with a slight hunchback, confided to me that Montenegro was the cradle of Serbian culture, language, and songs. Her mother was the sister of Varnava's father, who founded the Saint Sava Church in Gary, and Emily herself had taken care of the boy, a few years her junior. It was clear that the bishop's tragedy was her obsession. She showed me a photograph of Varnava—ascetic, bespectacled, talking to another bishop, with a dim figure from the Udba, Tito's secret police, in the background beside an automobile—and another of his funeral (sent her by her uncle), his body resting in a plain open casket, while the patriarch-german can be seen in white cap instead of black, an obvious mark of disrespect. Emily told of the cruel "accident" planned by the Communists in 1949 when Varnava was being taken from the prison of Sjenica to that at Srem. The guards placed the prisoners in a car on a siding, and at about 1:00 A.M. the engine rammed into it at full steam. All but eleven were killed. Varnava was thrown out of the window with both legs and one arm broken. A witness immediately telephoned his brother. However the militia put a guard at the scene of the accident, and the Udba prevented medication being given or the insertion of metal pins in his heels. Varnava was placed in an army train without mattresses or covers and taken to a hospital in Srem.

Emily and her fellow Serbs in Gary had worked ceaselessly to obtain the release and return of the bishop, through pressure on the State Department and the Indiana senators. The Saint Sava group hoped that Varnava might even succeed Dionisije as the American bishop at Libertyville. After the 1963 edict of the mother church creating three North American bishops, Varnava entered the controversy with letters supporting the anti-Communist stand of the Serbian Free Church. Emily showed me some of his letters, written in mixed Serbian and English; the English prose was eloquent and idiomatic. Varnava never lost his American spirit, Emily said; when he first went to Yugoslavia he wrote how he missed his movie idols Tom Mix and William S. Hart, chewing gum, the funny papers, and electric light switches.

Had a *gusle* song been written about the Bishop? I asked Emily. She produced a three-and-a-half-page typescript, running fifty-seven lines a page, titled *Smrt Vladike Varnave,* "The Death of Bishop Varnava," composed by Milisav Maksimovich, of Cincinnati, Ohio, and dated April 3, 1965.

The mother church group with whom I met at Rade Z.'s house in East Chicago promptly deflated Varnava, saying the Gary people had made a legendary figure out of hot air. It was a myth that the Communists beat him up; actually he had jumped off a train. He was not a true diocesan bishop but an assistant vicar bishop. The fact was that by his fruitless outcries he had proved an embarrassment to the Serbian Church.

In the life story of Bishop Varnava Nastich, all the elements of Serbian-American tradition fuse. He was born in Gary and died in Beocin, reversing the usual immigrant process. Letters and visitors kept his memory green in Gary. He recited *gusle* legendary songs as a youthful singer, and after his death he became the subject of a *guslar* bard. A play was produced in Gary about his martyrdom. His life and death struggle against the Communist oppressor reenact the heroic tragedies of earlier Serbians against the Turkish tyrants. He has become a potent symbol in the fateful church issue now splitting friends and families in Gary and East Chicago.

Croatians (from diary)

My next appointment was with Nick E., seventy-eight, retired, a great-grand-father. He lived out in the Glen Park section beyond the Northwest Campus. Nick was in the center of organized Croatian activities; he had been president of the Croatian Fraternal Union for a dozen years and was still honorary president. Although Nick called the Serbs Oriental and the Croats Western, he had an Oriental look about him, with a large oval face. He did not speak or volunteer readily but seemed content to answer questions. Finally he remembered a ghost story he had heard on one of his five visits to Croatia. The spark ignited when I asked him about the Serbs. Now he uttered all the counter-charges to refute Walter T.'s venom of the day before, and I got this on tape. The Serbs had assassinated Stepan Radich, leader of the Peasant Party for an independent Croatia, in Congress House in Belgrade. Serbia was trying to dominate Croatia, which had formerly held Bosnia-Hercegovina and Dalmatia, within the second Yugoslavia. The Serbs were taking over the Croatian language. Serbia took the money from Croatian factories to rebuild Belgrade at the expense of Zagreb. Croatians pay twice as much tax as the Serbians, and in Yugoslavia a friend had denied this publicly but told him privately it was true. Nick would not associate with Serbians in Gary. They were fanatic royalists for Peter, the son of King Alexander now living in Paris. Alexander was assassinated in Marseille by Croats in revenge for Radich. Serbia had taken the rich Vojvodina from Croatia. Nick showed me the "Croatian Voice," *Hrvatski Glas*, published in Winnipeg. An issue of February 10, 1968, had an article about a Croatian priest, Professor Draganovich, being kidnapped by the Serbs from Rome and taken to Belgrade, and another entitled "Separation of Croatia from Yugoslavia," all in Croatian.

As I was getting ready to leave, Nick put on records of sweet *tamburitza* music he had purchased in Zagreb, brought out two *tamburs* he had ordered from Kos Slavko, near Zagreb, and showed me large color photographs of the *tamburitzan* groups he directed, about thirty young people. They would take part in a national festival in Des Plaines, Illinois, on July 7. He rehearsed them every Friday night in the Croatian Hall and also gave lessons in Croatian. A man in Gary, Milan Opacich, made *tamburs,* but Nick could get one from Yugoslavia for $50 instead of paying $175 for one here. The name of one song on the record was "Three Days She Was Picking the Corn," and Nick said most were folksongs.

A phone call came and Nick said he had to witness the signature of the will of an old friend of eighty-two, Zlatko K., who would be dead of cancer within three months. He insisted on taking me to the house nearby. Zlatko was toothpick thin, his skin tight; he was gaunt, hollow, emaciated, hairless, but spry of mind and ready to be interviewed. He began telling of his immigrant experiences, being fired the first day on his job in a sausage factory in Chicago for stepping on a lever that sent the meat flying all over the room. An attorney showed up to draw up the will, and after the business advised me to leave, but with the understanding that if Zlatko felt in the mood I could return. Two middle-aged tearful daughters were present. (*end diary*)

Croatian tradition proved a good deal thinner than Serbian. One Croatian told me that he had married a Lithuanian and that his children were ethnic mongrels; but the Serbs remained clannish and tended to marry among themselves. The comic experience recounted by Zlatko K. belongs not to Croatian but to general immigrant lore about mishaps on first landing in America. Bessie M., of Serbian descent, related how her father ate a banana, skin and all, his first day in New York and exclaimed he had never tasted anything so horrible. A Romanian restaurant owner, John N., recounted an involved saga of his arriving in Detroit in the middle of the night with forty dollars strapped around his waist, not a word of English at his command, and waiting for the cab driver to locate a Romanian speaker. These comparable incidents, at once ludicrous and pathetic, in totality comprise one large chapter of immigrant folk history.

Greeks

At the International Institute I met the staff member who dealt with Greek families, Mrs. Stella D., a short, matronly, worried-looking woman born in Chicago but raised in Gary and active in Greek organizations there. Her father had been born in Athens and her mother in Smyrna. As president of the local Ahepa chapter, Stella had gone to Athens for the international congress in 1964. She enumerated a long list of Greek societies and clubs in town, saying they were often organized according to the regions or islands from which people came. I asked her about the evil eye, and she responded excitedly, saying she had learned the prayer to overcome its effects from her grandmother, but indirectly, by overhearing, since the prayer could only pass from man to woman and woman to man. It was necessary to burn three cloves and repeat the prayer; when the clove sparked, the spell was broken.[7]

"I've tried it on my daughters," Mrs. D. continued.

When I was young my grandmother did it to me often. I was sick and I'd perk up right away. Grandmother told me that a horse had fallen down on the street in Smyrna because someone had put the evil eye on it, without meaning to; she said the prayer and the horse got up. In Chicago a doctor friend used to come when he was feeling low and say, "Stella, tell me the prayer," and after it was said he'd feel better right away. Three cloves should be burned and placed in a little wine glass of water. Then say the prayer, bless the water with the sign of the cross and sprinkle it around. The prayer is repeated three times, with a count, 5–10–15–20–25 and so on. She could not utter the prayer.

On another occasion Stella introduced me to a client of hers, Emmanuel V., a friendly, clean-featured newcomer of thirty-eight who had been in Gary only four years, joining his father who had come from the isle of Kalymnos in the eastern Aegean in 1923. Emmanuel sold sponges and worked part time in the steel mills. In halting English, with the aid of Stella, he related an event that had caused a great stir on Kalymnos.

It happened in 1908 or 1909. There was a diver named Latare, he has a big rock in his hand weighing over thirty pounds, to weight him down, and no clothes. They drop him over the side of the ship, and he goes straight down about 175 feet. And a big shark was lying on its side, and its mouth was open. Latare went right through the mouth and the rock hit the stomach. And the shark threw the man out. The man on top pulls up the rope, so Latare came up, with marks all over his back. They had a big picture of him and the fish in the city hall. The king went to see him. People paid one Italian lira to look at him. Jim Z.,

7 See Richard M. Dorson, *American Folklore* (New York, 1959), 163, for a similar account.

who came here six years ago from Kalymnos, when he was 27, saw the picture. It was a miracle, the only time it ever happened.

Emmanuel invited me to the East Side Coffee House off 7th Avenue that evening, where Greek men met to play cards, talk, and have light refreshment. When I arrived, he had stepped out, and I sat conspicuously alone, eying and being eyed by the groups of dark-haired, dark-complexioned men sitting around tables reading Greek newspapers, conversing in Greek, and eating a sweet Greek pastry called *galakton baurike*. The men were all ages, in working-class clothes; women were not permitted, and one came to the door, but no further, to signal her husband. After a while the owner, Denos K., heavy-set and serious of mien, sat at my table and began conversing in passable English. Denos had been born in 1918 in Tarpon Springs, Florida, the transplanted community of Greek sponge fishermen, but lived in Kalymnos from 1921 to 1933, when he returned to Tarpon Springs and became captain of a sponge fishing boat. He moved to Gary with his brother in 1947, when some chemical killed off the sponge beds.

While we talked, Emmanuel entered and joined us. Then others crowded around, and suddenly our table was the center of excited conversation about Kalymnos, about Latare the lucky diver, about Saint Nicholas, patron saint of fishermen. A pleasant young barber, the Jim Z. who had seen the picture of Latare, counted twenty men from Kalymnos around the room. One was a famous diver, now converted into a railroad switchman, a cousin of Emmanuel, burly and impassive, and out of the conversation because he had no English. Over the mantel rested an elegant ship model called the *Kalymnos*. From somewhere in the room Jim brought a couple of prize sponges, one long and tufted and shaped like a helmet. Now Denos produced a treasured book with a torn blue paper cover showing a suited diver holding a large sponge in one hand and a claw-like instrument in the other. It was titled *Strangers at Ithaca, The Story of the Spongers of Tarpon Springs*, written by George Th. Frantzis and published by the Great Outdoors Publishing Company in St. Petersburg, Florida, in 1962. He looked through it lovingly, the others clustering around, as he pointed to persons he knew in the photographs. One was of his mother, "Eleni Georgious K., one of the first Greek beauties to come to Tarpon Springs," showing just her head. She was strikingly beautiful, with madonna-like features framed in black hair. In an emotional gesture Denos gave me the book, along with a postcard picturing a rugged peak and sheltered bay of Kalymnos.

In my notebook Denos drew a rough map of the inland coast of Florida to illustrate how in 1935 the hurricane had hit every city from Palmyra to Pensacola save Tarpon Springs.

The sponge fishermen in Kalymnos give the sponges they get on their last day to Saint Nicholas. In Tarpon Springs they say Saint Nicholas saved them from the hurricane. In 1935 my uncle, who was in the Bahamas as a sponge buyer, came to visit us in Tarpon Springs. The radio announced the hurricane coming. My uncle had had experience with the hurricane every year in the Bahamas. He called my father, "Get up and get prepared." And my father said, "Don't worry, Saint Nicholas is going to take care of that. Go back to bed." And the hurricane hit all the other cities, went out to sea about a hundred and fifty miles and came back and hit Pensacola, below Tarpon Springs.

These Gary Greeks no longer knew the *paramythia*, the old folktales with which they used to while away evenings on the sponge boats. But traditions enveloped the East Side Coffee House, conveyed in the pictures of Kalymnos, the ship model, the sponges, the true tale of Latare, and the faith in Saint Nicholas.

Mexicans (from diary)

I was introduced to Victor L., a young, positive fellow with pockmarked skin, who promptly invited me to his Adult Citizens English class at Riley School that evening. Then I was off to William M., who had invited me to a Mexican meal when I called at 4:00 P.M. His wife, Tilly, was an attractive dark-haired girl about thirty years of age, with boys of two and four. Bill was sturdy, full-faced, serious, darker than she. Tilly did not look Mexican, except for a slight olive complexion. They were second generation but filled with tradition, or aware of it. Tilly was one of thirteen children. Her dad had come from Mexico at twenty-six, fifty-three years before, from Yuriria, Guanajauto, which she had visited, and was thankful she had been born in the States. Her mother came from Jalisco, and recalled being helped off a train by Pancho Villa. Tilly had once dated a Greek boy of means, but with the understanding that both their parents would arrange their marriages. Tilly and Bill began telling me various Mexican folklore matters: about the *mariachi*, popular singing groups with stringed instruments bringing seventy-five to one hundred dollars an hour in the area; how Thomas Alva Edison was really Mexican; an account of La Llorona mixed with the female ghost of Cline Avenue, actually seen by Tilly's brother, a cab driver, who was interviewed on TV; the potato water cure of Tilly's mother to preserve her black hair and save that of her brother-in-law, which was coming out in patches. "She advised him to use water from boiled potatoes for three months." I recorded them.

Dinner was a regular Mexican meal of stew beef, yellow rice, and beans. Tilly and Bill told me that *enchiladas* and *tacos* were only used on special occasions. Everything they said I found of interest. Their church, "Our Lady of Guadalupe," in the Harbor, was having trouble keeping its parishioners, though it was the only Mexican church in town. The priests were Irish (Father Flanagan) or English (Father Meade), and when Tilly's family sponsored Father Frias from Mexico, well-spoken and handsome, the people flocked to hear him. A substantial sum was raised to send to Mexico, for a church or hospital, whereupon Father Flanagan got mad and refused to let Father Frias speak again. Tilly said that at the *mariachi* dances the "Mexican would come out" even in Americans, in the *grito*, a protracted yell. The church was losing parishioners because the younger people —and older ones—were moving out, and the Texans planned only to stay ten years and then return. Her family kept going to the old church for sentimental reasons, although they were closer to St. Mary's. Tilly remarked that the Mexicans did not stick together, as did the Serbians. Two rivals had lost out in the election for state representative to a non-Mexican, by one hundred votes. She and Bill had had to leave their Ivy Street apartment because the Serbian landlord was renting to Serbs. Pride and stubbornness were downfall traits of the Mexicans. Tilly mentioned a University of California book, *Mexican-Americans in a Mid-*

west Metropolis, that was so inflammatory—it described Mexican laborers being loaded into boxcars—that it could not be sold locally.[3]

After dinner I followed Bill across town to his foster mother's, around the corner from the old church in Indiana Harbor. Mrs. Tomasita G., a tiny, wrinkled, Indian-featured old lady, had been born in 1893 in Doctor Arroyo, south of Monterrey, and had come to East Chicago in 1917. Later Bill told me that she took a raw egg with garlic every morning, washed her eyes with lemon juice, had all her teeth, and had begun to wear glasses only two years before. She was a *curandera*, and her cures were based on faith. "She must be a devout Catholic," I observed tritely. "No, she's a Mormon," said Bill. "She goes to Highland to services there twice on Sunday, morning and afternoon." And not to the Catholic church next door, that Bill and Tilly drove across town to attend.

Mrs. G. had raised Bill and his three siblings, Texas-born, by herself, since he was three. When he entered her miniature apartment, he kissed her respectfully on the hand and cheek. We sat in a tiny dressing area in front of her four-poster bed, and she related cures for *susto* in Spanish, which Bill then translated. He volunteered a cure she had done for him when he was eight ("I was leery of it until then"); she had bathed him in a raw egg at night, which was cooked in the morning, and the fever gone. Another charm, involving a prayer written on paper strips and placed on four corners of the bed, drove away cockroaches. We only had a little time before the 7:00 P.M. class, which by coincidence the old lady was attending. A friend came in, a funny old gal with expressive gestures, Elisa D., from Michoacan, Mexico, and she told a comical *cuento* into the tape, a noodle tale, which Bill translated. Then we all drove off to Riley School. It turned out that Victor L. and Bill M. had gone to school and worked in the mill together. Victor pulled out of the class a grizzled Mexican, and found a classroom for us to talk in. He was Ray A. of East Chicago, born in La Barca, Jalisco, in 1901; he came to Arizona in 1921 and to East Chicago the next year. His English was fair, but he preferred Spanish. After some questioning I struck responses with La Llorona, *susto, brujería,* and Pancho Villa. His mother had given him a cure for *biles*, a virulent kind of *susto* causing throwing up and eventually death. A main ingredient was sour tamarind. After he left, Bill M., who had been translating, spoke of his difficulty in following the Spanish; he was just too much out of practice, although he sometimes used it at the mill or with the old folks. But in Mexico he felt at a loss. Puerto Ricans spoke very rapidly when they first came. He mentioned hybrid words, English with Spanish endings, like *watcheli*. He had learned to read Spanish by reading the Bible three times in Spanish.

Now Victor L. joined us and spoke in a very interesting and informed way about the language business and Puerto Rican-Mexican conflicts. He was the son of old Mexicans; and his sister, two years older, had had a terrible time learning English in school until her teacher told her father to speak English to her. Victor then had no trouble. He had kept up his Spanish with his parents later, in the store and in the mill. He had an A.B. and an M.A. in Education from Indiana University. His wife of four years was Puerto Rican, of a high-rank family. He

<hr>

[3] Julian Samora and Richard A. Lamanna, *Mexican-Americans in a Midwest Metropolis: A Study of East Chicago* (Los Angeles, 1967).

had flown at Christmas time to San Juan to get parental consent, while his brothers-in-law on the island had been afraid to approach the father. A couple of aunts, who were around her constantly, were from Spain. Victor attacked a number of stereotypes: that the Puerto Ricans all had Negro blood (his wife was a redhead, and there were plenty of blondes), that they didn't practice discrimination (there were ghettos in Puerto Rico), that they spoke so rapidly. Every other Spanish-speaking group was supposed to talk rapidly. He agreed with Bill M. that Harbor Spanish was a thing unto itself (citing a master's thesis by a Freddie Maraville), and he gave examples. He would use *autobús* in San Juan and be corrected to *huahua* and then be laughed at back home. He spoke of the warmth and hospitality of the Puerto Ricans, and also of the Mexicans. He had never expected to marry a Puerto Rican girl. Mexicans felt they could look down on Puerto Ricans because of their Negro blood. All Latins loved their mother and their country. Pride was one reason for their not learning English, and another was housing discrimination forcing them into Mexican ghettos. Two-thirds of the Puerto Ricans put their country first; they were the nationalists and territorialists. Mexicans were good workers and could take the heat in Open Hearth #2 at Inland. (*end diary*)

Puerto Ricans (from diary)

In Gary I had an appointment with A. M. in the National Bank Building. I arrived before he did in his plush office on the 9th floor—one of the few such offices I had encountered. He turned out to be youngish, yellow-skinned, square-faced, deliberate, and slow-speaking. He was an upper-class Puerto Rican, with French and Spanish blood, he said. He had an A.B. from Northwest Campus of Indiana University and his law degree from Valparaiso University, with other education in Europe. Our conversation was halting; I asked questions and he gave slow answers. He did not see much difference between Puerto Ricans and Mexicans; the food was pretty much the same. (But Mrs. Carmen R., a Puerto Rican married to a doctor from the Dominican Republic, had given me a long list of typical Puerto Rican dishes.) Puerto Ricans were not used to cold weather when they came to Gary. Most came from the small towns, not San Juan, and had been agriculturists, but since the 1940s, under Operation Bootstrap, 185 new industries had opened in Puerto Rico. Mexicans were nationalistic; they think they will make money and return home. I began cautiously to ask him about *brujería,* and finally drew a spark. "I had a client the other day that said her husband's girl friend was trying to destroy her with the *brujería,* and that she had heard voices. They stick pins in a doll, with the person's name on it. I tried to talk her out of it." He knew of the *botánica* shop that sold herbs, seeds, candles, and *escapularios* of cotton with the Virgin or a saint on them, to use against the *brujería,* and gave me the name of a former owner, Mrs. Pilar F., who was herself accused of being a *bruja.* I asked about *susto,* and he did not know of any connection with *brujería* but called out to his secretary, a pretty young Mexican, if she knew of such a connection and was surprised to hear her say yes. He gave me a note of introduction to take to Mrs. F.

On the way out I asked the secretary, Carmen M., about *susto.* Her mother had a recipe: suspend the egg over the sick person, then place it in a glass of water, and drop in crosses made of broom straws or toothpicks, which will float. In the morning the egg may be cooked, depending on the sickness. But she had not tried it. "I don't want to get involved."

Now I decided to try Pilar F., who lived in the Brunswick section of Gary, a quiet neighborhood with small homes and plots of ground between them. An enormously fat, blubbery dark woman, slightly Oriental in aspect and somewhat sinister looking, was carrying a bundle of clothing out the door. She called Pilar when I showed her my letter. Pilar was a half-sister to this one, lighter, fat but not so fat, with more regular features, open and pleasant, and with good English. She took me right inside and after reading A. M.'s note answered everything I asked, while trying to silence an unquenchable two-year-old, an adopted son, Carlito. She gave me an LP record of Puerto Rican music, containing traditional *plena* songs (like calypsos), and said that a local orchestra played such songs at the Puerto Rico Demo Club at birthday parties—piano, trumpet, guitar, saxophone, soloist. Yes, they made up local *plenas*. Now I questioned Pilar about her life history. She was born in 1932 in Santurce del Barrio, in a very poor section called Tras Talleres, the only child of parents who had each been married before, giving her stepbrothers and stepsisters. In 1949 she went to live with her half-brother in New York, and attended P.S. 101, at 111th between Lexington and Madison. Pilar retraced her career in close detail: a return to Puerto Rico to attend her sick mother, a course in New York in practical nurse's training, while living with her half-brother, who was a cook's helper for twenty-five years in the Hotel Vanderbilt; a decision to move to Washington, because of unspecified trouble in her brother's family; her failure to get a nurse's position in Walter Reed Hospital because she arrived ten minutes late for the test, not knowing the Pentagon was across the Washington, D.C., boundary in Virginia; her loneliness in Washington, where there were only twenty to thirty Puerto Ricans; her job in charge of linen at the Shoreham Hotel—she was ever after soured against nursing; the return to New York, and her decision, because of the noise, to find another place where she could live with Puerto Ricans; the move to Gary in 1957, as a result of a letter from a home-town friend living there; her first income from using her fifteen-dollar jalopy to drive Puerto Ricans and colored people daily to a clinic at Michigan City, making fifteen dollars a day by charging each $3; a move to East Chicago and a job there as typist with the city; a year in Chicago at Oak Forest Hospital; a return to East Chicago to work in politics for Mayor Nicosia on behalf of the Puerto Ricans; laborer in Inland Steel, in the tin mill; marriage in 1963; present job as jail matron, which she enjoyed. Her husband Lorenzo had worked in Youngstown seventeen years, knew no English, and even spoke Spanish poorly, but he had made $11,000 the past year as second helper in the blast furnace, where only he could speak Spanish. When it was necessary to communicate in English, he wrote messages. While we were talking, he came in, a slender, sallow man with a small mustache and a furtive look, but he offered me a cup of coffee in friendly fashion.

In all this Pilar had not mentioned the *botánica,* so I brought it up, and she looked a little surprised but giggled and spoke most openly about the whole business. So I brought in the tape recorder, and she told all her secrets to it. A. M.

43

said I should not mention *brujería* but let Pilar bring it up, but she showed no hesitation at all in talking about the matter. "The Spanish people believe in voodoo, and they come buy herbs and take a bath in it and say it will bring good luck." There were about twenty-five *botanicas* in Chicago, and many in New York. Her own, run by her sister in East Chicago, had had to close as a result of the criticism of the churches, Catholic and Protestant. The Catholics imposed a course called *curcillistra* [*cursillo*], which cost $37 to $40 for three days, and which even her half-sister took. Pilar regarded the *botánica* as a drugstore, to sell supplies to people affected with *brujería*. While we were talking she brought out charcoal, incense, and seeds and burned them in a little dish, describing the procedure for the tape-recorder. Usually she did this Fridays at midnight, and she always stayed home Fridays (hence I had come on the right day). She said giggling—and she giggled all the way through—that her husband told her the incense was to make him stay at home. Pilar had learned about voodoo—she fumbled for the word on the tape—from a spiritual meeting she had attended as a young girl in Puerto Rico, which she described graphically. At the end she mentioned a fly from Spain, *moscas cantareas*, black and blue, which made a z-z-z sound, and was considered very lucky. Well, she and other *botánicas* would sell substitute flies, or substitute incense, when they couldn't get the real articles, and this led to a crackdown by the government. These articles were used to bring good luck in the numbers game; even snakes were sold, and she mentioned one good-luck snake that would curl up on the sofa. She said all this frankly into the tape. On leaving I offered to pay Pilar for the record, but she refused any money. (*end diary*)

Conclusions

A field trip of twenty-three days cannot of course answer the theoretical questions framed at the outset of this inquiry. Still from the numerous interviews and the data obtained in notebooks and on tape and in the form of donated publications and other materials, plus of course the strong impressions derived from personal observation, I put forward the following concepts of modern urban folklore. How well they will stand up after further work in the Gary-East Chicago area and to what extent they may apply in other metropolitan localities remains to be seen, but I advance them with some conviction.

1. PAUCITY OF CONVENTIONAL FOLKLORE. The old familiar genres of folklore, particularly the tale and song, do not seem abundant in the city. Even jokes, the modern folktale, are forbidden in the steel mills for fear their ethnic slurs may arouse hostility. One can of course find storytellers and folksingers in the city, and in the country village not every soul is an active tradition carrier by a long shot. But genre folklore has become increasingly displaced by other kinds of oral tradition, which deserve the attention of collectors. A good example was my evening in the Greek coffee-house, that might as well have been on the Aegean isle of Kalymnos, which indeed most of the men present claimed as their birthplace. They were eager to tell me all they knew of Greek life and lore, and other people had told me no group was so clannish as the Greeks. None could tell *paramythia*, the popular fictions with which the sponge fishermen had regaled each other in the old days and in the Old Country; yet traditions of other

kinds retained a powerful hold upon them. Among the Negroes and other ethnic groups I encountered a generally similar response. My closest Negro friend, Harold M., Mississippi born and bred, was exceedingly articulate but not on matters of southern lore. The steelworkers' union of which he was an official dominated his thoughts and conversation. He finally did tell me two anecdotes; one was a civil-rights joke and the other dealt with an eccentric millworker. When tales and songs are collected, as in the Polish folksongs recorded by Pawlowska and the Armenian folktales recorded by Hoogasian-Villa in Detroit, they may belong to an inactive memory culture rather than to a vigorous living growth.[9]

2. RICHNESS OF CULTURAL TRADITIONS AND PERSONAL HISTORIES. If the conventional genres are hard to come by, folklore, or perhaps better folk culture, is nevertheless present and pervasive. American folklorists—and this certainly includes myself—have sought for texts and largely overlooked other kinds and forms of cultural traditions less easy to report. Among the Negroes, the Baptist church is in most of its manifestations a folk institution transplanted from the South. I was told there were over two hundred such churches in Gary. The ethnomusicologist and student of folk music can have a field day analyzing the combination of choral and instrumental, country and city, gospel and rhythm elements in these church performances. For the Serbians, calendar feast days play a pivotal role in their lives, both the saints' day celebrations associated with each family and the great church holy days. In a number of ethnic societies, choral and dance groups perform regularly, such as the Croatian *tamburitzan* club. On my last evening in Gary I attended a Serbian entertainment in Saint Sava Hall, the basement auditorium of the church, and saw local girl dancers, a singer, and two flailing accordionists; and finally, with the chairs cleared, a circular *cola* dance with adults and children all joining hands. The whole program was in Serbian, and one could see before one's eyes youngsters absorbing Serbian traditional song, music, and dance. To the religious and social occasions should be added the celebration of national holidays, like the Mexican one on September 16, a festal pageant with floats and a proud team of *charros*, the costumed horsemen.

Ethnic cuisine is still another flourishing form of tradition among every sizable group: the southern whites, the southern Negroes, the east Europeans, the Latins. A truck driver for Inland Steel from Kentucky discoursed rhapsodically in Mrs. Green's hotel about the heaping platters of farm fare back home. As noted above, one Negro middle-class lady from Memphis said that soul food kept the colored people from getting the rare diseases of the whites. A Puerto Rican housewife indignantly denied that Puerto Ricans had no dishes of their own to compare with those nationally publicized by the Mexicans, and she reeled off a string of recipes. The best restaurant in Gary, now enveloped by the Negro ghetto, was Greek. Ethnic restaurants tended to take on the character of social clubs. From southern hillbilly to Romanian, the people of Steel City cherished their foods.

Another dimension of folk culture to be fathomed is personal history. There are thousands of sagas created from life experiences that deserve, indeed cry for, recording. The folklorist need not worry about their relation to the oral genres.

---

[9] Harriet M. Pawlowska, *Merrily We Sing: 105 Polish Folksongs* (Detroit, 1961); Susie Hoogasian-Villa, *One Hundred Armenian Folktales* (Detroit, 1966).

Here are precious oral narratives dealing with a series of great folk movements—from the southern states, from Mexico and Puerto Rico, from eastern Europe—and this migration should be described in terms of humanity as well as of mass statistics. No discipline other than folklore looks in this direction. Oral history is concerned with the elite, anthropology with underdeveloped countries, sociology with social organization. The personal history may well be a genre of its own, honed and structured through periodic retellings. It is at any rate a fluent oral form on the lips of a number of tellers. Several memorable life stories came to my ears with virtually no prompting. The relation by seventy-three-year-old Laura P., the frail mother of a double amputee, Bill, about the long travail and cheerful endurance of her son, fits into no known formula. It was a heart-rending account of hospitalization and surgery, despair and grief, but without particular overtones of prejudice or poverty. On reflection the history seems to belong with what Charles Keil has called the role of the Negro in America as one long sacrificial ritual. Victor L., who had come from Mexico in 1906; Edward B., who had been born in the Guiana forest; Zlatko K. from Croatia, dying of cancer at eighty-two—all launched promptly into detailed life histories. Certain incidents are clearly traditional, such as the comic misadventures of the newly arrived immigrant.

3. THE ROLE OF THE SPOKEN WORD. The culture of Gary-East Chicago is largely an oral culture, in the sense that talk flows freely. Television has not displaced conversation; the Book-of-the-Month Club pretensions of the middle class are little in evidence. Especially is this true for the Negro, bearing out the claims of Abrahams and Keil that the black ghetto is an auditory and tactile as opposed to a visual and literate culture, with the man of words as the culture hero. In the immigrant groups the potential man of words is often hampered by his inadequacy with English, although the desire to communicate will not be denied. I think of the long evening with Walter and Milly T. in which they conveyed all kinds of information through a limited English vocabulary. The Negro man of words appeared as preacher-entertainer, gospel singer turned preacher plus steelworker, athlete turned preacher plus steelworker, and preacher turned civil rights leader. The three superb speeches given in the Calvary Baptist Church during Negro history week, by a young bank manager, a lady sociologist, and a city official stand out in my mind in contrast to the suffocatingly dull seminar on Gary's Model City project held at Bloomington, at which professional educators mouthed their irrelevant jargon.

4. THE ROLE OF THE BOOK. If this is not a highly literate society, nevertheless it is a society that greatly values special book publications for their symbolic value. In one group after another I encountered references to, demonstration of, and sometimes even the bestowal of a cherished tome. These books shared two common factors: they were far off the main stream of American publishing, often being issued with obscure imprints, and they served to reinforce cherished elements of the folk inheritance. When Chetniks spoke of their sufferings at the hands of the hated Ustashis and recorded on tape examples of atrocities they had personally beheld, they regularly alluded to and produced printed evidence to substantiate their statements, such as the pamphlet Walter T. gave me, *The Crime of Genocide*, and the book, *Genocide in Satellite Croatia*, men-

tioned previously. My last evening in Gary I saw Walter at the dance entertainment in St. Sava Hall, again distributing paperback books in Serbian. They were by Lazo Kostich, now living in Switzerland, and author of over fifty books documenting the atrocities that had taken the lives of two million Serbs in World War II. "He is defending my blood," said Walter simply. In the Greek coffeehouse, owner Delos K. proudly brought forth a history of the Greek settlement of sponge fishermen at Tarpon Springs, Florida, *Strangers at Ithaca.*

Another kind of book reinforcement supported ethnic pride in historical achievements customarily ignored in majority group histories. An eloquent Polish patriot in Gary with his own Polish-language radio program, T. Stan Dubiak, told me that there were 127 Polish-American organizations in Lake County. He complained about the Poles being left out of American history and triumphantly produced a volume, *Jamestown Pioneers from Poland 1608–1958,* documenting the presence of Polish colonists at Jamestown. In my interview with seventy-year-old Todd R., a retired Negro steelworker born in Alabama, I was astonished at his ability to produce little-known facts, names, and dates of Negro history, coupled with his dearth of folklore. Eventually he showed me two battered booklets, an *Afro-American World Almanac* and *A Tribute to Achievement.* Similarly Elder George M. in his preaching at the Primitive Baptist Church, although he could not read, relied for his impressive citations of Negro accomplishments on a book his wife read to him, *World's Great Men of Color 3000 B.C. to 1946 A.D.*

Books could be feared as well as cherished. The study by Samora and Lamanna, *Mexican-Americans in a Midwest Metropolis: A Study of East Chicago,* is a case in point. The fury it aroused in the Mexican community made the sale of the work impossible. The concept of the book in these instances is wholly different from the attitude toward books of casual bookbuyers and book readers. These books have a talismanic character, and they are unique, not simply titles in a library.

5. OTHER ARTIFACTS OF TRADITION. If a symbolic book serves as an artifact tangibly reinforcing the traditional culture, it can be joined by many other artifacts of more than sentimental worth. These physical objects decorate the home or clubroom and fill the closets and drawers, and the ethnofolklorist should seek to inventory them. They may take the form of old country costumes for ceremonial occasions, portraits of national heroes like Draža Mihajlovich, musical instruments like the *gusle* and tambour, or recordings obtained from the old country. Walter T. played for me a tape recording he had made in Belgrade of a record of a Serbian folksong being played on a local radio station. In the Greek coffeehouse a ship model named *Kalymnos* and two giant sponges refreshed club members' memories of their island birthplace and occupation. As the folklorist today is enlarging his vision to include folklife, so in dealing with nationality groups he should pay special heed to the transported and imported items of material culture that help to bridge the chasm between the Old World and the New.

6. REINFORCEMENT. The two preceding points lead into a related matter, the idea of reinforcement of the parent culture through continuous contacts. This concept, which I earlier suggested in *American Folklore,* contradicts the stereotype of the immigrant, northern Negro, Appalachian white, urban Puerto Rican, or Mexican as cut off abruptly and irrevocably from his traditions in an

47

alien and hostile environment.[10] In one instance after another, in every one of these groups, the evidence accumulates as to the continuing links with the *heimat*, through visits—by the American-born as well as the foreign-born or northern-born—correspondence, bringing of relatives or mates to the metropolis, and subscription to foreign-language periodicals and newspapers. The case of Bishop Varnava Nastich is a classic example of the linkage between Europe and America, reversing the immigration pattern as the Gary-born Serb returned to Yugoslavia to become the first American bishop in the Serbian Orthodox Church and a rallying figure for Gary anti-Communists. The bishop's cousin in Gary, Emily B., possesses extensive files on Nastich—reams of eloquent letters, half in English, half in Serbian; photographs; and clippings from American newspapers and Serbian publications. Daisy Wuletich and her mother described to me in close detail their visit with the bishop in the monastery in Beocin. The Nastich episode of course involves high drama, but in the regular course of events the dwellers in Gary and East Chicago scheduled trips to their places of birth or those of their parents.

The effect of this intermittent but consistent reinforcement needs to be measured. Once Harold M. told me that the pastor at his church, Trinity Baptist, had noticeably reverted to southern-style preaching after a vacation in Arkansas. Further inquiry can lead to subdivisions within the transplanted cultures. The Gary Greeks meet in separate coffeehouses according to their islands or mainland communities of origin; the Negroes join churches whose pastors come from their own southern states; the Croats in northwest Indiana address each other by nicknames designating the valleys and hillsides of their youth. Presumably reinforcement from these distinguishable backgrounds will show different shadings, just as dialects vary between regions.

7. CULTURAL PLURALISM. The generalizations offered under the preceding headings must be countered by another generalization, that each cultural group is unique in terms of its folklore retentions and pattern of assimilation and acculturation. Negroes may look upon all white people as "Whitey," northerners may lump Mexicans and Puerto Ricans together as Latins, WASPs may speak in the aggregate of eastern Europeans, city dwellers may call all southern migrants hillbillies, and these terms themselves are revealing of cultural attitudes and stereotypes. One does not need to spend much time in the field to appreciate the considerable differences that exist between ethnic and racial groups in their degree of folk-cultural tenacity.

The Serbs and the Croats provide a good illustration, since they are usually conjoined in the minds of outsiders, and their language, although written in different alphabets, is called Serbo-Croatian. But the Serbs are much more tradition-oriented than the Croats. One reason is the Church and another is the State. The Serbian Orthodox Church unites the American Serbs—or disunites them into two warring factions in the present ecclesiastical dispute—but it at least keeps aflame their national conscience. The Croats are swallowed up in the Roman Catholic Church and will mingle more with other Catholic ethnic groups such as the Poles and Italians. Serbia has its history as an independent state and a subjugated

---

[10] *American Folklore*, 156.

nation under the Turks to inspire her expatriates with heroes, legends, and tragic epics; but Croatia was a province submerged in the Austro-Hungarian empire, with little historical tradition to call its own. As John Sertich put it, the Croats were tribal rather than national, never having had their own king. The legend of Bishop Varnava Nastich grew out of the Gary Serbian community and could never have developed among the Gary Croatians. This is not to deny the American Croats their ties to old country and their interest in folk music and costume, as in the *tamburitzan* ensembles. The question here is one of degree and density of cultural conservatism.

Similar contrasts came to the surface after some inquiries about differences between Mexicans and Puerto Ricans. The latter fitted more easily into Gary-East Chicago because they had already lived under the American flag. The former supposedly worked better in the steel mills because they were accustomed to heat. Mexicans wed Indians and Puerto Ricans wed Negroes. In terms of tradition, the Mexican seemed much stronger, again because of a national history as a frame of reference. Mexican ethnic cuisine has become part of the national restaurant business, while Puerto Rican dishes are unknown.

One factor in assessing cultural pluralism and its effect on folklore is the dilution that occurs, or may occur, through intermarriage. A Croat who had remarried to a Lithuanian said that his children had no tradition. A young Mexican woman related she had once dated a Greek boy, but with the understanding that they would never marry, for the Greeks always stayed together. Marty G., the son of a Mexican father and a southern Appalachian mother whom I recorded for a long pleasant hour, called himself a "Mexican hillbilly," but his inheritance appeared to be all on the hillbilly side. He spoke with intimate knowledge, sympathy, and wit about the "stumpjumpers," "ridgerunners," and "crackers" of the South. My own judgment, until other evidence appears, is that ethnic traditions do not blend in a mixed marriage but either cancel each other out or result in one triumphing.

8. ETHNIC SEPARATISM. The present urban field experience supports my previous findings in rural areas that the strong force of what I call ethnic separatism keeps the in-group folklores apart; they cannot cross into each other's zones. It is the individual who must cross into the life experience of another group to absorb the traditions of that group. Twice I recorded tales in East Chicago from Puerto Ricans married to Negro women who had never heard, and expressed astonishment at, their husbands' narrations. Puerto Ricans and Mexicans share the same language and faith, but their folklore follows different channels. The Puerto Rican *botánica* or magic-herb store and the Mexican *curandera* or magic healer are separate and distinct. *Susto* has special connotations to Mexicans and Mexican-Americans, who believe that *susto* is induced by some supernatural or magical means; but the Puerto Rican lawyer representing the Latin American organization of Gary and East Chicago and who knew all about the *botánica*. drew a blank on any special significance of *susto*, and was astonished to learn that his Mexican secretary did react to the word.

Folk prejudices as well as cultural inertia contribute to ethnic separatism. In a conversation with Katie S. about the soul food prized by the colored people, I thought to ask her if she had ever tried Mexican dishes. Yes, she had tried *tacos* and rather liked them until she heard they were made from dead cats. Calling on a Slovak celebrating his fiftieth wedding anniversary, I elicited no folklore but did receive one double-barreled folk hatred: "I never see a picture like mine [of his golden wedding] for a Czech; they have twenty wives, like niggers."

9. THE URBAN SYNTHESIS. Yet if the migrant groups in Steel City never penetrate each other's folklore, or perhaps even each other's homes, they do share the environment, the living experience, and perforce the lore of their new abode. People are marked by living in Gary or East Chicago, for these are uncommon cities, just as the Upper Peninsula of Michigan is an uncommon region leaving its imprint on all its inhabitants. The pervasive themes of Gary-East Chicago binding its people into a new folk community are steel, crime, and the racial-ethnic mix.

Steel created Gary, and the great mills whose furnaces must burn twenty-four hours a day is the number one fact of life in Gary and its environs. Some day perhaps an urban folklorist will write a "Folklore of the Steel Industry" to match Mody Boatright's *Folklore of the Oil Industry*. Meanwhile anyone can hear little stories about steelworkers, for instance about problems in communication. A Romanian crane operator worked for thirty-nine years in Inland Steel without learning English. During my stay an injured worker brought to the infirmary at Inland could not make his ailment known, although a nurse present tried speaking to him in Polish. The staff had to send back to the patient's unit to learn he was a Serb. These incidents get talked about and lay the ground for a new body of anecdotes based on the age-old motif of language misunderstanding. The human side of steel inevitably involves ethnic and racial humor and *blason populaire*. Crime stories and fears are an outgrowth of the contemporary industrial city and the Negro ghetto. Everyone is apprehensive—whites and blacks—and talk swirls around hold-ups, beatings, and murders. One of my informants, Marty G., father of seven, was murdered with his wife not long after I recorded him: no clues, no motives. One evening when I was interviewing a group of East Chicago Serb adherents to the mother church, one man present, a policeman, interrupted the thread of our discussion to tell about several recent crime incidents. At the time I was impatient to get back to our main topic, but now I realize that he was dealing with a central theme of Gary-East Chicago lore. One incident dealt with the refusal of a storeowner and his wife, who had just been robbed, to identify their Negro assailant, found with their goods and the owner's wallet in his car. After the suspect's release, the police officer asked the couple why they had refused to make the identification. "Well, we have to live there after you leave. Let them have a few bundles of clothes. Better than to have his friends come back and burn the place down."

A brief summary of a long evening's conversation with three southern-born Negroes, all steelworkers, may further illustrate the newly evolving urban synthesis. They were my friend Harold M., an official in a labor union; Ben D., a former professional gospel singer now preacher at the Macedonian Baptist Church; and Ben T., his former manager and now his deacon. The first half of the conversation turned on life in the South, on methods of cotton-picking, frauds in the poultry business run by Italians in New Orleans, and managing spiritual singers. During these recollections I was able to record half a dozen familiar folk-

50

tales, such as "Dividing Souls" and "Why the Fox Has a Short Tail." For the second part of the evening the talk shifted to northern life, the labor unions, the Syndicate, and the political machine. Ben T. made sweeping and authoritative pronouncements: eighty-five percent of the people in Gary were from the South; Gary, and the world at large, were run by syndicates. He and Harold fell to comparing personalities in the unions and swapped accounts of the attempt by Democratic party forces to bribe union officials to swing votes against Dick Hatcher. Union grievance committeemen had each been given $250; half of them simply pocketed the money without acting. Ben talked at length about "snitching." Down south the black snitcher ran to Uncle Charlie, who protected him from the law, but up north the whites were the worst snitchers. The snitchers often had done the job themselves. One who was caught begged not to be sent to the "Peniten" but to the State Prison, because he knew he would be killed by the people he had snitched on. Ben ended these remarks by saying that Gary is the city of steel and that life revolved around the pay check every two weeks. Harold, a good talker but no storyteller, did think of two steel mill stories, one about an eccentric worker called "Old Man Shouting Robertson" and another about a lazy dog named Superintendent.

This full measure of talk, grossly synopsized here, suggests the shift from southern memories to northern conditions in the minds of migrants from the South, and the dominant themes of the races—petty and major crime and work in the steel plants, generating factual and finally fictional anecdotes. In the course of my sojourn I heard two fantasies in what may be an evolving legend of Richard Hatcher, the first Negro mayor of Gary. The more naturalistic ascribed to him a romance with a Jewish woman in Glen Park, which had gained him the Jewish vote, ordinarily bitterly anti-Negro. The second, propounded by a visiting television personality calling himself Psychic, held that Hatcher was actually the reincarnation of a southern white slave owner. This I heard from Harold M. Separate and divided as are the ethnic-race groups of Gary, all share participation in, and reaction to, the election of their Negro mayor. From this shared experience emerges the lore of the city.

These currents of city talk sometimes carry floating seeds of legend. On three occasions I heard the related legends of the Vanishing Hitchhiker and La Llorona, localized on Cline Avenue in East Chicago and the swampy Cudahy strip between East Chicago and Gary. A young Mexican-American, Tilly L., told me that her brother, a cab-driver, had been interviewed on television after picking up a woman often sighted and picked up on Cline Avenue by passing motorists, who found her gone from their vehicles when they arrived at the address she gave them as her destination. The newspapers had publicized the story. The related incident concerned a passionate murder of a woman in Cudahy whose wraith was frequently seen and identified by the Mexicans with La Llorona, the weeping lady-ghost mourning her lost children. An elderly but vigorous Mexican, Victor L., who narrated to me his life story for two hours without drawing breath, knew at firsthand the Cudahy murderer, a fellow-worker in the mill, and had seen his shooting of a husky man who tried to stop him the night he ran amok. Victor's son, born in East Chicago, explained that La Llorona was adapted to local events.

10. EXCEPTIONS TO STEREOTYPES. A plurality of cultures exists in Steel

51

City, going their own ways and not simmering in a melting pot. But if it is a mistake to treat all these folk cultures as equal in their rate of acculturation, it is a comparable error to treat all the individuals in the same cultural group as interchangeable parts. In the American scene—with its high mobility and unexpected juxtapositions, accentuated in urban settings—endless surprises occur. The individual breaks out of his stereotype frequently enough so that deviation itself becomes an acceptable concept.

A number of examples came to my attention in the Gary-East Chicago field trip. The most dramatic involved the Polish precinct-worker of the Democratic party, Marion Tokarsky, who broke with her ethnic, political, and religious allegiances to make common cause with the ghetto Negroes and support the Negro mayoralty candidate. Here was an unpredictable phenomenon, the Polish Catholic immigrant befriending her Negro enemies and explaining to them the supernatural-Catholic basis of her decision, to which they responded in the style and manner of the Baptist congregation. Other illustrations of deviancy can be given. The seventy-five-year old Mexican *curandera* in Indiana Harbor, Mrs. Tomasita G., who dictated formulaic cures for *susto* in Spanish into my tape-recorder, proved to be a Mormon. On Sundays she made two trips to Highland to attend services at the Mormon church there, although the old Catholic church was just around the corner, and her foster-son and his wife came across town out of loyalty to that church, when they could have gone to a nearer Catholic church in East Chicago. The president of the Northern Indiana Political Action Alliance that Marion Tokarsky addressed was not a southern or northern Negro but a native of British Guiana, who in his youth identified with the British ruling class and looked down upon the East Indian servants on his plantation. When Edward B. came to the United States, he was astonished to discover that Negroes were second-class citizens. He had married a Negro woman from Georgia.

In the *Indiana Alumni Magazine* I read about Fedor C., who had come to America as a refugee from the Nazis and Communists, knowing no English. He had worked in the steel mills, taken courses, and become chairman of the political science department at the Northwest Campus of Indiana University. In Gary I spent an evening with Fedor and his wife Astrid and discovered that, while no fact in the magazine account was untrue, the stereotype presented was completely false. The couple were gifted and attractive intellectuals, university-trained, cosmopolitan, and sophisticated. Their life stories, which they told readily into the tape recorder, are extraordinary human documents; but they have no relation to the conventional saga of the immigrant. Again, from Victor L., Jr., I heard contradictions of the Puerto Rican stereotype, for instance, that all Puerto Ricans had Negro blood and hence would move into and marry within the American Negro community. There were indeed Puerto Rican Negro couples whom I met in East Chicago. But Victor knew whereof he spoke, for he was an Indiana-born Mexican married to a redhaired, fairskinned Puerto Rican girl, whom he had to court in the face of protective Castilian-type chaperones.

The answer to the original query, "Is there a folk in the city?" must clearly be yes. Perhaps it is best to say that there are many folk groups, who in Gary and East Chicago are becoming a city folk. But city folk are different from the country folk of yesteryear, and the folklorist exploring their ways must drastically revise

52

his own traditional concepts of the folk and their lore. Yet the city is indeed a proper field for him to cultivate. If in North Uist, with its population decimated and a century of intensive collecting already achieved, John MacInnes can still say that he will never plumb all the layers of tradition, imagine how many lifetimes would be needed to explore the multiple folk cultures of Gary and East Chicago.

APPENDIX

The tangible results of this field trip—on which this paper is based—are nine tapes of twelve hundred feet played at one and seven-eighths speed and one tape of choral singing played at seven and one-half; notes on some fifty-three interviews; a diary written each evening running to ninety typed pages; and a box of books, pamphlets, leaflets, typescripts, and even a Puerto Rican straw hat and record album, given me by my new acquaintances—often books cherished and dear to them—as evidences and documents of their traditions and assertions. The interviews are divided as follows: Negro 15, Serbian 8, Mexican 7, Puerto Rican 5, Croatian 5, Greek 3, other 10. "Other" includes a Romanian couple, three Poles, two Italians, two Slovaks, one "Mexican hillbilly," and a daughter of a Sioux Indian mother and an Italian father. "Interview" is a formal word covering all kinds of meetings, sometimes with one, sometimes with several persons present, sometimes a chance encounter, sometimes an arranged appointment. Besides personal talks of some intimacy, I should also include attendance at four Negro church services on successive Sunday mornings, at a Negro choral performance, and at a program on Negro history given in Negro churches on two Sunday afternoons; a tour through Inland Steel, a luncheon-seminar and convocation lecture for and by Mayor Hatcher, for which I flew from Gary to Bloomington and back one day on the Indiana University plane; a spirited local production of "The Roar of the Greasepaint, the Smell of the Crowd," which as a review pointed out, curiously fit into the Gary milieu; and a Serbian musical program at St. Sava Church.

MORTON LEEDS

The Process of Cultural Stripping and Reintegration

The Rural Migrant in the City

WHAT HAPPENS IN THE MIGRATION to the city of people from the farm, the hill lands, and the small towns of the South is of critical importance to those of us who must deal with the cities of today. What follows may serve as a brief sketch of the movement to urban areas by the rural or small-town resident, who comes to seek a new life. A few rough indexes of the change process will be reviewed, as physical and social measures of what happens to family life when a move occurs. The picture is complicated, of course, by the problem of color, since moving is obviously not identical for the white and the Negro. For purposes of this analysis, however, they will be treated as a single group, since some universal elements are being sought.

In analyzing the problem of poverty and color, we discover the interesting fact that in absolute numbers there are more than twice as many poor whites as there are poor Negroes. This in part derives from the fact that whites outnumber Negroes nine to one. As measured by income levels, only 10 percent of white families had incomes below poverty levels in 1966, whereas 35 percent of the nonwhite families fell in this bracket. In absolute figures, this comes to 20.1 million whites, and 9.6 million nonwhites. Incidence of poverty, therefore, is three and a half times as great among Negroes.[1] The Negro problem is complicated by the social factor of caste discrimination—which combined with poverty, poor housing, poor education, and other forms of economic discrimination produces the tensions being seen in the cities today. Poverty is bad enough; but social discrimination makes it unbearable, particularly when television makes the discrimination obvious. The effect of TV as a social equalizing and disturbing force probably has not been correctly assessed as yet.

The drift to the great cities derives from the agricultural revolution, more than likely as great an agent of social change as any our society has experienced, but one that is further complicated by the roaring upsurge of our industrial capacity.

[1] Herman P. Miller and Dorothy K. Newman, *Social and Economic Conditions of Negroes in the United States* (Washington, D. C., 1967) 22, 25.

JOURNAL OF AMERICAN FOLKLORE, 1970, Vol. 83, No. 328, pp. 259-267.

The problem we now face is not one of ability to produce enough for all, but rather how shall it be distributed equitably within the framework of a work-oriented society with not enough actual work for all. Fortunately, that problem is not our immediate concern. Rather, we are examining the social and cultural byproducts of the industrial change, as rural and small town residents enter the city and try to drop old ways for new.[2] This is not a new problem for us. It has been going on for more than a century as Europe's poor came here, assimilated into the culture, and raised their children to be middle-class Americans.[3] The difference this time is that we are trying to assimilate our own rural poor, who have a far stronger claim on the resources of the culture.

The driving force behind the move from rural to urban areas is largely economic, with some social pressures as well. A collapse of the small-farm economy has taken place during the past generation, in part triggered by large-scale industrial farming. City life has always served as a positive lure, but with the rapid development of industrialization, physical movement from the land has accelerated. For the rural poor, the city is a great, bright, noisy, exciting, and sinful place. Its rates of pay are far better, its facilities and services incomparably superior to that offered by the small, rural community or by farm life in general. The penalties and frustrations inherent in the process of a move into an urban society are always present in the back of the migrant's mind, but they tend to be subordinated when economic pressure becomes too great to bear.

The Movement From Rural Lower Class to Urban Lower Class

When the move occurs, it has its impact on all areas of social existence. The American rural family, based on the extended family, includes the nuclear parent-children group as well as the grandparents, unmarried siblings of the parents, and additional relatives, who may represent broken families or unmarried individuals. In the city this extended family may begin to break up, with the nuclear two-generation family tending to be the norm. Grandparents with sources of income, such as social security or old-age assistance payments, or unmarried mothers on relief can be prized for their economic contribution. In such instances, they may be a welcome addition to the nuclear group. The children are primarily occupied with school and spend much of their free time in the streets. For them the change in life style is almost as significant as it is for the men. Since the density of urban living produces a large group of peers with whom it is easy to identify, the norms of the children tend to separate from those of their parents, and their expectations rise rapidly, far outstripping those of the older generation.

The farm family works as a unit on the land. Farm duties are assigned to each

[2] Some of the better works on the subject include Nathan Glazer and D. P. Moynihan, *Beyond the Melting Pot* (Cambridge, Mass., 1963); M. M. Gordon, *Assimilation in American Life: The Role of Race, Religion and National Origins* (New York, 1964); John Gulich, C. E. Bowerman, and K. W. Bach, "Newcomer Enculturation in the City; Attitudes and Participation," in *Urban Growth Dynamics,* ed. F. S. Chapin, Jr., and S. F. Weis (New York, 1962), 315–358; Oscar Handlin, *The Uprooted,* (Boston, 1951); A. M. Rose and Leon Warshay, "The Adjustment of Migrants to Cities," *Social Forces,* 36 (1957), 72–76. Lee Taylor and A. R. Jones, Jr., *Rural Life and Urbanized Society* (New York, 1964).

[3] A surprising parallel to the current problems posed by the Southern migration to the cities appears in W. I. Thomas and Florian Znaniecki, *The Polish Peasant in Europe and America,* 2 vols. (New York, 1927).

physically capable member of the family, regardless of age or sex. Certain of the chores derive from physical limitations while others are traditionally assigned to certain types of individuals. The farm economy involves little cash and is tightly geared to the price of farm products, since the sale of these items is the chief cash income. There is a residual economic strength, however, for those living on the farm. Food can be raised directly; and where the talent, the land, and the weather are favorable, the family if nothing else is assured of food and shelter. For the share-cropper and the tenant farmer this is less true, of course, depending on individual circumstances, and for the migrant farm worker it does not apply at all. Upon the shift to the city everything changes rapidly. The sense of relatedness to the physical world is immediately severed. The men work when they can find employment. The women tend to work more regularly, finding employment in the more menial and poorer paying jobs—as domestics, laundry workers, and unskilled factory workers, for example. For the children there is little opportunity to work, except running itinerant errands and doing the small jobs that no adult would accept.

Farm food is usually home-grown and frequently adequate. For those living on the small farm especially, only certain types of foods have to be obtained from the grocery. Certain favorite foods tend to be repeatedly used on farms, particularly where the economic level is low. The city offers a much broader variety, but also a necessary reliance on canned and partially prepared foods. Quality is only fair in the poorer areas; although fresh vegetables and familiar farm foods are sought after, they are not always available. The price differential between the rural area and the city can be quite great, especially when price and quality gouging occurs.

The dialects of the southern farm or rural area vary locally. There is a very strong reliance on parochial, esoteric, and regional speech. Whole groups of consonants may vanish from the speech, so that it becomes almost unrecognizable to those in the North or Far West. The change in language usage on arrival in the city tends to be less drastic than changes involving other factors, because the family normally will follow other relatives to a given city. Since the immediate environment is parochial and protective, it is some time before language begins to change. When it does, it appears in the form of accretion and agglomeration on the rural linguistic base, although loss of regional accent does take place upon further acculturation. For the young, change can sometimes be very dramatic when peer-group contacts produce specialized in-group language forms. In school the child is subjected to stereotyped middle-class linguistic presentations that are assimilated with various degrees of effectiveness. For the child well-integrated into family life, school language becomes a second language that is used first in school and then in later life. For the ambitious, bright, or perceptive child, however, school language becomes a vehicle for leaving the family environment when this becomes desirable.

In rural areas work clothes are the daily norm, with the stress on cleanliness and durability rather than style, cut, color, or match. A special set of clothes is kept for Sunday, church, or holiday observance. Upon the family's moving to the city, the clothing pattern does not change very much, except that there is less reliance on jeans and more on cheap imitations of middle-class daily clothes.

Farm and rural life is monotonous with continuous work, particularly during the growing season, and long stretches of inactivity during cold weather. Special occasions include weekly dances, mainly on Saturday night, church picnics on Sunday afternoons, ritual holiday events, periodic fairs around the harvest time, plus some hunting and fishing in season. Alcohol, though used covertly, is overtly frowned upon. In the city this pattern changes—on Friday and Saturday nights there are parties, T.V. is the daily staple, and mass spectator events occur frequently. Holidays become less important. Alcohol is heavily used as a social catalyst, with less disapproval expressed over its use.

Rural education is inadequate, tends to be extremely short—generally for eight or fewer years—with the school year shorter than in the city because of the nature of farming and farm duties. In a thin population, several grades may be grouped simultaneously. Equipment and facilities tend to be inadequate, and there is not too much variety. The lower class urban school has some of the deficiencies of rural education, plus some additional ones.[4] Density is high instead of low, producing highly fractionized age groups. Peer group identification becomes very strong, and there is a weakening of interage relationships. Facilities and equipment are not particularly good. Classes tend to be much larger, with poor student discipline. Academic standards, however, tend to be somewhat more demanding than in rural areas, and schooling tends to be longer, without the special demands of family chores on the land.

The Penalties of Movement to the City

The family and the individuals composing it can move in several directions: either laterally, remaining in the lower class without major change; downward, with collapse of the family and the shattering of its social and economic role; or upward into the lower middle-class by dint of great effort and good fortune. Lateral movement essentially involves a treadmill status, producing no major forward movement. This can occur where the family slowly begins to perceive urban norms and expands its wants slowly, as it expands its earning ability, but never enough to accrue capital or skills that would permit its members to move ahead in a class sense. Such a family within a few years develops a real sense of frustration and in some ways is worse off than the rural family without aspirations. City life becomes an exhausting dead-end, and such families truly lead lives of quiet desperation. Their one source of strength is the knowledge that they are not at the bottom of the social heap. The future is dim in general, but they do have their self-respect and integrity as a family, and they can cling to these for whatever they are worth. Their children, at least, may break out of the mold, and in many cases they do.

For many families, migration to the city is destructive. Previously, the man was the center of the family, and around his daily farm work the fears and aspirations of his wife and children could revolve. Though poor, they at least drew upon a centuries-long heritage of male dominance and relatedness to the land that supported them. The family's structure was supported and rarely challenged. The city provides a different setting. The man frequently cannot find work, or what work he can find is part-time, unskilled, undemanding, and demeaning. The work, in a

---

[4] For the social and educational tragedies that can take place in urban lower-class schools see Jonathan Kozol, *Death at an Early Age* (Boston, 1967).

sense, demands only part of the man and thereby makes him less of a whole man. A vast job hierarchy looms over the unskilled man, and he is at the bottom of the structure. Worst of all, he is without education and committed to remain at the bottom for most of his job life. Where skills, intelligence, adaptability, emotional make-up, or physical handicap stand in the way, the picture is even bleaker, since the man begins with further hazards to adequate employment.

But the demands of the city are relentless. The children are trying to go to school and need city clothes. Television, that most subversive of technical developments, offers a fairy box of the unattainable. To help meet these pressures the wife goes to work, and still further family problems arise. Her earnings may be steadier than her husband's, despite the menial character of her work. But the children may be neglected most of the day, and slowly the family pattern is reshaped. In some families the man breaks away, and the fatherless household appears.[5] Temporary husbands, illegitimacy, and the attendant train of full family disorganization are thereby set into motion. Squalor, poverty, illness, and unemployment reinforce each other, and the disruptive cycle is in full operation.

Economic problems, then, are central to social disorganization and represent much of the difference between the lower-class working family and the disorganized slum family. Steady work and a regular source of income, in effect, mark the difference between the two groups. Welfare for the disorganized family is not only a holding action but frequently a future disorganizing force, since the essential thrust of current welfare programs is maintenance of the *status quo*. As a result, many families continue the cycle of disorganization through several generations.

The disorganized family gets food when it can, at levels that match the income. Food tends to be starchy and fatty, cheap and inadequate, a pale echo of the poor farmer's fare that at least could count on the standard staples of corn, hominy, fowl, and eggs. While there is famine much of the time, the sudden arrival of a check, a visiting relative, or a temporary break of good fortune, is the cause for feasting and a temporary abundance of the good edibles of life. On such occasions the extended family or guests may be invited to share one's fortune.

The slum language demonstrates the qualities of a genuine subculture. Slang predominates; there are a great many local references that derive from the community's character, industry, and immediate qualities. Colloquial forms are heavily used. The choice of words is concrete and extremely picturesque. Since the written forms are subordinated or absent, vernacular forms tend to take over. Speech, therefore, can evolve fairly rapidly, breaking out of the written mold. The slum culture is largely unrecorded; therefore, language becomes the mirror of a rapid evolution. This is one of the areas where the slum has a great deal to contribute to the upper levels of the society. Interpersonal relationships become important, and forms of verbal jousting and personal contending take on a structurally ritualized but verbally more creative content. This is especially true of male-female interactions, where one wishes to take advantage of or predominate over the other. At times, they resemble the parlor games of another leisure class, the upper class.

Clothing in the slums consists of hand-me-downs, the tired, worn clothes that may have been brought from the farm, were made available by more affluent rela-

[5] A highly personal example is shown in Dick Gregory's *Nigger* (New York, 1964).

58

tives, or were bought in second-hand stores. Sometimes, in moments of temporary affluence, there will be an expensive purchase of special shoes or a hat, standing as a kind of wild waving in the wind of human aspiration.

Recreation at this level takes on a special quality. Banter and street play become quite important. It is as if the challenge of everyday living has proved overwhelming and there has been a regression to childish norms and standards. The man whose role is shattered will very often engage in adolescent behavior or street corner play, messing or fooling around, deriving personal advantage through ability to show off or demonstrate his importance. This is highly ritualized behavior that provides many secondary gains. Saturday night remains important for formal recreation, although many recreation events may go on for days at a time depending upon new resources and assets and the influx of new personnel. Activity at this level interweaves with the marginal or illegal sector and becomes in part an economic standby for the slum dweller, while serving as recreation for the middle-class or lower-class person. This would include the numbers game, crap games, card playing, and race betting, since they may have economic overtones. The same events, then, can have different meanings for different classes. The participants, too, may feed off the illegal activities as suppliers of refreshments or as procurers and pimps. Successful members of such groups, of course, may have an opportunity for upward mobility, enabling them to break out of the slum.

The slum school can become a kind of babysitting service that in part serves to keep the children off the street. Teachers, schools, books, libraries, and equipment tend to be inadequate for the problems at hand, and the picture of hopelessness is tragic, since the school in our society represents the key to the future. A hopeless school means a hopeless younger generation, and a custodial school represents the illusion of progress. The education that comes through interpersonal peer group experience becomes transcendent and represents far more powerful norms than those of a discredited school system. When schooling is rejected, the teacher is seen as a model of failure, and the school experience is seen as something to be ridden through like a storm. For some children with fully disorganized families, however, school can be a refuge, if only because the child experiences less direct anger, frustrations, and aggression and more of a sense of searching for unknown answers than at home.

The Rewards of Movement to the City

For the farm family that maintains its sense of coherence—with strong parental guidance, a fortunate choice in economic skills, good ties to an ongoing business or industry, special personal characteristics, or just good fortune—the rewards of the city can be very great. The family trudges in the footsteps of those who have followed the American Dream. They dream the dreams of the past century, bearing special burdens but also winning the benefits that others have carved before them. The various socioeconomic cushions—such as unemployment insurance, social security benefits, medicare, and similar benefits—may help the family in its long march. A bright child can become the focus of the family's dreams. A hard-working mother can keep her fist in the dike of economic troubles and keep a family going through many vicissitudes. Family birth planning helps keep family needs under control, and church attendance does the same for personal aspirations, giving a sense of relatedness to the universe at large. Two generations under one roof become the norm. The family dreams of moving out of the slum neighborhood, and successively into better and better areas. Television serves as the constant spur, and the parents become quite choosy about a child's friends. Eventually, ownership of a car and of a home becomes the seal of the ascent into the middle class.

An interesting conflict comes into play with the choice of foods since attachment to early dietary fare is one of the most persistent of cultural traits. The grandparents most of all, but the parents too, may continue their interest in lower-class food, while the children express a yearning for the newer, processed, more expensive foods now available in great variety. With the shift from one neighborhood to another better one, lower-class foods become less available, and the more standard American foods become the norm. The parents may have a desire for the foods of the farm, the fresh satisfying foods that become less and less available. In time, of course, the family tends to complete the change and to depend heavily upon frozen or prepared foods that require little or no cooking.

Again there is a conflict of generations as the children become accustomed to two languages. Those that adapt to middle-class norms have the greatest opportunities for advancement. They are the ones who can quickly adapt to and take on the protective coloration of urban middle-class vocabulary and pronunciation. They learn to read and write earlier and are subjected to a variety of verbal and intellectual stimulants. They step into the broad stream of the written English language and begin to assimilate another part of its cultural heritage. A dual vision proceeds for some time, however, since these children continue to transact with strong parents. The verbal limitations of the parents, whose norms are still those of the farm, gradually become obvious to the children. Sometimes loyalty is strained, but for the successful family the ties of affection override embarrassment at parental inadequacies.

At this stage clothing becomes a badge of change itself, and the tremendous stress Americans place on the formal presentation of self begins to show. The power of the adaptive dream goes into successful generations of clothing changes, so that the family slides more and more into ideal type patterns. Clothing becomes an expression of success. Clothing can conceal past origins too, as well as inadequate living arrangements, since the bulk of contacts with significant others take place outside the home. Clothing improvement is commensurate with, if not ahead of, the family's income. It becomes a mirror in which the family can interpret its increasing success. Clothing is changed more frequently to fit the special activity; specific clothes for sports and recreation, for gardening, for partying, or for special events are worn in imitation of the more affluent upper class.

The excitement of the slum, with its disorganized and haphazard daily and weekly events, slowly gives way to the more routinized life of the middle class. Television can be watched after homework has been done. The football game becomes a reward for personal diligence, and the Saturday night party becomes more restrained and decorous. Refreshments are more expensive, the more esoteric sports come to be followed or imitated, and special hobbies are taken up after the latest fashions. The children may be taught dancing, where previously they learned it from each other, and art lessons are encouraged to bring out creativity.

Education becomes the means of salvation; children are seen as extensions of parental dreams about what might have been as well as what might be. Children are pushed, prodded, lured, and intimidated into absorbing as much education as their minds will tolerate. Such attendance becomes a criterion by which the child is judged, and the rewards of affection and love are doled out generously to those who follow middle-class norms. Pressure for success is high; children are encouraged to go on to college wherever possible or to take specialized schooling that will prepare them for a proper class career. Schools are better, in better neighborhoods, and the accomplishments of the children reflect this. The rural child slides in beside his city cousins and, if he is adaptable, assimilates into the urban landscape.

Research Needs

There are a number of questions that we would like to see answered by anthropologists, ethnologists, sociologists, and psychologists. To what extent, for example, are capitalistic acquisitiveness and emergence from slum life related? How important, for instance, were Jewish tendencies toward business enterprise in the 1930s and 1940s to the resultant broad acceptance of the Jew in middle-class American life during the 1950s and 1960s? What does this mean for the Puerto Rican, who seems to be following in the footsteps of the Jew? Turning the question around, what kind of penalty, if any, is being levied against the Negro for the absence of such acquisitiveness? That is to say, is the Protestant ethic a significant barrier to the emergence of a Negro middle class in America? A puzzling question, a corollary to this one, would be, why are Catholic Puerto Ricans oriented toward small capitalism, while Protestant Negroes are not?

One of the factors in slum family failure is related to the male role in the family. How do we reinforce the male role in the slum family? The most obvious answers, of course, involve successful employment and disrupting the patterns of discrimination. Above and beyond this, however, it should be possible to understand more about family dynamics and how they can be used to reinforce father images and husband roles. Should the Negro, for instance, try harder to attain the medical professional role, at the top of the social heap? To what extent can Big Brother movements provide transitional role models for the fatherless child?

We need longitudinal studies of the ghetto family with follow-ups every decade or so. These can follow the patterns of Oscar Lewis, or other styles as well. Such studies could be very useful in revealing the dynamics of break-out from the ghetto, as well as increasing understanding about further entrenchment into the ghetto system. The dynamics and the gestalt of the ghetto family as a functioning or malfunctioning support system need to be explored in great detail. Certainly the positive factors exposed by successful break-out should be understood and where uncovered should be publicized. Some of the resultant findings could be extremely useful for helping families break out of successive generational patterns of slum living.

What is the relation between creativity and ethnicity? How much creativeness derives from the fact that one is different from the majority group, from a need to justify one's differences or to rationalize or interpret the differences? How many books like *Native Son* or *Invisible Man* would have remained unwritten in the absence of racial prejudice? How much of the protest literature of the 1930s produced by Jewish authors would have been aborted in a more congenial atmosphere? The neutral climate regarding Jews in the 1960s suggests some of the answers, but they are not definitive. This problem is a real one because creativity represents a wellspring from which many of a society's greatest achievements are derived. Social and ethnic differences demand a heavy price, but one that may produce significant fruit.

Margaret Mead has suggested that the upwardly mobile family can be helped to keep together as a cultural unit if all members of the family share in the education process. Can this be used as a technique for narrowing the intergenerational gap between slum parents and children? What are the essential ethnic characteristics that help us distinguish a subcultural group? Is it language? Food? Dress? Religious practices? Family organization? A combination of these? How can we help retain the most meaningful aspects of ethnic differences in subgroups without disrupting the larger society? What elements are meaningful and satisfying, providing differences but not disruption? What are the minimal differences that can be tolerated or encouraged?

Can a community be transferred to different locations and still retain the social and cultural ties that mark it as unique? This has special meaning not only for the southern rural and small-town migrants but also for local urban relocation programs that may inadvertently damage a cultural community. What are the differences in urban assimilation between the rural Negro and the white? What are the handicaps and the advantages for membership in each ethnic group? What are the rates of change, the sources of insecurity? A series of comparative studies, analyzing similar components, could be very useful in understanding the assimilation of these two quite different groups.

CONDITIONS OF LIFE IN THE RACIAL GHETTO

National Advisory Commission on Civil Disorders

The conditions of life in the racial ghetto are strikingly different from those to which most Americans are accustomed—especially white, middle-class Americans. We believe it important to describe these conditions and their effect on the lives of people who cannot escape from the ghetto.[1]

CRIME AND INSECURITY

Nothing is more fundamental to the quality of life in any area than the sense of personal security of its residents, and nothing affects this more than crime.

In general, crime rates in large cities are much higher than in other areas of our country. Within such cities, crime rates are higher in disadvantaged Negro areas than any where else.

The most widely used measure of crime is the number of "index crimes" (homicide, forcible rape, aggravated assault, robbery, burglary, grand larceny, and auto theft) in relation to population. In 1966, 1,754 such crimes were reported to police for every 100,000 Americans. In cities over 250,000, the rate was 3,153, and in cities over 1 million, it was 3,630—or more than double the national average. In suburban areas alone, including suburban

---

[1] We have not attempted here to describe conditions relating to the fundamental problems of housing, education, and welfare, which are treated in detail in later chapters.

From: REPORT OF THE NATIONAL ADVISORY COMMISSION ON CIVIL DISORDERS, March 1, 1968 (Washington: U.S. Gov't. Printing Office, pp. 133-141.

cities, the rate was only 1,300, or just over one-third the rate in the largest cities.

Within larger cities, personal and property insecurity has consistently been highest in the older neighborhoods encircling the downtown business district. In most cities, crime rates for many decades have been higher in these inner areas than anywhere, except in downtown areas themselves, where they are inflated by the small number of residents.

High crime rates have persisted in these inner areas even though the ethnic character of their residents continually changed. Poor immigrants used these areas as "entry ports," then usually moved on to more desirable neighborhoods as soon as they acquired enough resources. Many "entry port" areas have now become racial ghettos.

The difference between crime rates in these disadvantaged neighborhoods and in other parts of the city is usually startling, as a comparison of crime rates in five police districts in Chicago for 1965 illustrates. These five include one high-income, all-white district at the periphery of the city, two very low-income, virtually all-Negro districts near the city core with numerous public housing projects, and two predominantly white districts, one with mainly lower middle-income families, the other containing a mixture of very high-income and relatively low-income households. The table shows crime rates against persons and against property in these five districts, plus the number of patrolmen assigned to them per 100,000 residents, as follows:

TABLE 26-1. INCIDENCE OF INDEX CRIMES AND PATROLMEN ASSIGN-MENTS PER 100,000 RESIDENTS IN 5 CHICAGO POLICE DISTRICTS, 1965

Number	High-income white district	Low-middle income white district	Mixed high- and low-income white district	Very low-income Negro district No. 1	Very low-income Negro district No. 2
Index crimes against persons	80	440	338	1,615	2,820
Index crimes against property	1,038	1,750	2,080	2,508	2,630
Patrolmen assigned	93	133	115	243	291

These data indicate that:

Variations in the crime rate against persons within the city

64

are extremely large. One very low-income Negro district had 35 times as many serious crimes against persons per 100,000 residents as did the high-income white district.

Variations in the crime rate against property are much smaller. The highest rate was only 2.5 times larger than the lowest.

The lower the income in an area, the higher the crime rate there. Yet low-income Negro areas have significantly higher crime rates than low-income white areas. This reflects the high degree of social disorganization in Negro areas described in the previous chapter, as well as the fact that poor Negroes as a group have lower incomes than poor whites as a group.

The presence of more police patrolmen per 100,000 residents does not necessarily offset high crime in certain parts of the city. Although the Chicago Police Department had assigned over three times as many patrolmen per 100,000 residents to the highest crime areas shown as to the lowest, crime rates in the highest crime area for offenses against both persons and property combined were 4.9 times as high as in the lowest crime area.

Because most middle-class Americans live in neighborhoods similar to the more crime-free district described above, they have little comprehension of the sense of insecurity that characterizes the ghetto resident. Moreover, official statistics normally greatly understate actual crime rates because the vast majority of crimes are not reported to the police. For example, studies conducted for the President's Crime Commission in Washington, D.C., Boston, and Chicago, showed that three to six times as many crimes were actually committed against persons and homes as were reported to the police.

Two facts are crucial to an understanding of the effects of high crime rates in racial ghettos; most of these crimes are committed by a small minority of the residents, and the principal victims are the residents themselves. Throughout the United States, the great majority of crimes committed by Negroes involve other Negroes as victims. A special tabulation made by the Chicago Police Department for the President's Crime Commission indicated that over 85 percent of the crimes committed against persons by Negroes between September, 1965, and March, 1966, involved Negro victims.

As a result, the majority of law-abiding citizens who live in disadvantaged Negro areas face much higher probabilities of being victimized than residents of most higher income areas, including almost all suburbs. For nonwhites, the probability of suffering from any index crime except larceny is 78 percent higher than for whites. The probability of being raped is 3.7 times higher among nonwhite women, and the probability of being robbed is 3.5 times higher for nonwhites in general.

The problems associated with high crime rates generate widespread hostility toward the police in these neighborhoods for reasons described elsewhere in this Report. Thus, crime not only creates an atmosphere of insecurity and fear throughout Negro neighborhoods but also causes continuing attrition of the relationship between Negro residents and police. This bears a direct relationship to civil disorder.

There are reasons to expect the crime situation in these areas to become worse in the future. First, crime rates throughout the United States have been rising rapidly in recent years. The rate of index crimes against persons rose 37 percent from 1960 to 1966, and the rate of index crimes against property rose 50 percent. In the first 9 months of 1967, the number of index crimes was up 16 percent over the same period in 1966, whereas the U.S. population rose about 1 percent. In cities of 250,000 to 1 million, index crime rose by over 20 percent, whereas it increased 4 percent in cities of over 1 million.[2]

Second, the number of police available to combat crime is rising much more slowly than the amount of crime. In 1966, there were about 20 percent more police employees in the United States than in 1960, and per capita expenditures for police rose from $15.29 in 1960 to $20.99 in 1966, a gain of 37 percent. But over the 6-year period, the number of reported index crimes had jumped 62 percent. In spite of significant improvements in police efficiency, it is clear that police will be unable to cope with their expanding workload unless there is a dramatic increase in the resources allocated by society to this task.

Third, in the next decade, the number of young Negroes aged 14 to 24 will increase rapidly, particularly in central cities. This group is responsible for a disproportionately high share of crimes in all parts of the Nation. In 1966, persons under 25 years of age comprised the following proportions of those arrested for various major crimes: murder, 37 percent; forcible rape, 64 percent; robbery, 71 percent; burglary, 81 percent; larceny, about 77 percent; and auto theft, 89 percent. For all index crimes together, the arrest rate for Negroes is about four times higher than that for whites.

[2] The problem of interpreting and evaluating "rising" crime rates is complicated by the changing age distribution of the population, improvements in reporting methods, and the increasing willingness of victims to report crimes. Despite these complications, there is general agreement on the serious increase in the incidence of crime in the United States.

Yet the number of young Negroes aged 14 to 24 in central cities will rise about 63 percent from 1966 to 1975, as compared to only 32 percent for the total Negro population of central cities.[3]

HEALTH AND SANITATION CONDITIONS

The residents of the racial ghetto are significantly less healthy than most other Americans. They suffer from higher mortality rates, higher incidence of major diseases, and lower availablility and utilization of medical services. They also experience higher admission rates to mental hospitals.

These conditions result from a number of factors.

Poverty

From the standpoint of health, poverty means deficient diets, lack of medical care, inadequate shelter and clothing and often lack of awareness of potential health needs. As a result, almost 30 percent of all persons with family incomes less than $2,000 per year suffer from chronic health conditions that adversely affect their employ- ment—as compared with less than 8 percent of the families with incomes of $7,000 or more.

Poor families have the greatest need for financial assistance in meeting medical expenses. Only about 34 percent of families with incomes of less than $2,000 per year use health insurance benefits, as compared to nearly 90 percent of those with incomes of $7,000 or more.[4]

These factors are aggravated for Negroes when compared to whites for the simple reason that the proportion of persons in the

---

[3] Assuming those cities will experience the same proportion of total United States Negro population growth that they did from 1960 to 1966. The calculations are derived from population projections in Bureau of the Census, *Population Estimates*, Current Population Reports, Series P-25, No. 381, p. 63 (Dec. 18, 1967).

[4] Public programs of various kinds have been providing significant financial assistance for medical care in recent years. In 1964, over $1.1 billion was paid out by various governments for such aid. About 52 percent of medical vendor payments came from Federal Government agencies, 33 percent from states, and 12 percent from local governments. The biggest contributions were made by the Old Age Assistance Program and the Medical Assistance for the Aged Program. The enactment of Medicare in 1965 has significantly added to this flow of public assistance for medical aid. However, it is too early to evaluate the results upon health conditions among the poor.

United States who are poor is 3.5 times as high among Negroes (41 percent in 1966) as among whites (12 percent in 1966).

Maternal Mortality

Mortality rates for nonwhite mothers are four times as high as those for white mothers. There has been a sharp decline in such rates since 1940, when 774 nonwhite and 320 white mothers died for each 100,000 live births. In 1965, only 84 nonwhite and 21 white mothers died per 100,000 live births—but the gap between non-whites and whites actually increased.

Infant Mortality

Mortality rates among nonwhite babies are 58 percent higher than among whites for those under 1 month old and almost three times as high among those from 1 month to 1 year old. This is true in spite of a large drop in infant mortality rates in both groups since 1940.

TABLE 26-2. NUMBER OF INFANTS WHO DIED PER 1,000 LIVE BIRTHS

Year	Less than 1 month old		1 month to 1 year old	
	White	Nonwhite	White	Nonwhite
1940	27.2	39.7	16.0	34.1
1950	19.4	27.5	7.4	17.0
1960	17.2	26.9	5.7	16.4
1965	16.1	25.4	5.4	14.9

Life Expectancy

To some extent because of infant mortality rates, life expectancy at birth was 6.9 years longer for whites (71.0) than for nonwhites (64.1 years) in 1965. Even in the prime working ages, life expectancy is significantly lower among nonwhites than among whites. In 1965, white persons 25 years old could expect to live an average of 48.6 more years, whereas nonwhites 25 years old could expect to live another 43.3 years, or 11 percent less. Similar but smaller discrepancies existed at all ages from 25 through 55; some actually increased slightly between 1960 and 1965.

A fact that also contributes to poorer health conditions in the ghetto is that Negro families with incomes similar to those of whites spend less on medical services and visit medical specialists less often.

TABLE 26-3. PERCENT OF FAMILY EXPENDITURES SPENT FOR MEDICAL CARE, 1960-61

Income group	White	Nonwhite	Ratio, white to nonwhite
Under $3,000	9	5	1.8:1
$3,000 to $7,499	7	5	1.4:1
$7,500 and over	6	4	1.5:1

Since the lowest income group contains a much larger proportion of nonwhite families than white families, the overall discrepancy in medical care spending between these two groups is very significant, as shown by the following table:

TABLE 26-4. HEALTH EXPENSES PER PERSON PER YEAR FOR THE PERIOD FROM JULY TO DECEMBER 1962

Income by racial group	Total medical	Hospital	Doctor	Dental	Medicine	Other
Under $2,000 per family per year:						
White	$130	$33	$41	$11	$32	$13
Nonwhite	63	15	23	5	16	5
$10,000 and more per family per year:						
White	179	34	61	37	31	16
Nonwhite	133	34	50	19	23	8

These data indicate that nonwhite families in the lower income group spent less than half as much per person on medical services as white families with similar incomes. This discrepancy sharply declines but is still significant in the higher income group, where total nonwhite medical expenditures per person equal, on the average, 74.3 percent of white expenditures.

Negroes spend less on medical care for several reasons. Negro households generally are larger, requiring greater nonmedical expenses for each household and leaving less money for meeting medical expenses. Thus, lower expenditures per person would result even if expenditures per household were the same. Negroes also often pay more for other basic necessities such as food and consumer durables, as discussed in the next part of this chapter. In addition, fewer doctors, dentists, and medical facilities are conveniently available to Negroes than to most whites—a result both of geographic concentration of doctors in higher income areas in large cities and of discrimination against Negroes by doctors and hospitals. A survey in Cleveland indicated that there were 0.45 physicians per 1,000 people in poor neighborhoods, compared to 1.13 per 1,000 in nonpoverty areas. The result nationally is fewer visits to physicians and dentists.

TABLE 26-5. PERCENT OF POPULATION MAKING ONE OR MORE VISITS TO INDICATED TYPE OF MEDICAL SPECIALIST FROM JULY 1963 TO JUNE 1964

Type of Medical Specialist	Family incomes of $2,000-$3,999		Family incomes of $7,000-$9,999	
	White	Nonwhite	White	Nonwhite
Physician	64	56	70	64
Dentist	31	20	52	33

Although widespread use of health insurance has led many hospitals to adopt nondiscriminatory policies, some private hospitals still refuse to admit Negro patients or to accept doctors with Negro patients. As a result, Negroes are more likely to be treated in hospital clinics than whites and they are less likely to receive personalized service. This conclusion is confirmed by the following data:

TABLE 26-6. PERCENT OF ALL VISITS TO PHYSICIANS FROM JULY, 1963 TO JUNE, 1964, MADE IN INDICATED WAYS

Type of visit to physician	Family incomes of $2,000-$3,999		Family incomes of $7,000-$9,999	
	White	Nonwhite	White	Nonwhite
In physician's office	68	56	73	66
Hospital clinic	17	35	7	16
Other (mainly telephone)	15	9	20	18
Total	100	100	100	100

Environmental Factors

Environmental conditions in disadvantaged Negro neighborhoods create further reasons for poor health conditions there. The level of sanitation is strikingly below that which is prevalent in most higher income areas. One simple reason is that residents often lack proper storage facilities for food—adequate refrigerators, freezers, even garbage cans, which are sometimes stolen as fast as landlords can replace them.

In areas where garbage collection and other sanitation services are grossly inadequate—commonly in the poorer parts of our large cities—rats proliferate. It is estimated that in 1965, there were over 14,000 cases of ratbite in the United States, mostly in such neighborhoods.

The importance of these conditions was outlined for the Commission as follows:[5]

Sanitation Commissioners of New York City and Chicago both feel this [sanitation] to be an important community problem and report themselves as being under substantial pressure to improve conditions. *It must be concluded that slum sanitation is a serious problem in the minds of the urban poor and well merits, at least on that ground, the attention of the Commission.* A related problem, according to one Sanitation Commissioner, is the fact that residents of areas bordering on slums feel that sanitation and neighborhood cleanliness is a crucial issue, relating to the stability of their blocks and constituting an important psychological index of "how far gone" their area is.

* * * There is no known study comparing sanitation services between slum and non-slum areas. The experts agree, however, that there are more services in the slums on a quantitative basis, although perhaps not a per capita basis. In New York, for example, garbage pickups are supposedly scheduled for about six times a week in slums, compared to three times a week in other areas of the city; the comparable figures in Chicago are two to three times a week versus once a week.

The point, therefore, is not the relative quantitative level of services but the peculiarly intense needs of ghetto areas for sanitation services. This high demand is the product of numerous factors including: (1) higher population density; (2) lack of well managed buildings and adequate garbage services provided by landlords, number of receptacles, carrying to curbside, number of electric garbage disposals; (3) high relocation rates of tenants and businesses, producing heavy volume of bulk refuse left on streets and in buildings; (4) different uses of the streets—as outdoor living rooms in summer, recreation areas—producing high visibility and sensitivity to garbage problems; (5) large numbers of abandoned cars; (6) severe rodent and pest problems; (7) traffic congestion blocking garbage collection; and (8) obstructed street cleaning and snow removal on crowded, car-choked streets. Each of these elements adds to the problem and suggests a different possible line of attack.

[5] Memorandum to the Commission dated Nov. 16, 1967, from Robert Patricelli, minority counsel, Subcommittee on Employment Manpower and Poverty, U.S. Senate.

71

EXPLOITATION OF DISADVANTAGED CONSUMERS BY RETAIL MERCHANTS

Much of the violence in recent civil disorders has been directed at stores and other commercial establishments in disadvantaged Negro areas. In some cases, rioters focused on stores operated by white merchants who, they apparently believed, had been charging exorbitant prices or selling inferior goods. Not all the violence against these stores can be attributed to "revenge" for such practices. Yet it is clear that many residents of disadvantaged Negro neighborhoods believe they suffer constant abuses by local merchants.

Significant grievances concerning unfair commercial practices affecting Negro consumers were found in 11 of the 20 cities studied by the Commission. The fact that most of the merchants who operate stores in Negro areas are white undoubtedly contributes to the conclusion among Negroes that they are exploited by white society.

It is difficult to assess the precise degree and extent of exploitation. No systematic and reliable survey comparing consumer pricing and credit practices in all-Negro and other neighborhoods has ever been conducted on a nationwide basis. Differences in prices and credit practices between white middle-income areas and Negro low-income areas to some extent reflect differences in the real costs of serving these two markets (such as differential losses from pilferage in supermarkets), but the exact extent of these cost differences has never been estimated accurately. Finally, an examination of exploitative consumer practices must consider the particular structure and functions of the low-income consumer durables market.

Installment Buying

This complex situation can best be understood by first considering certain basic facts:

Various cultural factors generate constant pressure on low-income families to buy many relatively expensive durable goods and display them in their homes. This pressure comes in part from continuous exposure to commercial advertising, especially on television. In January, 1967, over 88 percent of all Negro households had TV sets. A 1961 study of 464 low-income families in New York City showed that 95 percent of these relatively poor families had TV sets.

72

Many poor families have extremely low incomes, bad previous credit records, unstable sources of income, or other attributes which make it virtually impossible for them to buy merchandise from established large national or local retail firms. These families lack enough savings to pay cash, and they cannot meet the standard credit requirements of established general merchants because they are too likely to fall behind in their payments.

Poor families in urban areas are far less mobile than others. A 1967 Chicago study of low-income Negro households indicated their low automobile ownership compelled them to patronize neighborhood merchants. These merchants typically provided smaller selection, poorer services, and higher prices than big national outlets. The 1961 New York study also indicated that families who shopped outside their own neighborhoods were far less likely to pay exorbitant prices.

Most low-income families are uneducated concerning the nature of credit purchase contracts, the legal rights and obligations of both buyers and sellers, sources of advice for consumers who are having difficulties with merchants, and the operation of the courts concerned with these matters. In contrast, merchants engaged in selling goods to them are very well informed.

In most states, the laws governing relations between consumers and merchants in effect offer protection only to informed, sophisticated parties with understanding of each other's rights and obligations. Consequently, these laws are little suited to protect the rights of most low-income consumers.

In this situation, exploitative practices flourish. Ghetto residents who want to buy relatively expensive goods cannot do so from standard retail outlets and are thus restricted to local stores. Forced to use credit, they have little understanding of the pitfalls of credit buying. But because they have unstable incomes and frequently fail to make payments, the cost to the merchants of serving them is significantly above that of serving middle-income consumers. Consequently, a special kind of merchant appears to sell them goods on terms designed to cover the high cost of doing business in ghetto neighborhoods.

Whether they actually gain higher profits, these merchants charge higher prices than those in other parts of the city to cover the greater credit risks and other higher operating costs inherent in neighborhood outlets. A recent study conducted by the Federal Trade Commission in Washington, D.C., illustrates this conclusion dramatically. The FTC identified a number of stores specializing in selling furniture and appliances to low-income households. About

73

92 percent of the sales of these stores were credit sales involving installment purchases, as compared to 27 percent of the sales in general retail outlets handling the same merchandise.

The median income annually of a sample of 486 customers of these stores was about $4,200, but one-third had annual incomes below $3,600, about 6 percent were receiving welfare payments, and another 76 percent were employed in the lowest-paying occupations (service workers, operatives, laborers and domestics), as compared to 36 percent of the total labor force in Washington in those occupations.

Definitely catering to a low-income group, these stores charged significantly higher prices than general merchandise outlets in the Washington area. According to testimony by Paul Rand Dixon, Chairman of the FTC, an item selling wholesale at $100 would retail on the average for $165 in a general merchandise store and for $250 in a low-income specialty store. Thus, the customers of these outlets were paying an average price premium of about 52 percent.

While higher prices are not necessarily exploitative in themselves, many merchants in ghetto neighborhoods take advantage of their superior knowledge of credit buying by engaging in various exploitative tactics—high-pressure salesmanship, "bait advertising," misrepresentation of prices, substitution of used goods for promised new ones, failure to notify consumers of legal actions against them, refusal to repair or replace substandard goods, exorbitant prices or credit charges, and use of shoddy merchandise. Such tactics affect a great many low-income consumers. In the New York study, 60 percent of all households had suffered from consumer problems (some of which were purely their own fault). About 23 percent had experienced serious exploitation. Another 20 percent, many of whom were also exploited, had experienced repossession, garnishment, or threat of garnishment.

Garnishment

Garnishment practices in many states allow creditors to deprive individuals of their wages through court action, without hearing or trial. In about 20 states, the wages of an employee can be diverted to a creditor merely upon the latter's deposition, with no advance hearing where the employee can defend himself. He often receives no prior notice of such action and is usually unaware of the law's operation and too poor to hire legal defense. Moreover, consumers

74

may find themselves still owing money on a sales contract even after the creditor has repossessed the goods. The New York study cited earlier in this chapter indicated that 20 percent of a sample of low-income families had been subjected to legal action regarding consumer purchases. And the Federal Trade Commission study in Washington, D.C., showed that, on the average, retailers specializing in credit sales of furniture and appliances to low-income consumers resorted to court action once for every $2,200 of sales. Since their average sale was for $207, this amounted to using the courts to collect from one of every 11 customers. In contrast, department stores in the same area used court action against approximately one of every 14,500 customers.[6]

Variations in Food Prices

Residents of low-income Negro neighborhoods frequently claim that they pay higher prices for food in local markets than wealthier white suburbanites and receive inferior quality meat and produce. Statistically reliable information comparing prices and quality in these two kinds of areas is generally unavailable. The U.S. Bureau of Labor Statistics, studying food prices in six cities in 1966, compared prices of a standard list of 18 items in low-income areas and higher income areas in each city. In a total of 180 stores, including independent and chain stores, and for items of the same type sold in the same types of stores, there were no significant differences in prices between low-income and high-income areas. However, stores in low-income areas were more likely to be small independents (which had somewhat higher prices), to sell low-quality produce and meat at any given price, and to be patronized by people who typically bought smaller sized packages which are more expensive per unit of measure. In other words, many low-income consumers in fact pay higher prices, although the situation varies greatly from place to place.

Although these findings must be considered inconclusive, there are significant reasons to believe that poor households generally pay higher prices for the food they buy and receive lower quality food. Low-income consumers buy more food at local groceries because they are less mobile. Prices in these small stores are significantly higher than in major supermarkets because they cannot achieve economies of scale and because real operating costs are higher in low-income Negro areas than in outlying suburbs. For instance, inventory "shrinkage" from pilfering and other causes is

* Assuming their sales also averaged $207 per customer.

75

normally under 2 percent of sales but can run twice as much in high-crime areas. Managers seek to make up for these added costs by charging higher prices for food or by substituting lower grades.

These practices do not necessarily involve exploitation, but they are often perceived as exploitative and unfair by those who are aware of the price and quality differences involved but unaware of operating costs. In addition, it is probable that genuinely exploitative pricing practices exist in some areas. In either case, differential food prices constitute another factor convincing urban Negroes in low-income neighborhoods that whites discriminate against them.

CHAPTER II: EQUAL EDUCATIONAL OPPORTUNITY

The advent of the "War on Poverty" brought to the attention of the country that gross inequality existed everywhere in the United States and that actual hunger was the rule for many Americans. Once the country discovered poverty the task for eradicating it was left largely up to the schools that would produce educated people who would then become employed and move into the mainstream of American life. Unfortunately, this has been far from the case in the past decade. More people are living in poverty today than were ten years ago. Too many have little hope for the immediate future. The 1970's will probably be labeled by the social historians as the "Era of Benign Neglect," when the country once again spent many millions on wars and defense establishment instruments while millions went uneducated, unemployed, and hungry.

American education had never been studied on a national scale until the 1966 Coleman Study funded by the U.S. Office of Education. This first national study raised several serious questions about public education in the country, especially that provided members of various culture groups such as American Indians, Blacks, and Mexican-Americans.

Although the Coleman Study has been interpreted by various groups to mean various things, the articles included in this chapter seem to give an adequate presentation of the main findings and their importance to the future of American education.

The question facing America today regarding equality of educational opportunity is whether the country really believes in equality of all people as stated in the Constitution or whether some people are more equal than others.

COMPENSATORY EDUCATION IN THE EQUALIZATION OF EDUCATIONAL OPPORTUNITY, I*

EDMUND W. GORDON

and

ADELAIDE JABLONSKY

Compensatory education is a term which has come into use since 1960 to refer to those pedagogical efforts directed at overcoming or circumventing assumed deficiencies in the background, functioning, and current experiences of children from economically deprived, culturally isolated, and/or ethnically segregated families. A wide variety of elements have been introduced under this banner. They include: (1) modifications in training, recruitment, and utilization of staff; (2) remedial reading and language development; (3) enrichment and modification of curriculum; (4) expanded guidance services; (5) enrichment of extracurricular activities; (6) increased parental and peer involvement; (7) extended reciprocal involvement of school and community; and (8) extensions and appendages to the school day and school year. Particular emphasis has been given to the prevention and salvaging of school dropouts and to the preparation for school through preschool programs. Although most of these programs have concentrated on improved or increased cognitive input, some have sought to introduce affective experiences or affect laden materials designed to improve self-concept and motivation. Compensatory education models have been widely and enthusiastically accepted. However, when one looks at their impact on academic performance in the target population, it is obvious that compensatory education as presently practiced is either insufficient or irrelevant to the needs of disadvantaged young people. There are some aspects of compensatory education which seem to have some promise with some children. There are other aspects projected — but not yet tried — which would logically seem to have good potential for success. Some of these more promising elements are in the direction of what we might expect excellent programs of education to be. Others are in the direction of what we might expect of a good and humane social order. Both of these utopian but obtainable goals are costly in terms of material resources and humanitarian concern; however, they may be prohibitive in cost in competition with distorted national values.

In this paper we review a number of primary and secondary sources for data and information concerning the nature, effectiveness and cost of compensatory ed-

----

* This chapter is based on a paper prepared under contract with the U. S. Commission on Civil Rights. It was undertaken independently from the Commission and is the responsibility of the authors alone.

JOURNAL OF NEGRO EDUCATION, 1968, Vol. 37, pp. 268-279.

ucation. From identifiable programs and practices and from implicit needs and theoretical projections, we have outlined what might be an adequate program (continued in the next chapter). From too limited information and even more limited experience, we have estimated the cost of such a program based upon the cost of present efforts.

EVALUATION OF CURRENT PROGRAMS

The several programs of special education for the disadvantaged have been described as compensatory because they are usually attempts to compensate, to make up for or to overcome, the effects of hostile, insufficient, different and/or indifferent conditions of prior experience and stimulation. The aim of these programs is to bring children from these backgrounds up to a level where they can be reached or served by existing educational practices. To the degree that these young people improve in academic achievement and approach the mean age-grade achievement levels established for the general population, compensatory education would be said to be effective or successful. It has been this standard which has guided practically all of our efforts at evaluating compensatory education.

For all of these programs the question is asked, "What changes can be observed in the academic achievement or intelligence test scores of the children served?" Although many aspects of these programs have been directed at other categories of function, and despite the growing skepticism that cognitive function is the optimal system through which immediate gains are reflected, the prime criterion of success or failure of these programs is academic achievement. Whether one likes this circumstance or not, it is at least understandable since the central thrust has been focused on bringing these children up to levels of performance comparable to those of the children with whom the school feels it succeeds.

Project Head Start

The largest compensatory education program undertaken to date is Project Head Start. This nationwide program has served almost one million children since its inception. It was designed to take children immediately preceding school entry, and through a broad-based program of educational, medical, and social services to better prepare them for primary school. Despite the broad-based program, the many efforts at evaluating Head Start have emphasized changes in children's intelligence scores. These evaluation efforts have resulted in varied findings.

In general, the test scores of children served by the program have been higher at the end of the program than they were when the children entered. When compared to expected growth patterns, the Head Start children tended to be performing better than would have been expected without the program. When compared to children not served by Head Start, the children in the program tended to show better progress. Although the dominant trend was in the direction of improved performance, there were many instances in which Head Start children showed no significant differences in scores from children not served by Head Start.

In several attempts to determine the persistence of these gains, equivocal findings are reported. In some of these studies children served by Head Start continued to show higher achievement levels throughout the first grade (the longest period reported so far). At the other extreme there are studies which indicate no persistent difference in achievement levels after two, four or six months in kindergarten or first grade. In the latter studies, which are often cited when "fade out" is discussed, it should be noted that it is the difference between the two groups that fades and not the prior gains. Equalization of performance seems to be a function of the non-Head Start children having caught up, rather than of Head Start children having lost some of their developmental gains.

After reviewing almost 100 major and minor studies of Head Start as an approach to compensatory education, it is clear that the introduction of broad-based but highly diversified services at the three to four year old level is associated with some gains in intellectual function for the population served. These gains are reflected in higher performance levels by these children than by children not served. The persistence of these gains is not consistent. Subjectively assessed changes in social-emotional maturation and in general readiness to benefit from the formal learning experiences of the primary school are more universally reported and are perceived by teachers as being more persistent. However, the long term impact of Head Start as an antidote to the destructive influence of poverty and inferior status on educational and social development is yet to be established.

Title I and Title III Projects

A second category of program is that which has been developed with support from Titles I and III of the Elementary and Secondary Education Act. With even more diversity with respect to program elements and quality than is true of Project Head Start, the Title I program in particular has been directed at improving the capabilities of the schools, in areas where disadvantaged children are concentrated. The legislation and regulations give the states and school systems wide degrees of freedom to develop programs and resources directed at the needs of poor children. Most of the eligible school systems have eagerly accepted this challenge. Some have mounted elaborate programs. Practically all of the 50 states have done something under one or both of these titles.

Reports on these efforts are available for 1965 and 1966. The review of these data is not encouraging. The reports indicate that: (1) In most instances money was made available in such haste that the quality of planning and development of programs was severely limited. (2) Many programs have been operative for too brief a period to be effectively evaluated. (3) Many programs were funded at levels insufficient to meet the requirements necessary to do an adequate job. (4) Most programs could not find adequate and appropriate specialized personnel to mount major efforts. (5) Most programs were unable to report appreciable improvement in academic achievement for the target populations. (6) Most programs tended to increase the quantity of services available without any substantive change in content and quality.

Among programs reporting positive findings, the tendency was toward improved morale, higher teacher expectation, improved staff-perceived climates for learning, improved attendance, and reduced school dropout rates. These gains are not to be demeaned. But the development of compensatory education under support from Titles I and III has not yet resulted in a major change in the schools' success patterns with children from disadvantaged backgrounds.

Upward Bound

Upward Bound is a national program designed to assist and increase the number of disadvantaged youth who enroll in some sort of post-secondary education. The program's primary focus is on developing interest in higher education among tenth and eleventh grade pupils from poor families.

In the summer of 1965, pilot programs were conducted on eighteen college campuses. In 1966 the program was expanded to include two hundred twenty colleges, universities, and residential secondary schools, and the number of students increased from 2,000 to 20,000. Elements common to these programs are (a) a six to eight week residential summer phase designed to remedy poor academic preparation and increase the pupils' possibilities for acceptance and success in college and (b) a follow-up phase conducted during the regular academic year which is designed to sustain the gains made during the summer months. In general, both phases include academic content that does not make an attempt to parallel the regular secondary school work. Both phases also include cultural enrichment experiences designed to increase total effectiveness.

Data from six of the original programs indicate that 80 per cent of students enrolled continued their education; 78 per cent of the students entered college in contrast to the 8 per cent who would normally have gone on to college. Data on college retention rates show that the dropout rate for Upward Bound youth in college is the same rate as for all other college youth. In 1965 the freshman year dropout was 12 per cent, the sophomore year dropout was 21 per cent, and the retention rate was 67 per cent. The project staff feels that the impact of Upward Bound should be judged not only on its short term effect on students but also on long term influences, e. g., sensitizing the secondary education system, bringing the most effective teachers into Upward Bound related secondary schools, and making the schools responsible for "brokering" their students into appropriate employment or higher education. It is, of course, too early to evaluate such structural impact.

School Dropout Programs

In the early 1960s considerable national attention was directed at the problems of the school dropout. In the summer of 1963 President Kennedy set into motion a large scale national campaign focused on 63 of the larger cities in this country. Almost 60,000 young people were contacted in that initial effort. Other school dropout projects have expanded on that crash program. They have generally been organized by high schools, community groups and by private industry. These projects have included intensive guidance services, remedial education, specific job training in and out of formal school settings and large scale "Stay in School — Return to School" publicity campaigns.

Data on the initial effort in 1963 indicate that 52 per cent of the youth contacted actually returned to formal school affiliations. National figures on the total effort subsequent to that time are not available. The need for large scale programs which combine intensive guidance services with remedial education, specific job training and remunerated work is clear. A review of the nation's attempt at doing this indicates that money and resources, when applied, are seldom sufficiently concentrated to achieve the obvious goal.

Project 100,000, United States Department of Defense

Project 100,000 was designed as an attempt by the armed services to become involved with and to help alleviate social and educational problems of the poor. In October 1966, 40,000 young men were taken into the armed services under lowered entrance standards. These men fell between the tenth and thirteenth percentile on Defense Department qualifying tests.

The 40,000 soldiers were tested in July on the Metropolitan Word Recognition, Reading and Arithmetic Fundamentals sections. The average was grade 6.5 on word recognition and arithmetic fundamentals, and grade six on reading. Seventeen per cent of this group were reading below the fourth grade level.

The first program which is basic training takes eight weeks for the majority of soldiers. In the total army population 98 per cent of these are expected to pass the performance and academic tests given at the end of the program. Of the 2 per cent that fail, one-half fail because of medical reasons.

In the special program, 95 per cent are expected to succeed in passing the performance and academic tests. However, about 8 per cent of this group require re-cycling, which means doing a week or several weeks' work over again,

before they can be passed; 4 per cent are discharged for physical and academic reasons.

After basic training some soldiers are sent directly into a combat area; most go through advanced training. For many of these advanced training courses, the language used by the instructors and in printed materials has had to be simplified in order to accommodate the program to the low reading level of these soldiers. In addition to the change in language, there are programmed texts in basic arithmetic skills, video tape and simulators with which it is hoped that soldiers will be trained to do a specific job in the service. For the individuals in this project, however, instructors in the practical courses such as automobile mechanics take the slow learners for after-hours tutoring. This tutoring may include either mechanical or basic academic assistance. In a recent speech, former Secretary of Defense, Robert McNamara, indicated that the earlier estimates of anticipated success were, in general, consistent with the performances of these men.

Banneker Project of St. Louis, Missouri

"Operation Motivation" was initiated in the Banneker School District of St. Louis, Missouri, in 1957, under the direction of Dr. Samuel Shepard. The program is an attempt to raise the academic achievement of children in kindergarten through eighth grade by concentrating on attitude change on the part of pupils, teachers, and parents rather than through specific curriculum modification.

The Banneker Project attempted to appeal directly to the sense of pride and competitive spirit of the pupils. Techniques employed were pep rallies, honor assemblies, competition contests, a radio program giving children suggestions on "how to succeed in school," and ungraded classes with heavy emphasis on reading. Teachers were encouraged to give pupils a sense of the direct relation between present day school work and future employment, to "quit teaching by I.Q. . . . quit their attitudes of condescension . . . assign homework . . . and visit the homes of the parents." Meetings were held with parents at which they were persuaded to look forward to a better future for their children and to inspire their children to regard school as the best means of self-fulfillment and upward mobility.

In the evaluation of the Banneker Project, student performance was compared with national norms and with norms found in other nearly all-Negro and all-white schools. When compared with other all-Negro schools, the Banneker school's academic standing showed no advance during the Project years. In 1965-66 the position of the Banneker schools relative to nearly all-white schools remained inferior. In looking at more than academic achievement test scores, Dr. Shepard has reported that the children have been more interested in school, have been better behaved, and have had better attendance, that teachers have been working harder, and that there has been excellent cooperation from parents.

More Effective Schools Program
of New York, New York

The More Effective Schools program was initiated in 1964 in ten New York City elementary schools and expanded in September 1965 to include eleven additional city schools. The Program was intended to create basic changes in curriculum, personnel, school plant and organization and school-community relations. Specific program elements were to include provision of teacher specialists, team teaching, reduced class size, heterogeneous grouping, and intensive work with parents and community.

Attention has recently been turned to the evaluation of the More Effective Schools program. Perhaps the most important finding of one such study was that despite certain administrative and organizational changes "little has happened in the way of innovation or restructuring in the basic teaching process." There was general agreement among both observers and school staff that "teachers have not revised techniques of instruction to obtain the presumed instructional advantages" of reduced class size and the availability of specialized services.

In reviewing the data on cognitive and attitudinal changes in MES classes, one must note both the provision of reduced pupil/teacher ratios and specialized psychological, social, and health services and the absence of any radical revision in instructional practices. On the basis of standardized tests and classroom observations, children in some ME schools made significant achievement gains over children in designated control schools and in other special service schools. In general, reading retardation was reduced in ME schools more so than in control schools. Comparisons of achievement in reading grade show some MES classes scoring from 2 to 5 months above control and comparison classes. It should be noted, however, that these findings are derived from a longitudinal analysis of MES pupil data.

On an earlier cross-sectional analysis the gains of MES pupils were less obvious.

In addition to measured cognitive gains, a clear sense of "enthusiasm, interest, and hope" has been reported among administrative staff and teaching faculty as well as parents and the community in general. As indicated in one evaluation, "The creation of such positive feelings and climates in a school system which in recent years has evidenced considerable internal stress and school-community conflict is an important accomplishment" and, we might add, a rather ironic one.

Higher Horizons Program of New York, New York

The Higher Horizons Program was conceived in large measure as an extension of the "successful" Demonstration Guidance Project. The Demonstration Guidance Project involved approximately 700 junior and senior high school students in Harlem. Counseling and remedial education staffs were significantly increased in the schools involved to provide a high concentration of supplementary help. The results were quite dramatic. Approximately 60 per cent of the students who had joined the Project in seventh grade gained an average of 4.3 years in reading achievement after 2.6 years in the Project; the dropout rate from high school for these children decreased from 40 to 20 per cent, and a significant portion were motivated to continue their education beyond high school.

The Higher Horizons Program was an attempt to replicate the Demonstration Guidance Project on a much wider scale and at minimum extra cost. Higher Horizons was begun in 1959 to serve 12,000 children from 31 elementary schools and 13 junior high schools, and was expanded in 1962 to include 64,000 children. The major purpose of Higher Horizons was to "develop techniques for the identification, motivation, enrichment, and education of the culturally disadvantaged children and to perfect means for stimulating them and their families to pursue higher educational and vocational goals." The foci of the program were intensive individual and group counseling, cultural and occupational experiences, remedial services and parent education. Several hundred specialized personnel were added to the staffs of the project schools. The extra teachers were used as curriculum assistants, teacher training specialists, or subject matter (particularly reading) specialists; each teacher was expected to spend a good part of his time on parent and community education, cultural activities, and inservice training, as well as on curriculum improvement and remedial work.

Any evaluation of the Higher Horizons Program must take into account that at least as far as budgeting was concerned, the Program was not supported financially to the extent originally planned. For example, in 1959 one additional teacher or counselor was provided for every 108 children, but by 1962 there was only one teacher or counselor provided for every 143 children. On a per capita basis, more than three times as much money was spent on the Demonstration Guidance Project as on Higher Horizons. In 1964 an evaluation was completed for the New York City Board of Education. The study concentrated on students in eight Higher Horizons schools matched on a one-to-one basis (on I.Q., reading comprehension, ethnic composition, geographic location, and size of school) with non-Higher Horizons students. For the period of the study (1959-62), the Higher Horizons schools had a somewhat smaller average class size, lower rates of pupil and teacher transiency, and larger percentages of regular teachers. The evaluation reported that there were no significant differences between Higher Horizons and control group children on reading and arithmetic achievement, ratings of school attitudes, self-image, and educational-vocational aspirations. The only significant differences noted were gains made by Higher Horizons elementary school children in arithmetic. Despite these disappointing results, the professional staff in the program were observed to be favorably disposed to the Program. They felt that it was most successful in providing cultural opportunities and extra remedial guidance services and that its least effect was on students' behavior, study habits, and educational goals.

Project Case II: MODEL

The Institute for Behavioral Research began its project Case II: MODEL (Contingencies Applicable to Special Education-Motivationally Oriented Designs for an Ecology of Learning) in February 1966 under the direction of Harold Cohen. Twenty-eight young men in the National Training School for Boys were involved. The basic goals of the project were to improve the academic behavior of all twenty-eight and to prepare as many as possible within a one-year time schedule for their return to school. The age range of the group was fourteen to eighteen, their average I.Q. was 93.8; 85 per cent were dropouts from school, and only three had never been sentenced and institutionalized before.

Case II was based on the idea that each learning experience should have built into it a series of reinforcing steps to maintain the students' interest. This meant direct tangible reinforcement as well as an individual sense of success and group approval. Cohen used money as an extrinsic immediate reinforcement — ". . . our student-inmates want to know, 'Man, what's the payoff now?' For them, as well as for the bulk of Americans, they work for money." Students became Educational Researcher's and went to work on 140 programmed educational courses in 18 programmed classes. When they performed on tests at 90 per cent or better, they were paid off. A point system was utilized, each point representing one penny. With his money earned, the student provided for his room, food, clothing, gifts and an entrance fee and tuition for special classes. "A student who does not have sufficient funds goes on relief — sleeps on an open bunk and eats food on a metal tray. No student has ever been on relief more than two weeks."

A specially designed 24-hour contingency-oriented educational laboratory was designed to provide, in effect, 24 hours of educational therapy. "Where and when a student sleeps, eats, makes contact with another student, with a machine, with a group, a program or a teacher is part of the educational ecology. . . . Every student in this program is being counseled by those people he selects during the day. He talks to his friends, to the librarian, the teacher, the cook, the secretary, the research staff and visitors. He can select a particular counselor on request, e. g., his minister, psychologist, or caseworker, for which he pays a small professional service fee."

The vital aspect of the structured environment is that it programs the individual for success. This is attained basically by (1) structuring each curriculum unit at a level where the individual can perform successfully step by step and (2) providing direct pay-off for achievement. This work is primarily directed at developing new and more appropriate behaviors under a schedule of reinforcement while eliminating inappropriate antisocial behaviors by a schedule which is non-reinforcing.

Cohen's intermediate findings are quite impressive. Increases of the I.Q.'s of the students have averaged 12.09 points. For every 90 hours of academic work, there was an average increase of 1.89 grade levels on the Stanford Achievement Test and 2.7 grade levels on the Gates Reading Survey.

GENERAL CRITERIA AND PROMISING MODELS

The rather modest success of these and many other efforts at compensatory education, when combined with the Coleman findings indicating that school factors account for a small amount of the variation in school achievement, could lead to the conclusion that improvements in the equality of education are hardly worth our effort. But just as the Coleman finding is based upon an examination of several factors which are probably not crucial in the determination of the quality of education, much that we see in the several approaches to compensatory education consists of educational features which may be necessary to the educational process, but evidently are not sufficient to make the difference in terms of greatly improved academic achievement in socially disadvantaged children.

Most of these programs have either attempted to modify basic cognitive processes, to change levels of content mastery, or to change the motivation of the young people served. However, most of these programs represent vast increases in the *quantity* of effort directed at improving function with very little improvement in the *quality* of program offered. The efforts directed at changed cognitive function are very traditional and have brought little that is new or changed in pedagogy. One does not see in these programs any reflection of current thinking relative to learning theory and behavioral organization. With but one exception, there is no representation in the programs reviewed of the application of behavioral analysis and contingency management to the learning experiences of these youngsters. Yet, as we have indicated, this is one of the few approaches to compensatory education which seems to be bearing fruit. In approaching improved content mastery, the programs seem to have concentrated on either an enriched or watered-down presentation of material to pupils. Again, drastic reorganization in the presentation of material, the quality of material and the conditions under which materials are presented are not present in these programs. At the level of increased motivation and attitude change, we have somewhat more promising signs in the effort of many of these programs. Several programs have sought more active involvement of parents and representatives of the communities from which these children come in the planning and conduct of educational programs. This emphasis, however, is by no means a widely accepted and dominant one. At least at the level of meaningful participation there continues to be strong resistance on the part of the education establishment. This has been particularly exhibited in recent struggles between school personnel and community groups. Despite the tradition of community control of the public school, when that control is likely to pass into the hands of poor and minority group persons the school resists strongly. If compensatory education is to compensate for the learning problems of young people who are thought to come to school without the necessary background of experience to optimally benefit from school, of youngsters who come to school poorly motivated toward the goals of the school, of youngsters who come to school lacking certain cognitive habits and skills, and of young people who come to the school attitudinally unprepared to participate or to sustain participation in academic learning tasks, there are then several criteria which might guide the development of compensatory education.

1. Effective instructional programs and practices must be a part of such an effort. If this is to be achieved, we will need to give greater attention to the dynamics of group interaction in their relationship to the teaching-learning process. Professionals concerned with such fields as psychotherapy and decision processes have developed elaborate systems of theory and practice based upon concepts of group dynamics. This sophistication has not yet been appropriately applied to education. Effective instruction will also require that we explore different ways of organizing learning experiences to meet individual differences in readiness and style. Readiness and style may vary with respect to the functional capacity to discriminate between things seen, heard, tasted, or felt. They may vary with respect to habit patterns that have been established around these sensory functions. They may vary based upon the dominance of one aspect of sensory function over another. It may well be that children whose life experiences vary drastically may also have significant variations in the hierarchical organization of sensory function and response modalities. Furthermore, if individuals, independently of experience or station in life, differ with respect to the degree to which they are inclined to respond with one or another of the senses, it may be that one of the significant variables in learning ability and disability is the quality of support provided when the learning task presented does not complement the sensory organization of the learner.

Another emphasis deserving of attention in our efforts at more effective instruction involves the utilization of behavioral analysis and contingency management in the design of learning experiences. In another context, one of the authors, (Edmund W. Gordon) has stressed the importance of qualitative as opposed to quantitative analysis of intellectual and other behavioral functions as a prerequisite for the development of prescriptions for learning. In behavioral analysis one is concerned with the detailed analysis and description of behavioral function, so that strength, weakness, style, preference, etc., are identified and a course of action for directed learning may be established. In contingency management, one is concerned with limiting the contingencies surrounding behavior so that the possible outcomes can be controlled, enabling the anticipation of consequences of the behavior. Such understanding and manipulation permit us to tie consequences of behavior to the antecedents of behavior and to use these consequences as reinforcers of desired behaviors.

2. If effective instructional programs can be achieved, compensatory education will need to reach children earlier, serve them over longer periods of the day, week, and year, and possibly follow them later into life. This latter need may increase as the need for continued learning and instruction as lifetime processes becomes more accepted in our society. The program then must provide for intensive and extensive care from the cradle until at least productive work or college. In many instances, it will need to provide, through the school, child care and instructional services ten to twelve hours a day, six or seven days a week, and twelve months of the year. If we are concerned with insulating the child from many of the destructive elements in disorganized communities and families, there is little choice but to drastically expand the periods for which the school is responsible for the child.

3. The enriched school experience will have little effect unless it can come to be valued and respected by the children and families served. Unless involvement in the school and respect for its values can become positive norms in the lives of the children, the productiveness of the school will be impaired. There is mounting evidence suggestive of the relationship between goal determination and task involvement. It would appear that participation in the determination of the policies of schools which these children attend by their parents and community members with whom they identify would be positively reflected in increased commitment to the objectives and programs of the school. A corollary of this involvement

is another attitudinal asset. The increasingly recognized sense of environmental control would seem also to be a potential product of this increased involvement in decision-making in school affairs. Participation in decision-making is by no means the only road to personal involvement. Of equal importance is the need that the school, the curriculum, and the materials it uses provide points of identification for the learner. In this connection, materials which are widely representative of the variety of cultural, economic, and ethnic groups in this country are essential. Staff members who also represent this variety of backgrounds are necessary.

4. If the school is to meet the special needs of youngsters who are handicapped by lower economic status, special attention and provision will need to be made to protect and insure good health, adequate nutritional status, and the material resources necessary for effective school learning. In some instances this will mean elaborate programs of health care. In other situations food supplements will be required. In many situations, stipends may be necessary to enable the youngster to provide the necessary supplemental school materials and pocket money for minimal social interaction. For these children, the school must alleviate or circumvent economic, cultural, social, experiential, and educational deficiencies in their environment. Many of these are functions the school was not originally designed to perform.

5. The influence of the school is by no means limited to the period during which the youngster is responsible to the school. What the youngster perceives as opportunity to utilize the school's products and

to participate in the mainstream of the society may be as important to his adjustment and progress within the school as it is to his development in the post-school period. Again, in reference to the all-important sense of environmental control, it may be that in the absence of perceived opportunity to do something with his life, all of our innovations and educational improvements will be for naught.

6. Since so much of the school's influence is mediated through verbal interaction, its program for these children will have to reflect respect for the languages with which these children come to school. In some instances, basic education may have to be provided in the vernacular of the child until development has progressed to a point where a transition to standard language forms may be achieved.

7. Since high degrees of mobility and transiency are characteristic of many families in the target populations, special provisions to accommodate transiency must be made. This may require comparability of basic goals and programs at each level of instruction and sufficient intimacy in teacher-pupil relationships to provide for emotional and physical security particularly at points of transition. This goal can be partially achieved through the provision of sufficiently small organizational units so that each child is enabled to achieve a sense of identity and involvement in the essential aspects of the educational process. In this setting the child will need to experience a real sense that what he does and what he decides can influence his progress, achievement, and future.

8. The implementation of programs which approach these criteria will to a large extent depend upon the availability of excellent school staffs. In the achievement of this goal special attention will need to be given to the preparation, supervision, and circumstances of work of the school's personnel. The dimensions of the necessary training programs have not yet been specified. Wide variations are possible in the backgrounds and training of persons utilized if emphasis is placed upon supervision and accountability. Nonprofessionals and paraprofessionals indigenous to the backgrounds from which the children come should be utilized, and these persons like all other staff members should be actively represented along with non-school employed members of the target community in decision-making in all aspects of the school's functioning.

9. The school must be adequately provided for in terms of material support. For the target population, facilities and resources do make a difference. Quality of teachers is important. There must be available the monetary and status rewards necessary to attract and hold able teachers in classroom instruction.

10. Cultural, economic, and ethnic integration in education is often viewed as alternative to compensatory education. Increasingly, it must be viewed as integral parts of compensatory or quality education. Probably more efficient than all the above stated factors excellently provided would be the mixing of children from more limited backgrounds in schools where the majority of pupils come from more privileged circumstances of life. Instead of a choice between integration and compensatory education, we advocate integration as an essential feature in compensatory education.

Equal schools
or
equal students?

JAMES S. COLEMAN

The Civil Rights Act of 1964 contains a section numbered 402, which went largely unnoticed at the time. This section instructs the Commissioner of Education to carry out a survey of "concerning the lack of availability of equal educational opportunities" by reason of race, religion or national origin, and to report to Congress and the President within two years. The Congressional intent in this section is somewhat unclear. But if, as is probable, the survey was initially intended as a means of finding areas of continued intentional discrimination, the intent later became less punitive-oriented and more future-oriented: *i.e.*, to provide a basis for public policy, at the local, state, and national levels, which might overcome inequalities of educational opportunity.

In the two years that have intervened (but mostly in the second), a remarkably vast and comprehensive survey was conducted, focussing principally on the inequalities of educational opportunity experienced by five racial and ethnic minorities: Negroes, Puerto Ricans, Mexican Americans, American Indians, and Oriental Americans. In the central and largest portion of the survey, nearly 600,000 children at grades 1, 3, 6, 9, and 12, in 4000 schools in all 50 states and the District of Columbia, were tested and questioned; 60,000 teachers in these schools were questioned and self-tested; and principals of these schools were also questioned about their schools. The tests and questionnaires (administered in the fall of 1965 by Educational Testing

THE PUBLIC INTEREST, Summer 1966, pp. 70-75.

Service) raised a considerable controversy in public school circles and among some parents, with concern ranging from Federal encroachment on the local education system to the spectre of invasion of privacy. Nevertheless, with a participation rate of about 70% of all the schools sampled, the survey was conducted; and on July 1, 1966, Commissioner Howe presented a summary report of this survey. On July 31, the total report, *Equality of Educational Opportunity*, 737 pages, was made available (Government Printing Office, $4.25).

The summary of the report has appeared to many who have read it to be curiously "flat," lacking in emphases and policy implications. Much of the same flatness can be found in the larger report. The seeming flatness probably derives from three sources: the research analyst's uneasiness in moving from description to implications; the government agency's uneasiness with survey findings that may have political repercussions; and, perhaps more important than either of these, the fact that the survey results do not lend themselves to the provision of simple answers. Nevertheless, the report is not so uncontroversial as it appears. And some of its findings, though cautiously presented, have sharp implications.

Perhaps the greatest virtue of this survey — though it has many faults — is that it did not take a simple or politically expedient view of educational opportunity. To have done so would have meant to measure (a) the objective characteristics of schools — number of books in the library, age of buildings, educational level of teachers, accreditation of the schools, and so on; and (b) the actual extent of racial segregation in the schools. The survey did look into these matters (and found less inequity in school facilities and resources, more in the extent of segregation, than is commonly supposed); but its principal focus of attention was not on what resources go into education, but on what product comes out. It did this in a relatively uncomplicated way, which is probably adequate for the task at hand: by tests which measured those areas of achievement most necessary for further progress in school, in higher education, and in successful competition in the labor market — that is, verbal and reading skills, and analytical and mathematical skills. Such a criterion does not allow statements about absolute levels of inequality or equality of education provided by the schools, because obviously there are more influences than the school's on a child's level of achievement in school, and there are more effects of schools than in these areas of achievement. What it does do is to broaden the question beyond the school to all those educational influences that have their results in the level of verbal and mathematical skill a young person is equipped with when he or she enters the adult world. In effect, it takes the perspective of this young adult, and says that what matters to him is, not how "equal" his school is, but rather whether he is equipped at the end of school to compete on an equal basis with others, whatever his social origins. From the perspective of society, it assumes that what is important is not to "equalize the schools" in some formal sense, but to insure that children from all groups come into adult society so equipped as to insure their full participation in this society.

Another way of putting this is to say that the schools are successful only insofar as they reduce the dependence of a child's opportunities upon his social origins. We can think of a set of conditional probabilities: the probability of being prepared for a given occupation or for a given college at the end of high school, conditional upon the child's social origins. The effectiveness of the schools consists, in part, of making the conditional probabilities less conditional — that is, less dependent upon social origins. Thus, equality of educational opportunity implies, not merely "equal" schools, but equally effective schools, whose influences will overcome the differences in starting point of children from different social groups.

The widening educational gap

This approach to educational opportunity, using as it does achievement on standardized tests, treads on sensitive ground. Differences in average achievement between racial groups can lend themselves to racist arguments of genetic differences in intelligence; even apart from this, they can lead to invidious comparisons between groups which show different average levels of achievement. But it is precisely the avoidance of such sensitive areas that can perpetuate the educational deficiencies with which some minorities are equipped at the end of schooling.

What, then, does the survey find with regard to effects of schooling on test achievement? Children were tested at the beginning of grades 1, 3, 6, 9, and 12. Achievement of the average American Indian, Mexican American, Puerto Rican, and Negro (in this descending order) was much lower than the average white or Oriental American, at all grade levels. The amount of difference ranges from about half a standard deviation to one standard deviation at early grade levels. At the 12th grade, it increases to beyond one standard deviation. (One standard deviation difference means that about 85% of the minority group children score below the average of the whites, while if the groups were equal only about 50% would score below this average.) The grade levels of difference range up to 5 years of deficiency (in math achievement) or 4 years (in reading skills) at the 12th grade. In short, the differences are large to begin with, and they are even larger at higher grades.

Two points, then, are clear: (1) *these minority children have a serious educational deficiency at the start of school, which is obviously not a result of school;* and (2) *they have an even more serious*

93

deficiency at the end of school, which is obviously in part a result of school.

Thus, by the criterion stated earlier — that the effectiveness of schools in creating equality of educational opportunity lies in making the conditional probabilities of success less conditional — the schools appear to fail. At the end of school, the conditional probabilities of high achievement are even *more* conditional upon racial or ethnic background than they are at the beginning of school.

There are a number of results from the survey which give further evidence on this matter. First, within each racial group, the strong relation of family economic and educational background to achievement does not diminish over the period of school, and may even increase over the elementary years. Second, most of the variation in student achievement lies within the same school, very little of it is between schools. The implication of these last two results is clear: family background differences account for much more variation in achievement than do school differences.

Even the school-to-school variation in achievement, though relatively small, is itself almost wholly due to the *social* environment provided by the school: the educational backgrounds and aspirations of other students in the school, and the educational backgrounds and attainments of the teachers in the school. *Per pupil expenditure, books in the library, and a host of other facilities and curricular measures show virtually no relation to achievment if the "social" environment of the school — the educational backgrounds of other students and teachers — is held constant.*

The importance of this last result lies, of course, in the fact that schools, as currently organized, are quite culturally homogeneous as well as quite racially segregated: teachers tend to come from the same cultural groups (and especially from the same race) as their students, and the student bodies are themselves relatively homogeneous. Given this homogeneity, the principal agents of effectiveness in the schools — teachers and other students — act to maintain or reinforce the initial differences imposed by social origins.

One element illustrates well the way in which the current organization of schools maintains the differences over generations: a Negro prospective teacher leaves a Negro teacher's college with a much lower level of academic competence (as measured by the National Teacher's Examination) than does his white counterpart leaving his largely white college; then he teaches Negro children (in school with other Negro children, ordinarily from educationally deficient backgrounds), who learn at a lower level, in part because of his lesser competence; some of these students, in turn, go into teacher training institutions to become poorly-trained teachers of the next generation.

Altogether, *the sources of inequality of educational opportunity*

94

appear to lie first in the home itself and the cultural influences immediately surrounding the home; then they lie in the schools' ineffectiveness to free achievement from the impact of the home, and in the schools' cultural homogeneity which perpetuates the social influences of the home and its environs.

A modest, yet radical proposal

Given these results, what do they suggest as to avenues to equality of educational opportunity? Several elements seem clear:

a) For those children whose family and neighborhood are educationally disadvantaged, it is important to replace this family environment as much as possible with an educational environment — by starting school at an earlier age, and by having a school which begins very early in the day and ends very late.

b) It is important to reduce the social and racial homogeneity of the school environment, so that those agents of education that do show some effectiveness — teachers and other students — are not mere replicas of the student himself. In the present organization of schools, it is the neighborhood school that most insures such homogeneity.

c) The educational program of the school should be made more effective than it is at present. The weakness of this program is apparent in its inability to overcome initial differences. It is hard to believe that we are so inept in educating our young that we can do no more than leave young adults in the same relative competitive positions we found them in as children.

Several points are obvious: It is not a solution simply to pour money into improvement of the physical plants, books, teaching aids, of schools attended by educationally disadvantaged children. For other reasons, it will not suffice merely to bus children or otherwise achieve pro forma integration. (One incidental effect of this would be to increase the segregation within schools, through an increase in tracking.)

The only kinds of policies that appear in any way viable are those which do not seek to improve the education of Negroes and other educationally disadvantaged at the expense of those who are educationally advantaged. This implies new kinds of educational institutions, with a vast increase in expenditures for education — not merely for the disadvantaged, but for all children. The solutions might be in the form of educational parks, or in the form of private schools paid by tuition grants (with Federal regulations to insure racial heterogeneity), public (or publicly-subsidized) boarding schools (like the North Carolina Advancement School), or still other innovations. This approach also implies reorganization of the curriculum within schools. One of the major reasons for "tracking" is the narrowness of our teaching methods — they can tolerate only a narrow range of skill in

95

the same classroom. Methods which greatly widen the range are necessary to make possible racial and cultural integration within a school – and thus to make possible the informal learning that other students of higher educational levels can provide. Such curricular innovations are possible – but, again, only through the investment of vastly greater sums in education than currently occurs.

It should be recognized, of course, that the goal described here – of equality of educational opportunity through the schools – is far more ambitious than has ever been posed in our society before. The schools were once seen as a supplement to the family in bringing a child into his place in adult society, and they still function largely as such a supplement, merely perpetuating the inequalities of birth. Yet the conditions imposed by technological change, and by our post-industrial society, quite apart from any ideals of equal opportunity, require a far more primary role for the school, if society's children are to be equipped for adulthood.

Self-confidence and performance

One final result of the survey gives an indication of still another – and perhaps the most important – element necessary for equality of educational opportunity for Negroes. One attitude of students was measured at grades 9 and 12 – an attitude which indicated the degree to which the student felt in control of his own fate. For example, one question was: "Agree or disagree: good luck is more important than hard work for success." Another was: "Agree or disagree: every time I try to get ahead someone or something stops me." Negroes much less often than whites had such a sense of control of their fate –a difference which corresponds directly to reality, and which corresponds even more markedly to the Negro's historical position in American society. However, despite the very large achievement differences between whites and Negroes at the 9th and 12th grades, *those Negroes who gave responses indicating a sense of control of their own fate achieved higher on the tests than those whites who gave the opposite responses. This attitude was more highly related to achievement than any other factor in the student's background or school.*

This result suggests that internal changes in the Negro, changes in his conception of himself in relation to his environment, may have more effect on Negro achievement than any other single factor. The determination to overcome relevant obstacles, and the belief that he will overcome them – attitudes that have appeared in an organized way among Negroes only in recent years in some civil rights groups – may be the most crucial elements in achieving equality of opportunity – not because of changes they will create in the white community, but principally because of the changes they create in the Negro himself.

96

Alternative Public School Systems*

KENNETH B. CLARK

It is now clear that American public education is organized and functions along social and economic class lines. A bi-racial public school system wherein approximately 90 per cent of American children are required to attend segregated schools is one of the clearest manifestations of this basic fact. The difficulties encountered in attempting to desegregate public schools in the South as well as in the North point to the tenacity of the forces seeking to prevent any basic change in the system.

The class and social organization of American public schools is consistently associated with a lower level of educational efficiency in the less privileged schools.

* This paper was originally presented at the National Conference on Equal Educational Opportunity in America's Cities, sponsored by the U. S. Commission on Civil Rights, November 16-18, 1967.

HARVARD EDUCATIONAL REVIEW, 1968, Vol. 38, pp. 100-113.

This lower efficiency is expressed in terms of the fact that the schools attended by Negro and poor children have less adequate educational facilities than those attended by more privileged children. Teachers tend to resist assignments in Negro and other underprivileged schools and generally function less adequately in these schools. Their morale is generally lower; they are not adequately supervised; they tend to see their students as less capable of learning. The parents of the children in these schools are usually unable to bring about any positive changes in the conditions of these schools.

The pervasive and persistent educational inefficiency which characterizes these schools results in:

(1) marked and cumulative academic retardation in a disproportionately high percentage of these children, beginning in the third or fourth grade and increasing through the eighth grade;

(2) a high percentage of dropouts in the junior and senior high schools of students unequipped academically and occupationally for a constructive role in society;

(3) a pattern of rejection and despair and hopelessness resulting in massive human wastage.

Given these conditions, American public schools have become significant instruments in the blocking of economic mobility and in the intensification of class distinctions rather than fulfilling their historic function of facilitating such mobility. In effect, the public schools have become captives of a middle class who have failed to use them to aid others to move into the middle class. It might even be possible to interpret the role of the controlling middle class as that of using the public schools to block further mobility.

What are the implications of this existing educational inefficiency? In the national interest, it is a serious question whether the United States Government can afford the continuation of the wastage of human resources at this period of world history. Although we cannot conclusively demonstrate a relation between educational inefficiency and other symptoms of personal and social pathology such as crime, delinquency, and pervasive urban decay, there is strong evidence that these are correlates.

Increasing industrialization and automation of our economy will demand larger numbers of skilled and educated and fewer uneducated workers. The manpower needs of contemporary America require business and industry to pay for the added burden of re-educating the mis-educated. This is a double taxation. The burdens of the present inefficient public education include this double taxation in addition to the high cost of crime and family stability and the artificial constriction of the labor and consumer market.

Beyond these material disadvantages are the human costs inherent in the failure to achieve equality of educational opportunity. This dehumanization contributes significantly to the cycle of pathology—poor education, menial jobs or unemployment, family instability, group and personal powerlessness. This passive pathology weakens the fabric of the entire society.

Obstacles to the Attainment of Efficient Education

The obstacles which interfere with the attainment of efficient public education fall into many categories. Among them are those obstacles which reflect historical premises and dogmas about education, administrative realities, and psychological assumptions and prejudices.

The historical premises and dogmas include such fetishes as the inviolability of the "neighborhood school" concept which might include the belief that schools should be economically and racially homogeneous. The administrative barriers involve such problems as those incurred in the transportation of children from residential neighborhoods to other areas of the city. Here again the issue is one of relative advantages of the *status quo* versus the imperatives for change.

The residual psychological prejudices take many forms and probably underlie the apparent inability of society to resolve the historical and administrative problems. Initially the academic retardation of Negro children was explained in terms of their inherent racial inferiority. The existence of segregated schools was supported either by law or explained in terms of the existence of segregated neighborhoods. More recently the racial inferiority or legal and custom interpretations have given way to more subtle explanations and support for continued inefficient education. Examples are theories of "cultural deprivation" and related beliefs that the culturally determined educational inferiority of Negro children will impair the ability of white children to learn if they are taught in the same classes. It is assumed that because of their background, Negro children and their parents are poorly motivated for academic achievement and will not only be unable to compete with white children but will also retard the white children. The implicit and at times explicit assumption of these cultural deprivation theories is that the environmental deficits which Negro children bring with them to school make it difficult, if not impossible, for them to be educated either in racially homogeneous or heterogeneous schools.

This point of view, intentionally or not, tends to support the pervasive rejection of Negro children and obscures and intensifies the basic problem.

There are more flagrant sources of opposition to any effective desegregation of American public schools. White Citizens' Councils in the South, parents' and taxpayers' groups in the North, and the control of boards of education by whites who identify either overtly or covertly with the more vehement opposition to change are examples of effective resistance. School officials and professional educators have defaulted in their responsibility for providing educational leadership. They have tended, for the most part, to go along with the level of community readiness and the "political realities." They have been accessories to the development and use of various subterfuges and devices for giving the appearance of change without its substance and, in doing so, have failed to present the problem of the necessary school reorganization in educational terms. This seems equally true of teachers and teachers' organizations. In some cases, teachers, textbooks, and other teaching materials have either contributed to or failed to counteract racism.

Within the past two years another formidable and insidious barrier in the way of the movement towards effective, desegregated public schools has emerged in the form of the black power movement and its demands for racial separatism. Some of the more vocal of the black power advocates who have addressed themselves to the problems of education have explicitly and implicitly argued for Negroes' control of "Negro Schools." Some have asserted that there should be separate school districts organized to control the schools in all-Negro residential areas; that there should be Negro Boards of Education, Negro superintendents of schools, Negro faculty, and Negro curricula and materials. These demands are clearly a rejection of the goals of integrated education and a return to the pursuit of the myth of an efficient "separate but equal"—or the pathetic wish for a separate and superior —racially-organized system of education. One may view this current trend whereby some Negroes themselves seem to be asking for a racially segregated system of education as a reflection of the frustration resulting from white resistance to genuine desegregation of the public schools since the *Brown* decision and as a reaction to the reality that the quality of education in the *de facto* segregated Negro schools in the North and the Negro schools in the South has steadily deteriorated under the present system of white control.

In spite of these explanations, the demands for segregated schools can be no more acceptable coming from Negroes than they are coming from white segregationists. There is no reason to believe and certainly there is no evidence to support

100

the contention that all-Negro schools, controlled by Negroes, will be any more efficient in preparing American children to contribute constructively to the realities of the present and future world. The damage inherent in racially isolated schools was persuasively documented by the comprehensive study conducted by the United States Commission on Civil Rights.[1]

Furthermore, the more subtle and insidious educational deprivation for white children who are required to attend all-white schools is furthered by both the black and the white advocates of racially homogeneous schools.

Attempts at Remedies

In spite of these obstacles in the path of genuine desegregation of American public schools and the attainment of effective, nonracially constrained education for all American children, there have been persistent attempts to compensate for the deficits of racial isolation in the American public schools. A tremendous amount of energy and money has been expended in the attempt to develop special programs designed to improve the academic achievement of Negro children, who are the most obvious victims of inferior, racially segregated public schools.

The United States Commission on Civil Rights report, *Racial Isolation in the Public Schools,* has presented facts which raise questions concerning the long-range effectiveness of these programs. There is some evidence that these special programs do some good and help some children; but they clearly underline the inadequacy of the regular education these children receive. In addition to the fact that they obscure the overriding reality that underprivileged children are being systematically short-changed in their regular segregated and inferior schools, these programs may also be seen as a type of commitment to the continuation of segregated education.

If one accepts the premise which seems supported by all available evidence, and above all by the reasoning of the *Brown* decision, that racially segregated schools are inherently inferior, it would seem to follow that all attempts to improve the quality of education in all-Negro and all-white schools would have necessarily limited positive effects. All programs designed to raise the quality of education in racially homogeneous schools would therefore have to be seen as essentially evasive programs or as the first stage in an inferior approach to a serious plan for ef-

[1] U.S. Commission on Civil Rights, *Racial Isolation in the Public Schools* (Washington: U.S. Government Printing Office, 1967).

101

fective desegregation of public schools. Given the resistance to an immediate reorganization of the present system of racially organized schools so as to create a more effective system of racially heterogeneous schools, however, one may be required to attempt to increase the efficiency of education in all-Negro schools as a necessary battle in the larger struggle for racially desegregated schools.

The problem of the extent to which it is possible to provide excellent education in a predominantly Negro school should be re-examined thoroughly in spite of the basic premise of the *Brown* decision that racially segregated schools are inherently inferior. Some questions which we must now dare to ask and seek to answer as the basis for a new strategy in the assault against the inhumanity of the American system of racial segregation are:

(1) Is the present pattern of massive educational inferiority and inefficiency which is found in predominantly Negro schools inherent and inevitable in racially segregated schools?

(2) Is there anything which can be done within the Negro schools to raise them to a tolerable level of educational efficiency—or to raise them to a level of educational excellence?

If the answer to the first question is *yes* and to the second question is *no,* then the strategy of continued and intensified assault on the system of segregated schools is justified and should continue unabated since there is no hope of raising the quality of education for Negro children as long as they are condemned to segregated schools—there is no hope of salvaging them. If, on the other hand, the answers to the above questions are reversed, it would suggest that a shift in strategy and tactics, without giving up the ultimate goals of eliminating the dehumanizing force of racial segregation from American life, would be indicated. This shift would suggest that given the present strong and persistent resistance to any serious and effective desegregation of our public schools, that the bulk of the available organizational, human, and financial resources and specialized skills be mobilized and directed toward obtaining the highest quality of education for Negro students without regard to the racial composition of the schools which they attend. This attempt would demand a massive, system-wide educational enrichment program designed to obtain educational excellence in the schools attended by Negro children.

Recent experiences in New York City, Boston, Chicago, Philadelphia and other northern cities reveal that this temporary shift in the battleground will not in itself lead to any easier victory. School boards and public school officials seem as resistant to developing or implementing programs designed to improve the quality and efficiency of education provided for Negro children in segregated schools as they are deaf to all requests for effective desegregation plans and programs. The interests and desires of white middle-class parents, and the interests of the increasingly powerful teachers' federations and professional supervisory associations are invariably given priority over the desire of Negro parents for nonsegregated quality education for their children. The interests of the white parents, teachers, and supervisors are often perceived by them as inimical to the desires of the Negro parents. Furthermore, the capture and control of the public schools by the white middle-class parents and teachers provided the climate within which the system of racially segregated and inferior schools could be developed, expanded and reinforced and within which the public schools became instruments for blocking rather than facilitating the upward mobility of Negroes and other lower-status groups. One, therefore, could not expect these individuals and groups to be sympathetic and responsive to the pleas of Negro parents for higher quality education for their children. Negro parents and organizations must accept and plan their strategy in terms of the fact that adversaries in the battle for higher quality education for Negro children will be as numerous and as formidable as the adversaries in the battle for nonsegregated schools. Indeed they will be the same individuals, officials, and groups in different disguises and with different excuses for inaction but with the same powerful weapons of evasion, equivocation, inaction, or tokenism.

An effective strategy for the present and the future requires rigorous and honest appraisal of all of the realities, a tough-minded diagnosis of the strengths and weaknesses of the Negro and his allies. We cannot now permit ourselves to be deluded by wishful thinking, sentimental optimism, or rigid and oversimplified ideological postures. We must be tough-mindedly pragmatic and flexible as we seek to free our children from the cruel and dehumanizing, inferior and segregated education inflicted upon them by the insensitive, indifferent, affable, and at times callously rigid custodians of American public education.

In developing an appropriate strategy and the related flexible tactics, it must be clearly understood that the objective of improving the quality of education provided for Negro children is not a substitute for or a retreat from the fundamental goal of removing the anachronism of racially segregated schools from American life. The objective of excellent education for Negro and other lower-status children is inextricably linked with the continuing struggle to desegregate public education. All of the public school, college, and professional school civil-rights litigation instituted by the legal staff of the NAACP arose from recognition of the obvious fact that the segregated schools which Negroes were forced by law to attend were inferior and therefore damaging and violative of the equal protection clause in the 14th amendment of the United States Constitution.

The suggested shift in emphasis from desegregation to quality of education is not a retreat into the blind alley of accepting racial separation as advocated by the Negro nationalist groups, nor is it the acceptance of defeat in the battle for desegregation. It is rather a regrouping of forces, a shift in battle plans and an attempt to determine the most vulnerable flanks of the opposition as the basis for major attack. The resisting educational bureaucracies, their professional staffs, and the segment of the white public which has not yet been infected fatally by the American racist disease are most vulnerable to attack on the issue of the inferior quality of education found in Negro schools and the need to institute a plan immediately to raise the educational level of these schools. The economic, political, military, social-stability, international democratic, humane, and self-interest arguments in favor of an immediate massive program for educational excellence in predominantly Negro schools are so persuasive as to be irrefutable. The expected resistance should be overcome with intelligently planned and sustained efforts.

The first phase of an all-out attack on the inferior education now found in racially segregated schools should be coordinated with a strategy and program for massive and realistic desegregation of entire school systems. This more complicated phase of the over-all struggle will continue to meet the resistances of the past with increased intensity. It will be necessary, therefore, to break this task down into its significant components and determine the timing and phasing of the attack on each or combinations of the components. For example:

The evidence and arguments demonstrating the detrimental effects of segregated schools on the personality and effectiveness of white children should be gathered, evaluated, and widely disseminated in ways understandable to the mases of whites.

The need to reorganize large public school systems away from the presently inefficient and uneconomic neighborhood schools to more modern and viable systems of organization such as educational parks, campuses, or clusters must be sold to the general public in terms of hard dollars and cents and educational efficiency benefiting all children rather than in terms of public-school desegregation.

The need to consolidate small, uneconomic, and relatively ineffective school districts into larger educational and fiscal systems in order to obtain more efficient education for suburban and exurban children must also be sold in direct practical terms rather than in terms of desegregation of schools.

The need to involve large metropolitan regional planning in the mobilization, utilization, and distribution of limited educational resources on a more efficient level must also be explored and discussed publicly.

The movement toward decentralization of large urban school systems must be carefully monitored in order to see that decentralization does not reinforce or concretize urban public school segregation—and to assure that decentralization is consistent with the more economically determined trend toward consolidation and regional planning allocation of resources and cooperation.

A final indication that phase one, the struggle for excellent education for Negro children in ghetto schools, is not inconsistent with phase two, the struggle for nonsegregated education for all children, is to be seen in the fact that if it were possible to raise the quality of education provided for Negro children who attend the urban schools to a level of unquestioned excellence, the flight of middle-class whites to the suburbs might be stemmed and some who have left might be attracted back to the city. Hence, phase one activity would increase the chances of obtaining nonsegregated education in our cities. Similarly, some of the program suggestions of phase two such as educational parks and campuses and the possibilities of regional planning and educational cooperation across present municipal boundaries could lead to substantial improvements in the quality of education offered to inner-city children.

The goal of high quality education for Negro and lower-status children and the goal of public school desegregation are inextricable; the attainment of the one will lead to the attainment of the other. It is not likely that there could be effective desegregation of the schools without a marked increase in the academic achievement and personal and social effectiveness of Negro and white children. Neither is it possible to have a marked increase in the educational efficiency of Negro schools and the resulting dramatic increase in the academic performance of Negro children without directly and indirectly facilitating the process of public school desegregation.

Problems of Educational Monopoly

It is possible that all attempts to improve the quality of education in our present racially segregated public schools and all attempts to desegregate these schools will have minimal positive results. The rigidity of present patterns of public school organization and the concomitant stagnation in quality of education and academic performance of children may not be amenable to any attempts at change working through and within the present system.

Until the influx of Negro and Puerto Rican youngsters into urban public schools, the American public school system was justifiably credited with being the chief instrument for making the American dream of upward social, economic, and political mobility a reality. The depressed immigrants from southern and eastern Europe could use American public schools as the ladder toward the goals of assimilation and success. The past successes of American public education seem undebatable. The fact that American public schools were effective mobility vehicles for white American immigrants makes even more stark and intolerable their present ineffectiveness for Negro and Puerto Rican children. Now it appears that the present system of organization and functioning of urban public schools is a chief blockage in the mobility of the masses of Negro and other lower-status minority group children. The inefficiency of their schools and the persistence and acceptance of the explanations for this generalized inefficiency are clear threats to the viability of our cities and national stability. The relationship between long-standing urban problems of poverty, crime and delinquency, broken homes—the total cycle of pathology, powerlessness, and personal and social destructiveness which haunts our urban ghettos—and the breakdown in the efficiency of our public schools is now unavoidably clear. It is not enough that those responsible for our public schools should assert passively that the schools merely reflect the pathologies and injustices of our society. Public schools and their administrators must assert boldly that education must dare to challenge and change society toward social justice as the basis for democratic stability.

There remains the disturbing question—a most relevant question probably too painful for educators themselves to ask—whether the selection process involved in training and promoting educators and administrators for our public schools emphasizes qualities of passivity, conformity, caution, smoothness, and superficial affability rather than boldness, creativity, substance, and the ability to demand and obtain those things which are essential for solid and effective public education for all children. If the former is true and if we are dependent upon the present educational establishment, then all hopes for the imperative reforms which must be made so that city public schools can return to a level of innovation and excellence are reduced to a minimum, if not totally eliminated.

The racial components of the present crisis in urban public education clearly make the possibilities of solution more difficult and may contribute to the passivity and pervading sense of hopelessness of school administrators. Aside from any latent or subtle racism which might infect school personnel themselves, they are hampered by the gnawing awareness that with the continuing flight of middle-class whites from urban public schools and with the increasing competition which education must engage in for a fair share of the tax dollar, it is quite possible that Americans will decide deliberately or by default to sacrifice urban public schools on the altars of its historic and contemporary forms of racism. If this can be done without any real threat to the important segments of economic and political power in the society and with only Negro children as the victims, then there is no realistic basis for hope that our urban public schools will be saved.

The hope for a realistic approach to saving public education in American cities seems to this observer to be found in a formula whereby it can be demonstrated to the public at large that the present level of public school inefficiency has reached an intolerable stage of public calamity. It must be demonstrated that minority group children are not the only victims of the monopolistic inefficiency of the present pattern of organization and functioning of our public schools.

It must be demonstrated that white children—privileged white children whose parents understandably seek to protect them by moving to suburbs or by sending them to private and parochial schools—also suffer both potentially and immediately.

It must be demonstrated that business and industry suffer intolerable financial burdens of double and triple taxation in seeking to maintain a stable economy in the face of the public school inefficiency which produces human casualties rather than constructive human beings.

It must be demonstrated that the cost in correctional, welfare, and health services are intolerably high in seeking to cope with consequences of educational inefficiency—that it would be more economical, even for an affluent society, to pay the price and meet the demands of efficient public education.

It must be demonstrated that a nation which presents itself to the world as the guardian of democracy and the protector of human values throughout the world cannot itself make a mockery of these significant ethical principles by dooming one-tenth of its own population to a lifetime of inhumane futility because of remediable educational deficiencies in its public schools.

These must be understood and there must be the commitment to make the average American understand them if our public schools and our cities are to be effective. But it does not seem likely that the changes necessary for increased efficiency of our urban public schools will come about because they should. Our urban public school systems seem muscle-bound with tradition. They seem to represent the most rigid forms of bureaucracies which, paradoxically, are most resilient in their ability and use of devices to resist rational or irrational demands for change. What is most important in understanding the ability of the educational establishment to resist change is the fact that public school systems are protected public monopolies with only minimal competition from private and parochial schools. Few critics of the American urban public schools—even severe ones such as myself—dare to question the givens of the present organization of public education in terms of local control of public schools, in terms of existing municipal or political boundaries, or in terms of the rights and prerogatives of boards of education to establish policy and select professional staff—at least nominally or titularly if not actually. Nor dare the critics question the relevance of the criteria and standards for selecting superintendents, principals, and teachers, or the relevance of all of these to the objectives of public education—producing a literate and informed public to carry on the business of democracy—and to the goal of producing human beings with social sensitivity and dignity and creativity and a respect for the humanity of others.

A monopoly need not genuinely concern itself with these matters. As long as local school systems can be assured of state aid and increasing federal aid without the accountability which inevitably comes with aggressive competition, it would be sentimental, wishful thinking to expect any significant increase in the efficiency of our public schools. If there are no alternatives to the present system—short of present private and parochial schools which are approaching their limit of expansion—then the possibilities of improvement in public education are limited.

Alternative Forms of Public Education

Alternatives—realistic, aggressive, and viable competitors—to the present public school systems must be found. The development of such competitive public school systems will be attacked by the defenders of the present system as attempts to weaken the present system and thereby weaken, if not destroy, public education. This type of expected self-serving argument can be briefly and accurately disposed of by asserting and demonstrating that truly effective competition strengthens rather than weakens that which deserves to survive. I would argue further that public education need not be identified with the present system of organization of public schools. Public education can be more broadly and pragmatically defined in terms of that form of organization and functioning of an educational system which is in the public interest. Given this definition, it becomes clear that an inefficient system of public systems is not in the public interest:

108

—a system of public schools which destroys rather than develops positive human potentialities is not in the public interest;

—a system which consumes funds without demonstrating effective returns is not in the public interest;

—a system which insists that its standards of performance should not or cannot be judged by those who must pay the cost is not in the public interest;

—a system which says that the public has no competence to assert that a patently defective product is a sign of the system's inefficiency and demands radical reforms is not in the public interest;

—a system which blames its human resources and its society while it quietly acquiesces in, and inadvertently perpetuates, the very injustices which it claims limit its efficiency is not in the public interest.

Given these assumptions, therefore, it follows that alternative forms of public education must be developed if the children of our cities are to be educated and made constructive members of our society. In the development of alternatives, all attempts must at the same time be made to strengthen our present urban public schools. Such attempts would involve re-examination, revision, and strengthening of curricula, methods, personnel selection, and evaluation; the development of more rigorous procedures of supervision, reward of superior performance, and the institution of a realistic and tough system of accountability, and the provision of meaningful ways of involving the parents and the community in the activities of the school.

The above measures, however, will not suffice. The following are suggested as possible, realistic, and practical competitors to the present form of urban public school systems:

Regional State Schools. These schools would be financed by the states and would cut across present urban-suburban boundaries.

Federal Regional Schools. These schools would be financed by the Federal Government out of present state aid funds or with additional federal funds. These schools would be able to cut through state boundaries and could make provisions for residential students.

College- and University-Related Open Schools. These schools would be financed by colleges and universities as part of their laboratories in education. They would be open to the public and not restricted to children of faculty and students. Obviously, students would be selected in terms of constitutional criteria and their percentage determined by realistic considerations.

Industrial Demonstration Schools. These schools would be financed by industrial, business, and commercial firms for their employees and selected members of the public. These would not be vocational schools—but elementary and comprehensive high schools of quality. They would be sponsored by combinations of business and industrial firms in much the same way as churches and denominations sponsor and support parochial or sectarian schools.

Labor Union Sponsored Schools. These schools would be financed and sponsored by labor unions largely, but not exclusively, for the children of their members.

Army Schools. The Defense Department has been quietly effective in educating some of the casualties of our present public schools. It is hereby suggested that they now go into the business of repairing hundreds of thousands of these human casualties with affirmation rather than apology. Schools for adolescent drop-outs or educational rejects could be set up by the Defense Department adjacent to camps—but not necessarily as an integral part of the military. If this is necessary, it should not block the attainment of the goal of rescuing as many of these young people as possible. They are not expendable on the altar of anti-militarism rhetoric.

With strong, efficient, and demonstrably excellent parallel systems of public schools, organized and operated on a quasi-private level, and with quality control and professional accountability maintained and determined by Federal and State educational standards and supervision, it would be possible to bring back into public education a vitality and dynamism which are now clearly missing. Even the public discussion of these possibilities might clear away some of the dank stagnation which seems to be suffocating urban education today. American industrial and material wealth was made possible through industrial competition. American educational health may be made possible through educational competition.

If we succeed, we will have returned to the dynamic, affirmative goal of education; namely, to free man of irrational fears, superstitions, and hatreds. Specifically, in America the goal of democratic education must be to free Americans of the blinding and atrophying shackles of racism. A fearful, passive, apologetic, and inefficient educational system cannot help in the attainment of these goals.

If we succeed in finding and developing these and better alternatives to the present educational inefficiency, we will not only save countless Negro children from lives of despair and hopelessness; and thousands and thousands of white children from cynicism, moral emptiness, and social ineptness—but we will also demonstrate the validity of our democratic promises. We also will have saved our civilization through saving our cities.

110

CHAPTER III: ETHNICITY AND EDUCATION

Why do culturally different children learn less in school than white middle-class children? This question is often asked and seldom definitively answered. First, what are the variables that tend to depress academic achievement of this group of children? Is it lower intelligence, poor home environment, poor nutrition, or just plain apathy toward the school and its mission? This chapter deals with several of these variables of underachievement of culturally different children. American Indians, Mexican-Americans, Orientals, and Black children and their problems with the American school are discussed. The bias of the white oriented school serving the culturally different child is covered in an article by Maurie Hillson in great detail and this may provide a few clues to new teachers of culturally different children.

Unfortunately, few programs or pieces of curriculum have been specifically designed to take into account the socialization process of the culturally different children in the urban slums. Few, if any, reading programs have been built around the types of speech known to ghetto children and the vocabularies they possess. In the case of Black children, the dialect they speak is usually discarded as being a

depressor of learning how to read standard English.
Great efforts are then exerted to eradicate this "bad"
speech in favor of standard English found in the textbooks and in the speech of the teacher. However, what
would be the effect if Black dialect were used as a
positive reinforcer of learning to speak and read
standard English?

The child with English as a second language has
an exceptionally difficult problem in school because
learning how to read and speak English are new games
to him along with the ethos of his middle-class oriented
school.

Quality education, equal educational opportunity,
and separate schools are three terms currently in question
in educational circles in this country. Actually, they
apply almost solely to the culturally different child
living in the slums of the inner cities and in the rural,
socially isolated areas of the rest of America. Can
quality education of equal proportions be obtained by
culturally different children in separate or segregated
schools? Or, is it necessary for our pluralistic
society to be integrated at least in the schools, if not
in the residential and employment spheres? The question
of race constantly enters this question, especially in

Northern cities such as Detroit, Chicago, Cleveland, and Philadelphia as bussing looms over the metropolitan schools. The history of America has advocated the melting pot theory where ethnic groups become homogenized Americans after several generations and the schools have been a leading agent of social mobility for these groups. However, today we see that melted Americans do not desire that other Americans with different colored skins be melted down into homogenized Americans. The "rightness of whiteness" still reigns supreme in this country and its school systems. The culturally different child sees this. And as he passes through the school system, he becomes more frustrated and alienated and finally becomes so disgusted that he just drops out. Educators often claim he is not future oriented; however, why should he be? It would seem that one would have to perceive a significant future to be future oriented.

In summary, this chapter says that the deck is stacked against culturally different children in this country and little is being done at present to even up the odds. It seems strange that a country with all of the resources for erasing poverty and actually providing an ample amount of opportunity for its citizens would be so selfish as to let people go hungry in the midst of plenty.

By MAURIE HILLSON

The Reorganization of the School: Bringing About a Remission in the Problems Faced by Minority Children

T HE SCHOOL IN AMERICA is the major social institution that serves as the acculturation agency for the society. The school is a middle-class agency. Friedenberg observed that lower-class, and for the most part minority group, adolescents "are helpless in the meshes of middle-class administrative procedure and are rapidly neutralized and eliminated by it . . . they cannot defend themselves against the covert, lingering hostility of teachers and school administrators."[1] There is no question in the minds of observers and students of the educational scene that the school discriminates against lower-class students, minorities, and in many instances, any who deviate slightly from the established and imposed middle-class norm behavior patterns and performances. This is recorded middle-class social behavior. It is substantially evident in all geographical sections of the country. Even though the schools are publicly supported and are maintained supposedly for all peoples, classes, and groups, the lower-class and especially minority group populations benefit less.

As Clark points out, "The Northern Negro is clearly not suffering from a lack of laws. But he is suffering — rejected, segregated, discriminated against in employment, in housing, his children subjugated in de facto segregated and inferior schools in spite of a plethora of laws that imply the contrary."[2] The lower classes seem to be permitted merely to attend schools and must adapt themselves to what is to many of them the "phony" but existing system. Functional programs of significance which could offer lower-class youth opportunities for rehabilitation are essentially absent from the curricula and teaching procedures in the present middle-class oriented schools.

The mind set of this middle-class orientation toward minority children is one that sets into motion actions that attempt to bring about a conversion to middle-class ways of life. The widely used term culturally deprived for purposes of identifying minority or lower-class children is a middle-class stereotype. This stereotype feeds the reform or conversion orientation embraced by the school and encompasses the attitudes

---

[1] Edgar Z. Friedenberg, The Vanishing Adolescent (Boston, 1959), p. 112.
[2] Kenneth B. Clark, "The Wonder Is There Have Been So Few Riots," New York Times, September 5, 1965, Section 6, p. 38.

PHYLON, 1967, Vol. 28, pp. 230-245.

of teachers, administrators, and active patrons who control school boards, school organizations, and offices in parent-teacher associations. The attempts to reorganize the school as a social institution, so it will better serve minority children as they face problems attendant to acculturation are practically nil. There are the exceptions of the few who have made enlightened thrusts. Their work and commitment stand out like beacons in this otherwise dark morass of inaction.

It is not within the purview of this article to adduce the evidence that supports the general validity of the conclusions concerning the middle-class hold and determination of the aims and policies of the school. The intent is to reveal the manner in which extant programs, albeit scarce in number, produce more effective educational opportunity and success when focused on the strengths and relevant needs of the lower-class and minority populations. In addition, some approaches to minority group and lower-class education based on the sociological and psychological correlates of this population will be considered.

Prior to an accounting or analysis of the situation concerning lower-class or minority children, the school they attend, and their problems, an assumption concerning the attitude toward these children needs to be made. Much of the problem of discontinuity experienced in school exists because the middle class runs the school. They operate it on the idea that the middle-class existence, as they experience it, is superior to the lower-class way of life. The composition of the lower class relies heavily on minority groups for its makeup and a large part of its population.

This is especially true in urban areas whose slums are made up of a coalition, or at the least a collocation, of minorities. Simply stated, a "natural" superiority over minority groups is assumed by many of those of the middle class. Functioning with this point of view in mind, it becomes evident that middle-class people can perceive that the school (their school) has no obligation to meet the irrelevant expectations of the lower class. This Procrustean attitude has been the circumstance for years. It continues, only mildly abated, to be the condition in many of the "crash" compensatory education and job training programs being mounted in the present war on poverty. It takes on an even more intense nature in those activities that are directly supervised by business enterprises which see the poverty money windfall as their own natural common market.

If, on the other hand, along with Ruth Benedict, A. L. Kroeber, Franz Boas, and Melville Herskovits, one can assume that no particular way of life is superior, but rather that all culture is functional in nature (including lower-class or minority group culture), it is legitimate to expect, nay insist, that the public school of America meet the expectations of the youth of any given social class. These expectations can be "aspirationally" middle class in nature, or they can be those that will enable youth to cope better, in a highly relevant way, with their present life situation. If the life styles of minority groups and the lower class are granted functional validity, and if the school as a social institution creates programs based on the environmental and motivational correlates of this culture, then by this action the school would truly reflect the most cherished wishes of an operational democracy.

The simple truth is that, with rare exception, the American school has discriminated against the lower-class and minority group youth from early childhood education programs on through to all areas of higher education where the so-called enlightened and leadership community should have known better. This youth has been offered less in facilities, quality of teaching, challenging and relevant curricula, worthwhile organizational changes and innovations, and favorable pupil-teacher ratios. Moreover, teacher education programs rarely recognize the aspects of education attendant to the problems of various social classes. By implication, unwittingly or maybe by purpose, colleges fail to create a trained and viable corps of teachers who want to involve themselves in the education of the lower-class or minority children.

Even as awareness grows concerning the needs of lower-class youth, the educational programs and approaches being proffered are frequently unimaginative. They habitually smack of the supercilious middle-class proselytism. This is reflected in the verbalisms of the curriculum documents and the less than enthusiastic teaching that accompanies these unrealistic forays into areas that cry for real action. Education at all levels suffers from a cumulative deficit in understanding and coming to grips with the problems of education for lower-class and minority children. These children do not evidence any deprivation of culture. Through the workings of a powerful middle-class majority they have been put in a clearly and distinctly disadvantageous position educationally as well as in almost every other way imaginable.

In America today there is a seeming shift of emphasis. The civil rights movement continues apace. The riots of the Northern ghettoes, the explosions of the social dynamite that reverberate through shaken communities, waken many. The responsible elements of the society need to ask themselves important and germane questions. Will education as it concerns minority groups become, in Clark's words, "an active center of cultural and social change as it grows in size and complexity and takes on new tasks?"[3] Will the colleges make an impact at the teacher education level? Will they create a teacher for these youngsters who will be "a cultural transmitter?"[4] Can teachers "achieve sufficient awareness of the multidimensional processes involved so that few-

[3] Burton R. Clark, *Educating the Expert Society* (San Francisco, 1962), p. 26.
[4] George D. Spindler, "The Transmission of American Culture," in George D. Spindler (ed.), *Education and Culture: Anthropological Approaches* (New York, 1963), p. 172.

er potentially creative channels of communication, of transmission, be blocked, with the consequence that more children can be effectively caught up in the educative process?"[5] Is the problem compounded so that "until the comprehensive school has been reassessed and until the lower-class schools are given autonomy, independent financing, and trained staffs to deal with their own problems, the social class problem will be glaring at the American educator, regardless of whether he is personally prejudiced?"[6] And can we grapple insightfully with the notions that "the method of organizing may either abort or enhance the possibility of fulfilling the school's aims... [that] the problem is not only a technical one, but a moral one . . . [and that] failure to consider the effects of organization on educational aims is to overlook one of the basic forces of modern life-complex organization?"[7]

Elements of all of these factors are involved in the problem of educating lower-class or minority children. The classic failure of the schools to educate successfully lower-class youth in general, and serve them as they served earlier generations, is due in large measure to attempting simple treatments of what are highly complex problems as compared to those faced by the immigrant society of the late nineteenth and early twentieth centuries. Many of the administrators, supervisors, and teachers in the schools have reduced the educational problem to one of motivation. This dooms most programs to failure because from this erroneous base various projects and activities are put into operation, miscarry, and gain little, if any, positive response from the pupils.

The school will not become an "active center" of change unless certain operant conditions change within the teaching profession and within the administrative and organizational scheme of the school itself.

What will be the process of enculturation or socialization when studies reveal that the teacher, the transmitter, is involved in the unequal distribution of school rewards from kindergarten through college? The distribution of those rewards is based on social class and the preponderance is received by the middle and upper classes.[8]

---

[5] *Ibid.*
[6] Ronald G. Corwin, *A Sociology of Education: Emerging Patterns of Class Status and Power in the Public Schools* (New York, 1965), p. 188.
[7] *Ibid.*, pp. 188-89.
[8] W. Lloyd Warner, Robert J. Havighurst, and Martin Loeb, *Who Shall Be Educated* (New York, 1944), p. 77; W. W. Charters, Jr., "Social Class Analysis and the Control of Public Education," *Harvard Educational Review*, XXIII (Fall, 1953), 272; August B. Hollingshead, *Elmtown's Youth* (New York, 1949), pp. 172-80; Patricia Cayo Sexton, *Education and Income* (New York, 1961), p. 163; Charles S. Benson, *The Cheerful Prospect* (Boston, 1965), pp. 19-28; Stephen Abrahamson, "School Rewards and Social Class Status," *Educational Research Bulletin*, XXXI (1952), 8-15; Burlyn Wade, "Social Class in a Teacher's College," *American Journal of Sociology* (November, 1954), 131-38; J. K. Coster, "Attitudes toward School of High School Pupils from Three Income Levels," *Journal of Educational Psychology*, XLIX (April, 1958), 61-66; Howard S. Becker, "Social-Class Variations in the Teacher Pupil Relationship," *Journal of Educational Sociology* (1952), *et passim*. These studies represent just a small part of the congeries of empirical materials extant and which clearly show the existence and continuous practice of unequal and discriminatory distribution of rewards in the educational life of minority or lower-class children. Cf Ben H. Bagdikian, *In the Midst of Plenty: The Poor in America* (Boston, 1964); Patricia Cayo Sexton, *Spanish Harlem: Anatomy of Poverty* (New York, 1965), and Simeon Booker, *Black Man's America* (Englewood Cliffs, 1964) who are insightful reporters and whose material corroborates the findings of the social scientists (Professor Sexton is also an able sociologist) concerning inequalities of educational opportunity for lower-class or minority children compared to the generality of the school population.

When school people fight with an almost evangelical fervor to retain the present organization of the schools (i.e., grade levels, learning tracks, subject matter orientation, neighborhood based, psychologically rather than sociologically teacher oriented), what hopes exist for enhancing the real "possibility of fulfilling the school's aims" through the effects of organizational innovation or change? Strong movements are taking shape in upper- and middle-class communities aimed at educational reorganization. Little is being done in schools that are populated by minority or lower-class children. Yet, it is patently obvious that where some of this innovation is being attempted, where elements of teacher collaboration, nongrading, and pupil-team learning exist, and where teachers possess a deeper knowledge of the anthropological, philosophical, and sociological correlates of minority or lower-class life, an impact is being made in meeting the functional needs of this population. And, it is important to note that this impact is being made in spite of the overwhelming political and economic pressures that mitigate such change that brings with it subsequent measures of success.[9]

There can be little doubt that an awareness of this whole problem is growing. There is evidence that a shift from the old social welfare concept of social work with its inherent inaction is giving way to a community involvement and development concept with its inherent positive action. There are many things that harbinger well for a real advance in the long march toward honest equality. A short, non-exhaustive listing would include the insistence of the United States Commissioner of Education on compliance with the law vis-à-vis desegregation in order to receive federal funds, the various new laws extending civil rights and voting rights, and the Economic Opportunity Act of 1964, with its insistence on the inclusion in decision-making capacities of those individuals for whom the Act is intended.

This new awareness coupled with the many pioneer efforts is reflected in the growing collection of material concerning educating lower-class or minority children. The category that usually identifies this material is called *The Education of the Disadvantaged or Culturally Deprived*. This kind of euphemism, or any other fastidious linguistic delicacy, cannot wipe away stark facts of reality. It is in one way just

[9] One such program is the "Madison Area Project" of the City School District of Syracuse, New York. This was directed by Dr. Mario D. Fantini and was supported by the New York Department of Education and the Ford Foundation. It is a hint and reflection of what committed and insightful leadership can create. See *Laboratory for Change: The Madison Area Project* (City School District, Syracuse, New York, October 1964). A similar, but limited, program was carried out in Passaic, New Jersey. See Maurie Hillson, "The Second Interim Report of the Grant to Fairleigh Dickinson University by the Ford Foundation on December 17, 1962" (July 15, 1965), pp. 37-49. See also "The First Interim Report of the Grant to Fairleigh Dickinson University by the Ford Foundation on December 17, 1962" (September 1, 1964, unpaged) for an overview of the problem prior to reorganizational and innovative projects. Other examples of similar activities are extant. See *Promising Practices from Projects for the Culturally Deprived* (Chicago: The Research Council of the Greater Cities Program for School Improvement, 1964). And for a picture of the New York State programs see Bernard A. Kaplan, "Issues in Educating the Culturally Disadvantaged," *Phi Delta Kappan*, XLV, No. 2 (November, 1963). These New York programs are basically oriented toward the principle of lower-class conversion rather than rehabilitation.

another indication that lower-class status, or poverty, or disadvantage is something that is difficult for the middle class to face up to when the social distance from this way of life is so great. Minority children of today are from the lower classes. They usually live in urban slums or rural poverty pockets. They suffer much deprivation. They are disadvantaged economically, socially, and educationally. This collection of circumstances makes the terms *disadvantaged children, minority children, lower-class children, deprived children,* or *culture of poverty children* frequently, if not always, interchangeable. Regardless of the terminology used, the material extant on the disadvantaged offers some insight into the present status of the actions concerning the education of this large and growing segment of the population. A careful reading and study of the programs allow for opportunities for evaluation, reflection, and, hopefully, for new and purposeful directions. Only an overview can be attempted in the space allowable.

There are certain kinds of head start programs. President Johnson's enthusiasm notwithstanding, a more socially scientific look must be taken at what he hailed in a political sense as a smashing success in reversing the problems of educational disadvantage. These programs do serve to equalize, to a degree, the needed readiness to learn some of the customary curricula of present middle-class schools. More are needed. Stronger curricula are needed. Many compensatory educational programs are now in operation in an attempt to compensate for that which was not offered or, if offered, not assimilated by the pupils the first time around. These are in existence, not only in slums, but in suburbs as well. Many minority groups who have escaped the ghettoes find themselves in new situations where their children are operating at academic levels below those found in well-established middle-class schools. Various programs encompassing tutorial activities, pre-school cooperative nurseries, study-center and study-skills aid projects, and other compensatory endeavors have been developed. These are aimed at closing the gap between the learning levels.

Fewer programs by far of really functional educational intervention are taking place. Intervening into the existing pattern of nonfunctional educational programs is the most difficult of techniques. It is an attempt at both structural and organizational change.[10] Few educators can train their own staffs to do this, nor, in many instances, are they interested. They have no desire to take on the political and social power structures which are against change. Even with backing developed from an awakened community spirit seeking positive action, the problem is one of almost insurmountable proportions if not of frustrating pros-

---

[10] "Laboratory for Change: The Madison Area Project," *op. cit.*, pp. 5-23.

pects.[11] Real educational intervention, which attempts to stop one trend and establish a counteraction, while still dealing with the other basic problems which plague this population, requires total involvement. It demands the implication or inclusion of every facet of a community at large, and in particular, the school as a social institution. It requires a different kind of teacher education. It insists on different kinds of methods of instruction, strategies of approach in teaching, and actions dealing with school organization. It mandates creative and vastly different insights concerning educational supervision and administration. Most importantly, intervention should bring with it the demand that teaching will be based on a concept of the learner gained from an in-depth knowledge of the psycho-sociological correlates or concomitant relationships of social class, ethnicity, and race. These actions will eliminate the blatant disjunctive, purposeless, and frequently irrelevant intuitively based educational programs being foisted upon these youth.

The strong influences that environmental factors play in education (especially in the creation of predispositions for or against it) may be minimized by well-planned educational interventions. If they cannot be accomplished with the backing of a community so that they are total in nature, at least the educational community within the confines of a school building, or a teacher within the classroom, can intervene to establish better educational opportunity.

Deutsch feels that although "some of the responsibility may be shared by the larger society, the school, as the institution of that society, offers the only mechanism by which the job can be done." [12] Recent studies reveal that giving a youngster a head start in a strong compensatory educational program may bring him only to a level of readiness for a customary nonfunctional school program. His constant return to the attitudes and deprivations of social opportunity and family cohesion, racial discrimination, and other social variables quickly erase that equalization. The overwhelming aspects of this kind of life reverse the educational trend started in the pre-school years, and increasing weeks and months of nonfunctional schooling bring poorer rather than better performance, retardation, and school leaving. Beyond the work of the school, Clark [13] points out that only a total alteration of the life situation of the slum and of the total community will eliminate what might be described as an educational pathology; and Sexton calls for an action to bring teachers, through special housing buys, back into the slums and at the same time organize for attitudinal change,

---

[11] Francis P. Purcell, "Action Programs in the War on Poverty," *Proceedings of the Institute on Poverty* (South Dakota University, October 12-13, 1964), pp. 22-24. This whole set of materials is worthy of careful consideration by any student of poverty and disadvantagement.
[12] Martin Deutsch, "The Disadvantaged Child and the Learning Process: Some Social, Psychological and Developmental Considerations," in A. H. Passow (ed.), *Education in Depressed Areas* (New York, 1963), p. 178.
[13] Kenneth B. Clark, *Dark Ghetto: Dilemmas of Social Power* (New York, 1965).

new instructional and organizational methods, and for community arousal.[14]

Even with a mounting war on poverty, along with what seems to be a greater national awareness of the problems of civil rights and racism, the depth of understanding necessary to hasten widespread social change makes it evident slum living, urban or rural, will exist for years to come. The self-generated plaudits of the public relationists concerning the activities of government, private industry, and other poverty agencies are indicative of the patina-like commitment and impoverishment of insight into the real needs of these people. The full cure for the social sickness of poverty, disadvantagement, unequal opportunity, and racism cannot be achieved immediately. But some basic thrusts through revised school programs can be achieved and are absolutely necessary. These could effect the first tentative steps toward a long overdue total restorative drive to reverse the desolation attendant to unequal treatment for lower-class and minority children.

One of the major aspects of concern, a major variable in educating the often nonliterate disadvantaged, and sometimes bilingual, children is the use of language. Language is a basic code. Through it, the necessary and appropriate insights and actions dealing with the larger social context take place. Outside of the neighborhood, wherein the functional patois allows for the coming to grips with life's needs, there exists a larger area of contact.

The study of language as behavior is not limited to the scholarly literature. George Bernard Shaw felt that language served as the social class cosmetic. It was in his play *Pygmalion* that we learn from Professor Higgins "the great secret . . . is not having bad manners or any other particular sort of manners, but having the same manner for all human souls; in short, behaving as if you were in heaven, where there are no third class carriages, and one soul is as good as another."

Bernstein,[15] an English sociologist, offers a viable socio-linguistic theory in which he sees language as the pivotal factor in socialization. He postulates the existence of two linguistic codes: elaborated and restricted. These, he contends, regulate behavior and are used differently by social classes. Each code requires distinct verbal planning. The middle classes manipulate the verbal symbols successfully in the elaborated code. Conversely, the lower classes operate in a restricted code and are restricted by it to a different level of opportunity. Teachers generally dea¹ with or speak an elaborated code. Theirs is a language, or verbalization scheme, representative of middle-class society.

[14] Sexton, *op. cit.*, p. 69.
[15] Basil Bernstein, "Social Class and Linguistic Development: A Theory of Social Class Learning," in A. H. Halsey *et al* (eds.), *Education, Economy and Society* (Glencoe, 1961), pp. 288-314. See Susan M. Ervin and Wick R. Miller, "Language Development, in *Child Psychology*, 62nd Yearbook of the Society for the Study of Education (Chicago, 1963), pp. 128-29.

The levels of abstraction along with the verbal manipulation rarely coincide with the restricted code knowledge held by the pupils. This lack of confluence between communication modalities increases the social distance between the middle-class teacher and lower-class minority children. If one accepts the school in society as a socializing agency offering a *weltanschauung*, then all children of all classes need to be in contact with the equipment to deal with the procedures of a total society. This is not a commitment to any particular class value structure or to class mobility as a basic aim of the educational enterprise. It creates familiarity with the operational items needed to deal with and understand the society. It seems reasonable that some of the strategies involved in teaching disadvantaged, minority, or lower-class youth require the creation of intense and constant activities that build or offer opportunities for both the knowledge and the acquisition of the elaborated language code. This allows children to function within their own culture or to subsist at a different cultural level if they so desire.

An excellent example of this clash of milieus, this linguistic inconsistency, is offered by an analysis of teacher verbal output in a classroom. The author used a "Two Stop Watch" technique as a means of apprising student teachers of the intensity of their verbosity. It was a simple method. The left pocket contained a watch that moved when the teachers spoke and the right pocket contained a watch that moved when the pupils participated. At the conclusion of a lesson a teacher was asked to estimate the amount of time he had spoken and the amount of time the pupils had spoken. The length of time for the lessons observed ranged from eleven minutes in the lower grades to sixty-five minutes in the upper grades. The assessments of the amounts of time for both teachers and students made by the teachers were woefully unrealistic. The teachers rarely came close to a realistic assessment of their prolixity, estimating it to be about one quarter or one third of what the stop watch revealed, and conversely assigned to pupil verbalization amounts of time far in excess of what they were.

In the context of a discussion concerning the restricted language code of children and their lack of appropriate symbols for verbal impression *vis-à-vis* middle-class teachers, the problem becomes clear. Couple this revelation with the usual inattentive behavior patterns of the youngsters of this milieu due to inappropriate learning settings and some obvious conclusions can be drawn. If seven or eight minutes of a twelve minute lesson represent teacher verbalization, even if the teacher moves into some of the restricted code patois, any impression on the part of the children is usually minuscule. In addition to the fact that the children lack certain kinds of language stimulation, there exists the real and more unfortunate situation that middle-class teachers scorn and denigrate the language patterns that are native to the lower class.[16]

These pupils usually come from homes where monosyllabic responses and commands are habitual, where physical action such as shrugs, nods, or facial expressions replace words, and where the premium may be placed on silence — or else. In the classroom there arises a clash of purposes rather than a congruity of aims. The educational implications are varied, but research seems to indicate that the most important thing is to prevent as much as possible the pejorative language acquisition in the home. This is difficult. The children hold strong emotional ties to this language that allows them to communicate with parents and friends and to disparage it is frequently to endanger the emotional security of the children.

In spite of the difficulty, the problem must be encountered. At least two approaches can be ventured: establish highly creative linguistic activities in spoken and written discourse with the emphasis on the spoken, and create much more concrete and related learning activities which serve as cues or leads to higher levels of abstractions in not only language but in learning in general. If one draws some insights from the vast collection of materials in cultural anthropology that show the understandable relationship and integration of work and play in the education of children, then the highly creative approaches to this whole area of education can soon be forthcoming.

The time for this is in the pre-school years. Where the accumulated learning deficits have intensified this problem over a period of years, various techniques can be employed to elevate the use of language through the use of "live case studies" that can lead to the creation of synonymical language patterns of the elaborated or standard language code. Ausubel recommends "an enriched program of pre-school education that would emphasize perceptual discrimination and language acquisition." [17] A simple nontechnical analysis of what is normally done in the middle-class home could serve as a teacher job description as it concerns some of the strategies to employ in teaching lower-class, disadvantaged minority children. Bloom, Davis, and Hess reflect this idea clearly in their observation that:

> The child in many middle-class homes is given a great deal of instruction about the world in which he lives, to use language to fix aspects of this world in his memory, and to think about similarities, differences, and relationships in this very complex environment.

---

[16] Two excellent discussions on this will serve to give the reader insight into the enormity of the problem as well as relevant suggestions for correction. See Bernard Hormann, Speech, "Prejudice, and the School in Hawaii," in B. Hormann (ed.), *Community Forces in Hawaii* (Honolulu, 1956), pp. 233-36, and Norman A. McQuown, "Language Learning from an Anthropological Point of View," *Elementary School Journal*, LIV (1954), pp. 402-08.

[17] David P. Ausubel, "How Reversible are the Cognitive and Motivational Effects of Cultural Deprivation? Implications for Teaching the Culturally Deprived Child," *Urban Education*, 1 (Summer, 1964), 25.

Such instruction is individual and is timed in relation to experiences, actions, and questions of the child. Parents make great efforts to motivate the child, to reward him, and to reinforce desired responses. The child is read to, spoken to, and is constantly subjected to a stimulating set of experiences in a very complex environment. In short, he 'learns to learn' very early. He comes to view the world as something he can master through a relatively enjoyable type of activity, a sort of game which is learning. In fact, much of the approval he gets is because of his rapid and accurate response to his formal instruction at home.[18]

A strong subscription to these things, things a teacher should be doing rather than lamenting the lacks children display because of their disadvantage, when appropriately adapted, could make up the content and method of a strong program. Moreover, "in addition to the pre-school activities much time would be spent in reading and talking to children, in furnishing an acceptable model of speech, in supplying corrective feedback with respect to grammar and pronunciation, in developing listening, memory, and attentivity skills, and in providing appropriate reading readiness, reading and writing instruction." [19]

It should be understood by anyone working with disadvantaged youth that to approach teaching and learning as it concerns linguistic or language needs in a customary traditional school manner dooms the program to failure. The almost rampant pragmatism of these youth insists on a different and creative teaching strategy. For example, structural linguistics, with its applied use of word forms and pattern sentences, offers a much better hope for teaching the knowledge and use of standard language than reliance on the classification of grammar and the various parts of speech. The emphasis should be placed through creative situations on the mastery of the forms and simple patterns. After establishing some mastery, various types of language-form substitutions can be made by the learner. In the later school years, new and different materials must be employed so that previously rejected customary materials do not reinforce the history of school failure which encumbers many lower-class or minority youth. These materials need to be highly related and should have, insofar as possible, immediate relevance for the learner. Some materials are now being produced commercially.[20] But the most important thing will be the methods the teachers employ.

----

[18] Benjamin S. Bloom *et al, Compensatory Education for Cultural Deprivation* (New York, 1965), p. 15.
[19] Ausubel, *op. cit.*, pp. 25-26.
[20] The publishers of children's trade books are lacking in producing materials related and germane. A national council is now working on this problem. Some very promising language experience readers for the lower grades and which are highly related to the culture have been produced (Chandler Publishing Company, San Francisco). *The Rochester Occupational Reading Series* (Science Research Associates, Inc., Chicago) are very readable and real life related materials for the upper levels. Project English at Hunter College, New York, produced some simple anthologies using writers and themes indigenous to the disadvantaged population. The patois frequently found in the materials serve as an aid to immediate identification and help motivate the youth to read or listen to the stories (Project English Curriculum Study Center, Hunter College of the City University of New York).

The author in his work with teachers of disadvantaged youth was dismayed more than once concerning this. When he answered the complaint that teachers had concerning the lack of materials and equipment by supplying it in abundance, he found that this was not the real problem. Even in Job Corps Centers, with equipment budgets that stagger the imagination, no impact is made if the administration, supervision, strategies, and methods of teaching reflect an impoverishment of both insight and commitment which for too long have plagued the teaching profession.

The methods employed in teaching that place an emphasis on the learner change behavior. This is very true in the kind of teaching that seeks a different kind of language behavior. Creative teachers apply various strategies, use various approaches, and move the learner from the idiomatic restricted code to a more nearly standard elaborated code. Weinstein's creative approach to teaching Langston Hughes' poem "Motto" is an excellent example of learner emphasis and how to move from a hip (restricted code) idiom to elements of standard English (elaborated code).[21] Riessman recounts a shortened version of this lesson and indicates that as a result of this kind of teaching, "the enthusiasm of the class session led the students into more of Hughes' poetry [and] later they moved into other kinds of literature in more conventional language."[22]

The collected research and insights in this area offer a premise which, to coin a term, could be called *psycho-socio-Shavian*. Disadvantaged or minority children display language behavior restricted in precision, scope, and range according to present middle-class norms. This language behavior must be one of the immediate areas of attack and must remain an on-going vital concern. Other areas, of course, represent problems of varying magnitude. But various enrichment programs, such as Higher Horizon activities as well as other programs of this character, without the essential background and readiness to "tune in" on the inherent values available, frequently result in behaviors portrayed in the trip to Wall Street in Warren Miller's *The Cool World*.

There are other methods of teaching that have proved successful in the education of disadvantaged and minority children. One simple strategy is built on the concept of centrality, which is teaching in such a way as to create, or contrive in the best sense of the word, a situation in which the child perceives himself as the focal concern. The teacher creates a situation so alive, so related, that it stimulates that felt need to learn how to live with it or function realistically in terms of the pre-

[21] General Weinstein, "Do You Dig All Jive?" (Unpublished transcript of a lesson, Madison Area Project, City School District, Syracuse, New York, no date), pp. 1-10.
[22] Frank Riessman, "The Lessons of Poverty," *American Education*, I, No. 2 (February, 1965), 23.

dicament. In this condition, that is "real," with teacher guidance the child can "make it." By producing subsequent successful steps of "making it," the beginning of the different self-concepts that could result in higher levels of aspiration or could bring successful life within the present culture are begun. These produce a history of reinforcement based on success rather than failure.[23]

The move from a disadvantaged life, one of poverty, failure, threat, instability, and insecurity, requires a self-conceptualization that allows for insight, with careful sociologically based guidance, into functionally realistic aspirational levels for all phases of existence. The generic idea needs to be: if youngsters try and are given the opportunity for success (and this can be defined in the relative cultural sense), they can make it! These youngsters do not need to be converted to any particular class value system. They need to be given the opportunities to rehabilitate all of the necessary personal equipment to handle their own life situations satisfactorily, with security, and with success. The schools can no longer rely on those old bromides, "they lack readiness," "they aren't motivated," "their parents don't care about schooling," and a dozen or more of the same genre, as the excuses for not teaching disadvantaged children. The job of the schools is to motivate, to build readiness, and to teach these youth.

They can be taught, and taught well. An organic or systematically coordinated approach to learning embracing the aforementioned concept of centrality can result in better learning. The concept of centrality is not synonymous with the concept that some of the "modern" teachers in a misunderstood fashion hold. It is not expediency, wherein everything that seems related is seized upon and made into a teaching or learning unit. Centrality means using the immediate environment for creating the opportunities for teaching the process of education. Process is extremely important because in this Protean society that which is factually correct today may be glaringly obsolete tomorrow. No linear predictions can be made. The expedient thing can fade or pass and thereby doom children to a reversion of the circumstances from which the attempt is being made to withdraw them.

Not only is process the most important thing to teach, regardless of the substantive matter involved, it is the most difficult aspect of educating the disadvantaged. The varying and various strategies of teaching which are employed when process is the focal point differ markedly from the teaching strategies that presently exist. Many teachers easily

---

[23] The importance of self-concept is so basic to sound mental health which in turn is one major correlate to learning that understandings about it concerning minority or disadvantaged populations are requisite for any who are involved in their education. Strongly recommended is William C. Kvaraceus *et al* (eds.), *Negro Self-Concept: Implications for School and Citizenship* (New York, 1965), pp. 1-80; and in a more popular but no less accurate vein Charles Silberman, *Crisis in Black and White* (New York, 1965).

verbalize about certain philosophically and psychologically sound methods or ideas in teaching. To use them successfully is quite another thing. If, for example, the creation of the abilities to use standard English is a worthy goal, the process of education involved in moving from the restricted to the elaborated code must be thought of as a collection of intellectual strategies and methodological approaches enveloping the pupils in the action. The action requires the most insightful guidance techniques, the most relevant techniques of motivation, and a profundity of ever growing knowledge about the psychological, sociological, and anthropological correlates attendant to this population.

Additionally, a basic concept that undergirds learning progress is a process of learning to learn. Few can quarrel with the assessment of life in the American society which indicates that to continue one's success there is a constant need and ability to learn throughout life so as to be able to cope with change. Fact gathering, rote learning, and dealing with educational minutiae constitute a grim program in preparation for change. What is mandated for the education of all, and particularly for the disadvantaged or minority population which is marked by less stability in terms of jobs and life in general, is a kind of teaching that relies on aspects of the various methods of inquiry. Because the members of this population frequently are imposed upon, it becomes obvious that their functional rehabilitation requires the ability to question, investigate, test, and achieve for themselves knowledge that is reliable and dependable. Teachers must be impelled to create classrooms that serve as a matrix in which learning can become self-satisfying, assimilative, and accommodative. They must be classrooms in which pupils can transform their perceptions to other situations. The strategies of teaching need to lead from problem-solving to a point of pupil achievement, shown by the ability of the pupils to make appropriate generalizations and by their skill in successfully extending these to a host of functional situations.

All of the strategies of teaching aimed at successfully educating this population depend in large measure on the insightful and imaginative innovations made in the organization or setting for learning in the schools. The customary graded school with its lock-step progress, delimited programs based on chronology, nonscientifically based retention policies, and limited commitment to individualized, unhampered integrated learning spans of time represent a static nonfunctional organizational framework for education. This framework is imposed on a population that needs a dynamic, evolving process and program of education. Asynchronies in growth, background, intellect, as well as other temporizations in learning, clearly indicate the difference between dullness and slowness, verbal manipulation and real understanding, and interest and agreeable assent. Many times disadvantaged children when slow to learn material that is being badly taught are branded dull. There are many other examples of this kind of rationalization. One is compelled to accept the fact that the customary school organization, rigid in its ideas of pupil progress, calcified in its segmentation of subject matter, and ossified, with the help of the publishing companies, into seeing vertical progression packaged into 180 school day units of increasing difficulty, is clearly obsolete, especially to serve this population. The author, during a visit to a third grade in a disadvantaged area school, in a discussion of some general problems, elicited the following statement from the teacher as a summary description of the problem she faced: "Everything would be all right and would move along nicely if only the other thirty in my class could keep up with the four who are working well on grade level." Hillson [24] offers a comprehensive view and collection of insights and assessments concerning elementary school reorganizational patterns. His lists of advantages and disadvantages allow for some tentative conclusions.

Clearly the advantages of certain innovations are worthwhile for any school population. They are especially worthwhile for educating the disadvantaged and would eliminate or mitigate some of the behavior of the third grade teacher reported above. The nongraded school, team teaching, coordinate teacher activities, teacher collaboration, multiage or multilevel grouping, and other variations allow for greater flexibility, greater individualization, greater coordination of diagnostic efforts, and more opportunity for better and creative teaching. Many of these innovations fruitfully support teacher efforts to become successful in educating the disadvantaged. In view of the present situation, the adoption of many are essential if widespread progress is to be made.

Finally, it is important to realize that innovations can become mere manipulations. Publicized new approaches may be only hollow verbalisms. New programs could represent only administrative tinkering. This will be so unless a much greater knowledge of this population is acquired by those who have governance over the primary agency of their socialization, the school. Those who operate the schools need to have greater familiarity with the variables that affect the life of this population. A better understanding of these lead to greater insights in setting up the needed educational priorities and strategies for creating and achieving worthwhile programs. Along with this, school reorganizational plans and innovations in grouping and in teaching approaches related to the life styles of this population will abet all the efforts needed in gaining success. If the school is not the only mechanism for the elimina-

[24] Maurie Hillson, *Change and Innovation in Elementary School Organization* (New York, 1965), pp. 163-380. See also Maurie Hillson and Harvey B. Scribner, *Readings in Collaborative and Team Approaches to Teaching and Learning* (New York, 1965).

tion or remission of the problems of disadvantaged, lower-class minority children, it is unquestionably the principal one. Certainly, given the situation in the United States, it could be doing a better job. Life in the United States is encompassed by a complex culture and involved in an even more complex universe beset by many problems. Wasted lives, wasted resources, and wasted talents are always frustrating. Faced by the complexities of life, this waste serves only to deprive the world of possible insights, answers, and opportunities hitherto unknown. Can anyone disagree that of all of the categories of wasted talent, "the one that must lie heaviest on our conscience is our disadvantaged minorities." [25]

---

[25] The Rockefeller Panel Reports, "The Use and Misuse of Human Abilities," in *Prospect for America* (Garden City, 1961), p. 380.

William F. Brazziel

QUALITY EDUCATION FOR MINORITIES

Several close observers of the American scene have speculated that the U.S. is going through some sort of nervous breakdown. Recent events seem to support this hypothesis. Some small symptoms: *The New York Times* presents its readers with a full page of text and pictures of the retired madame of a large and successful house of prostitution. The *Phi Delta Kappan* opens its pages to America's most celebrated racist to present his Las Vegas method of genetics research and to theorize on the worth in I.Q. points of a pint of white blood from certain American stock.*

W. D. Cash observed in his *Mind of the South* that race has a deeply unstabilizing effect on people and that all sorts of hallucinatory and bizarre behavior can be expected in times of heightened racial conflict. This may explain the magazine article. One hopes that the pressures of inflation in a time of recession, protracted war, and perhaps pollutants in the air can explain the society page treatment of the madame.

This article is not concerned with gene pools, I.Q. points, sunspots, or any of the other aspects of the current nature-nurture struggle. Henry Dyer stated recently that nature-nurture arguments were not worth the time and trouble they command and that the real problem in American education is to remove tests as a deterrent to teaching.[1] One could add that the spectacle of American educational leadership giving serious consideration to the proposition that half of the school children are genetically inferior to the other half because of marks on a heavily criticized test will not do much to restore badly needed confidence in schools and school leadership.

Dyer is vice president of the Educational Testing Corporation and acknowledged dean of American psychometrists. After reading his analysis of the testing situation ("I.Q. tests are the most useless source of controversy ever devised"), one can only put away his sword and channel his energies into more productive pursuits. This article, then, reviews some of the legacy of achievement of minorities in America, concentrating on black Americans because of the data available. We then turn to a consideration of strategies that minorities, school people, and people of good will generally can employ to consolidate and build on the rapid gains

---

*William Shockley, "Dysgenics, Geneticity, Raceology: A Challenge to the Intellectual Responsibility of Educators," January *Kappan*, adequately answered by N. L. Gage. — *The Editor*

PHI DELTA KAPPAN, May 1972, pp. 547-552.

minorities are making in education, jobs, and housing. Much of what is said has relevance for children of all races. It has special meaning for those unfortunate enough to be born poor and in the wrong school system.

Excellence in a Hostile Land

Minorities literally built a large part of America. All received less than their share of respect on coming to America; many still live in an atmosphere of hostility and are denied rights guaranteed by the Constitution. In all groups, however, excellence and genius have shone through in spite of adversity; with the lowering of racial and ethnic barriers, the future looks bright for minority achievers. We shall probably see another gene pool hassle at the next peak season for sunspots, but we are probably witnessing the death rattle of white and Aryan supremacy psychology. The record of achievement will speak for itself.

Most remarkable of the many minority groups in America have been the Americans from Africa. Subjected to 350 years of inhuman treatment, this hardy band has multiplied itself by a factor of six since its involuntary immigration was halted and is now working its way up the ladder in economic and political life. The legacy of achievement under stress of their more productive minds is instructive. White supremacists trying to make a case for their theories might consider a reverse hypothesis: To persevere and do as well as they have done, blacks may be superior to whites.

From 1865 until well into the 1930s, more than 300 black men were lynched and thousands murdered each year. The response of the power structure in America was to establish and support a center at a black university in the South to count and report the carnage. Each year (and this is 1972) more than 200,000 children, mostly black, eat lead paint in slum housing and become deathly ill or neurologically impaired for life. Sickle cell anemia affects another large number for which exact data is not available. Infant mortality, because of inability to secure medical care is three times higher for blacks than for whites and many remnants of sharecropper Southern agriculture are literally starving to death.

In spite of all this, black population is growing instead of receding and blacks show no signs of weakening. Indeed, the opposite may be true. Black athletes are six times more likely than whites to win an Olympic medal and their presence in athletics generally needs no explication to a television-viewing American public.

In the first 50 years after the abolition of slavery, blacks filed over a thousand patents, although fewer than 75 high schools and almost no colleges were open to them in the entire country. Over 3,000 patents have been filed by blacks since the inception of the Patent Office. Pioneering designs patented by blacks include the stoplight, the gas mask, blood plasma, plastics, ice cream, and potato chips.

The first clock entirely made in America was produced by a black inventor. This same genius published the first almanac. As a member of a commission appointed to plan our nation's capital city, he also finished the job from memory when the French designer named to head the group went back to Paris in a huff, taking most of the important documents with him.

A black scientist, born a slave and raised by Iowa whites, revolutionized a boll weevil-ridden Southern agriculture with the development of new fertilizers and new plastics from peanuts and soybeans. A black surgeon performed the first open heart operation and a black engineer developed an airframe which eliminated the need for second- and third-stage engines on rockets.

The census people record a 100% increase in black professional and technical workers since 1950. With the elimination of discrimination in employment, these figures should rise even further, especially if everything possible is done to improve schooling for children and youth now mangled by poverty and substandard schools.[2]

One could go on in this manner. Each week seems to bring a new success story of blacks surging forward to grasp the new opportunities extended them and attempting to consolidate their hard-won gains. There is even something for the history buffs: Black slaves who turned on the Spanish exploration party operating in the Peedee River Valley of South Carolina were the first permanent settlers in America. The Spaniards folded their tents and went home; the blacks stayed on. The year, 1526, was 39 years before St. Augustine, 80 years or so before Jamestown, and nearly 100 years before the Mayflower.

When they put their minds to it and when job, housing, and school conditions are favorable, blacks also do well on the culturally biased tests we hear so much about. Indeed, two of the most widely hailed papers at the 1971 convention of the American Psychological Association (Jane Mercer and A. J. Mayeske) involved the analysis of massive amounts of data (150,000 subjects) to show that there is little black-white difference on these tests when social class is held constant. It is interesting to note that these papers, read across the corridor from Mr. Shockley at the APA meeting, received as much or more attention in the press but were not selected for inclusion in the *Kappan* issue on race and I.Q. This was not an oversight, because the papers were brought to the attention of the editor. Vice-President Agnew may be right. There really may be something wrong with our media.

In the first massive testing ever done in America, black soldiers from several states in World War I out-tested their Southern counterparts. This was repeated in World War II testing and is true for draftees from both Northern and Southern states today.[3,4]

Some gene pool theorists seized on this information to "prove" that the South was settled by poorer stock (refugees from debtors' prisons, etc.) than the North and that this accounted for the lower test scores as well as the low incidence of college attendance and the boll weevils and pellagra and more. We now find that the problem was grinding poverty and bad schools. The South is now one of the fastest growing industrial regions in the country and some communities are matching their Northern counterparts in many arenas, including school integration and race relations.

A black school led the city of Los Angeles in I.Q. testing in 1969 and a black school in Virginia took top honors in reading in 1970. A black girl in Georgia made the highest score ever recorded on an I.Q. test.[5]

The National Merit Scholarship Corporation indicates that their black winners score in the top 20 of the nation; since discrimination was eliminated in the program, several black Rhodes Scholars have been selected each year.

Blacks at Stanford have compiled a higher graduation rate than their white counterparts over the last four years. At Northwestern, attrition in their special programs for minorities is only 5%, compared with a much larger rate generally.[6] One could continue in this vein for many pages. But let us now turn to strategies for a fuller development of minority resources through the delivery of quality education in depressed areas.

Strategies for the Seventies

The trend is generally up where minority progress is concerned in the drive for quality education, and school people must join with others to build on the momentum created in the sixties. Black high school graduation rates jumped from 36 to 63% during this period, for example, and college enrollment showed an 85% increase. Blacks are forging ahead in graduate studies and as members of the professional, technical, and crafts job cadres.[7]

Problems must not be obscured or swept under the table, but building on successes won by contention and a good measure of alarmism is far more productive than continued contention and alarmism. The public's mind boggles after a time and the feeling sets in that school people are perhaps inept and don't quite know how to deliver. The brief popularity of performance contracting may have been based on this feeling. The public is convinced that there are smarter, more able people at IBM and Westinghouse than in teaching and administrator ranks. This thinking must be reversed.

Quality education for minorities in depressed areas might well include the following thrusts for the seventies:

—A conscious effort to eliminate debilitating labels now attached to children in families with modest incomes

An effort to put the spotlight on schools that are succeeding with these children

Provision of state, local, and federal funds for large numbers of school personnel to visit and observe in these schools

Productions of films and film loops of these programs for nationwide distribution and for showing on nationwide TV

—Expansion of "cradle schools" for children of families where maternal teaching capabilities are inadequate

—Expansion of work-study and alternative school programs for high schools

—Initiation and perfection of the career education idea advanced by the commissioner of education

—Expansion of programs designed to develop the talents of gifted disadvantaged children and youth

Expansion of federal scholarships and assistance programs for college-bound minority group representatives

Elimination of I.Q. testing and normative-based achievement testing in all schools, to be replaced by sophisticated short-form diagnostic and criterion-referenced testing

Expansion of the drive to desegregate administrative ranks in schools and colleges

—An expanded effort to make clear to the public, and the business sector especially, the push-pull relationship of jobs, housing, schooling, and economic advancement

—Expansion of Title I (ESEA) aid to provide $1,000 per year to educate every child in families with incomes under $6,000 and $2,000 per year for every child in families with incomes under $4,500 (permitting cradle school education).

A few words of explication for some of the less obvious planks in this platform and our work will be done. It may first be noted that these are modest and attainable proposals. They may be considered as a base from which to build. They will deliver goodly results. More grandiose proposals can be advanced, such as 150 new towns in the next three decades, creation of a new research program to try to discover the secrets of learning, and so on. All of these can be done and should be done, but not at the expense of early and direct help to poor children and youth. The country has seen enough of using the plight of less fortunate people as a lever to mount programs which benefit them only tangentially. We also assume here that the states will do everything possible to bring about as much school integration as possible. Much of this program, then, would involve quality education for poor children everywhere.

Eliminating Hurtful Labels

Reginald Jones reports research to show the effects on children when the

133

press and the public use derogative labels.[8] The data showed that describing children as "culturally deprived" and "disadvantaged" turns them off and is counterproductive to government and schools' efforts to help them. Further, Jones showed data which indicated that teachers completing courses in urban education and on the "deprived" child had lower estimates of the children's capabilities than they had when they enrolled in the course. Jones, who is chairman of education at the University of California at Riverside, advises, "Just call them children."

Spotlighting, Emulating Success

Children in modest-income neighborhoods have been subjected to an amazing amount of experimentation. The wheel has been reinvented again and again in districts charged with improving schooling in these neighborhoods. More than a few entrepreneurs have come to the scene to bring salvation − for a fee.

We are indebted to George Weber and the Council for Basic Education for a careful and comprehensive study of the critical ingredients for success in such schools. In a year of searching, Weber identified 95 of these schools. He selected four for intensive study and identified critical ingredients of success as follows:

−A no-nonsense administrator determined to have success

−An air of expectancy for success on the part of teachers and children

−Competent and thorough teaching of phonics

−An atmosphere of quiet and industry in the schools

−Extra reading specialists located in the buildings

−Progress grouping after the first year with room for movement between groups

−A conscious effort to individualize instruction as much as possible

−A sophisticated use of diagnostic and criterion-referenced testing.[9]

The techniques of the Weber schools and the many others which are finally succeeding after casting about should be made available to schools everywhere by the sophisticated use of every modern technique for dissemination at our disposal.

Further, minority communities must insist that only high-impact programs be installed in their schools. Of the thousands of flying submarines tested in minority schools, only a few have been successful in delivering the goods. Minorities can count on David Wickart's High Scope program, Siegfried Engelmann's Academic Primary, Merle Karnes' KAC, and the BRL programs of Palo Alto, California, to be utterly dependable if their school boards do what they are supposed to do. There are surely other learning systems that can deliver, but a show of credentials is advisable before boards and parent advisory committees admit the healers.

Cradle Schools Deliver

Rick Heber enrolled 40 black kids in a Milwaukee slum in a cradle school at five days − yes, five days − of age in the mid-sixties. These children received one-to-one perception and language instruction by paraprofessionals for a year. At age two, the children were placed in small-group classes; at three they went to nursery schools and pre-K classes stressing the same skills. The average I.Q. on culturally biased I.Q. tests is now 115; some I.Q.'s went as high as 135. Heber further found that all kids in such a neighborhood would not need cradle schools. Many were quite bright before they went to school. Thus cradle schools can be limited to a rather small number of families, mainly where mothers have very limited schooling themselves, are retarded, or are so overburdened that children would have almost no maternal instruction.[10]

The schools and the various government agencies working in slums should expand cradle schools rapidly. The initial cost was $2,000 per child per year, but it is well worth the money. Some school heads will beg the issue with a recitation of school law, but it is the job of school leadership to change school law and school policy to make it administratively possible to do good. It is not to continue to wring their hands in print and at conferences about the loss of the most crucial years of a child's life. School systems ought to operate cradle schools.

Job-Oriented Education Pays Off

Well-off and well-connected people reward their children's efforts in school by assuring them good jobs upon completion of school and college. A vast system of interim rewards is used to spur effort in many homes where school programs may be deadly or the adolescent's interests are more on his developmental tasks.

Homes with modest incomes cannot match this reward system, but schools and businesses can team up more to make education meaningful and the carrot more tempting through work-study, alternative, and career-oriented education. The kid in the chartreuse pants will simply work harder at his books and stay on to finish school if there is a payoff at the end and if he can see himself gaining a high level of technical skill to assure these rewards.

Where local business and industry is too feeble or too bigoted to make a place for minority work-study youth, the federal government should provide a job for every four interested students, to be utilized on a quarterly rotating basis. To quiet those who might complain of a revival of the WPA, the government might provide that subcontracts from the aerospace corporation it recently subsidized be provided in these communities. The children might also help keep the books and

work on the formulas for the subsidies of the Department of Agriculture and other agencies.

The commissioner of education is pushing career education to eliminate all high school curricula except college prep and technical education. There is a danger of a return to Booker T. Washington where black slum youth is concerned in this approach; but a conscious effort to provide high-level technical education in both slum and suburb and the folding in of college education as career education will enable us to avoid this.

Desegregating Leadership Ranks

In 1969-70 the world was treated to the spectacle of a union and a supervisors' association in a large Eastern city using every stratagem possible to block the expansion of the tiny cadre of four minority principals then found in ranks totaling 900 whites. Little progress was made in this situation and the NAACP was forced to file suit in local courts to force change.

One would have to look to the unbelievable situation in the Bureau of Indian Affairs to find a worthy parallel. Because of behavior like this, many minorities regard white administrators in all-minority schools as Indian Affairs types – losers looking for a reservation, payroll to ride. This is not true for many dedicated, hard-working administrators, and it is sad that they must be stereotyped because of misadvised efforts of their colleagues. It is true for many, however, and the request for transfer files in the central offices belie protestations to the contrary. Quality education is impossible to achieve if such a situation exists.

The way to solve this problem is to integrate the administrative ranks across the board in the schools. Everybody, black and white, should be able to take leadership roles in all types of schools: black, white, and integrated. The black

135

youngster in the black school does not really need a black principal in order to learn well, if he knows that black **principals are in charge of schools in many instances in his system.**

In an improved situation, minority representatives would serve as superintendent from time to time. The administrative departments of the teacher training institutions would drop their gentlemen's agreements regarding minority administrators and prepare a much larger number than is presently the case. The state departments and the U.S. Office of Education would recruit minorities for general rather than ethnic slots.

Push-Pull Relationships

It is extremely difficult to deliver quality education to children of poor people and, conversely, it is extremely difficult to avoid delivery of quality education to the well-off. This axiom is not understood clearly by the American people and circumstances require that we use new strategies to make it clearer. The Coleman Report was a good effort in this direction, but its meaning was obscured by bad instrumentation and an overemphasis on racial differences.

American people must be able to understand that people work hard to improve the education of their children when they, themselves, get better jobs, make more money, are able to live in better houses, buy better food and medicine, break away from the community for trips and cultural events, and save a bit to make plans of the children for college and career more meaningful. Schooling for the children is always a high priority when the wolf is finally beaten away from the door. This is economic determinism and too little attention has been paid to it. I am convinced that all of the special programs in the schools could very well be eliminated and money placed in programs to generate economic activity.

The resulting well-being of the population involved would in turn generate an intensified effort to improve the schooling and aspirations of the children. Well-being *plus* special programs have a synergistic effect.

Two large studies, one recent and one quite old, offer insight into this dynamic. The recently released National Child Development Study of Britain shows that by age seven middle-class children are 17 months ahead of working-class children on tests. Upper-middle-class children are even further ahead if parents limit offspring to one or two. **Working-class children without toilet facilities are the worst off and working-class children generally** are six times more apt to be poor readers than middle-class children. They are 15 times more apt to not be able to read at all.[11]

Genetic elitists will try to make something of this, no doubt, as they tried to make something of the data from the 10-year longitudinal study completed by Lester Wheeler on mountain children in two counties of the Tennessee mountains.

Wheeler tested all the children in the counties involved in 1930 in a time of poor schools, poor homes, isolation, and grinding poverty. The children averaged in the low 80s on I.Q. tests, with accompanying deficits on achievement tests. Wheeler returned 10 years later and tested everybody again. In the interim, roads had lessened isolation in the mountains, new jobs had brought a better standard of living, and the schools had been improved. The children averaged nearly 16 points higher on I.Q. tests, with accompanying improvement on achievement tests. The rhetoric in Wheeler's report is reminiscent of things heard today: "Does the deviation of these children from the normal distribution indicate that they are inherently inferior?" Wheeler posed hypotheses of genetic deficits, dysgenic trends, and bad stock. Events forced him to abandon these speculations.[12]

136

One could recite the success story of the Osage Indians or the early black immigrants from Southern farms and villages documented by Klineberg and Lee; but perhaps the story of white children of English stock is more instructive for our audience.

There is a lesson for the government and the captains of finance and industry here, and if school people do not instruct these gentlemen in these mysteries no one else will. The lesson: If the country would have the schools push poor minorities into a more competitive position in the schools, they must do everything possible to pull with gusto on the other end.

There are 800,000 unemployed workers in the black community, for example. Expansion of public service jobs from the 200,000 already created by the Nixon Administration (for unemployed engineers and scientists) to absorb this surplus would boost the education of black street urchins as much as a huge new education program would. Again, the push-pull could become synergistic. An expansion of the remarkable strides made in housing in the last few years would help. So would added effort to speed the trend toward smaller families in poor neighborhoods.

The latter factor has not been given the attention it deserves in discussions and has seldom, if ever, been controlled for in research, thus rendering many cross-cultural studies invalid. As the British studies and studies by the National Merit Scholarship Corporation have shown, children in small families are simply better developed and first children and only children receive better development than all. Two-thirds of the NMSC winners are first-born or only children, as are Ivy League students, physicians, and so on. The cumulative average I.Q. of a family of children is inversely proportionate to its size, it seems. In a group comparison of children in, say, 2.3 and 3.6 birth-order families, the higher incidence of second-

and third-order children of the latter and the higher incidence of only children in the former skews the results.[13] A good study would be controlled for average family size, thus eliminating first-born and only children as factors.

Bad birth-order studies and the improper conclusions drawn from them remind one of cyclamates and high cholesterol foods people ingested before science discovered they were harmful. They are water under the bridge and there is little use in trying to rectify the situation. The future should bring controls for these factors in research studies.

Free family planning advice, devices, and pharmaceuticals, plus free or inexpensive abortion on demand will assure better development for minority children in families with modest incomes. The trend is already in this direction. Middle-class blacks have even fewer children than their white counterparts; white and black birthrates in depressed areas are dropping sharply.

More and Better-Utilized Money

When the smoke had cleared from the first two years of Title I operations, it was determined that funds spent had averaged out to about $93 per child. Further, it was found that some school districts in mildly depressed areas had been able to accomplish much with these funds, but others in very bad situations had not been able to deliver. In Virginia, for example, state officials reported that Title I schools were delivering an average of 1.06-month gain for each month taught in rural areas and small towns, up from about half that in pre-Title I days. The record was not as good in cities.[14] Disturbingly, instances were found in misuse of the funds across the nation.

Cradle schools, work-study programs, and high-impact curricula will cost more than $93 per child. A careful study of these programs will probably indicate the need for a combined federal-local outlay of about $1,500 to $2,000 per year. The government should assure districts that deliver high-quality programs whatever financing is necessary to get the job done.

Criterion-Referenced Testing

It is surely time that the "child racing" of normative-based testing is eliminated in schools. Minorities have been bellwethers in the drive against this sort of measurement, but it is detrimental to all children and the new criterion tests make it idiotic to continue the debacle.

Further, standardized tests have a hamstringing effect on efforts to update curricula to keep pace with exploding knowledge and changes in a supertechtronic society. More and more, school administrators find themselves faced with a choice between a modern, interesting course of study or hewing to a test-bound corpus defined by a commercial test corporation and its consultants.

Again we may turn to the wisdom of Henry Dyer. He believes the present testing scene is a disaster. He states that he has given up as impossible the task of making teachers and administrators, including many school psychologists, see that age-grade scores are not additive, that much of intelligence is a function of teachers and schools, that other misadvised individuals (not Binet) developed I.Q. tests, that most minorities and tests are not on the same wavelength, that only a miracle would produce I.Q. averages that are similar for *any* distinct cultural groups, and that tests are not "good" for children as a means of strengthening the mind and making youngsters study harder.[15]

Dyer proposes a new start by all hands. He recommends 20,000 or so school districts with programs based on the works of Jean Piaget. The result would be schools all over America employing sophisticated techniques to diagnose a child's stage of development,

whereupon a wide panoply of school experiences would be used to maximize this development. Schools would provide nongraded, continuous-stream experience. Criterion tests would measure development. There would be clear and rigorous, yet friendly standards toward which the teachers and their young charges could work.[16] The number of "smarter" children would increase instead of decrease, and the increase in saner children would be remarkable.

Dyer is right. Educational leaders cannot command the respect of the American public if they fail to take steps in the direction he suggests.

1. Henry Dyer, "Testing Little Children — Some Old Problems in a New Setting," technical paper delivered at National Leadership Institute/Teacher Education: Early Childhood, University of Connecticut, Storrs, Conn., 1971.

2. *Legacy For All: A Record of Achievement by Black American Scientists,* New York: Western Electric Corp., 1970.

3. Eli Ginsburg, *The Negro Potential.* New York: Columbia University Press, 1960.

4. *Health of the Army Supplement: Results of Examinations of Youths for Military Service.* Washington, D.C.: Department of the Army, 1971, pp. 138-39.

5. Olive Walker, "The Windsor Hills School Story," *Integrated Education,* May-June, 1970, p. 4.

6. *Chronicle of Higher Education,* June 7, 1971, p. 2.

7. *Social and Economic Conditions of the Negro,* Department of Labor, 1971.

8. Reginald Jones, paper read at USOE Teacher Education Conference, December, 1971.

9. George Weber, *Slum Children Can Learn to Read: Four Successful Schools.* Washington: Council for Basic Education, 1971.

10. Stephen Strickland, "Can Slum Children Learn?," *American Education,* July, 1971, pp. 3-7.

11. *National Child Development Study,* British Ministry of Education, 1971.

12. Lester Wheeler, "A Comparative Study of the Intelligence of East Tennessee Mountain Children," *Journal of Educational Psychology,* May, 1940, pp. 321-34.

13. Robert Nichols, *The Origin and Development of Talent,* National Merit Scholarship Corporation, 1966, pp. 18-19.

14. *Report of Title I Program,* Virginia Department of Education, 1969.

15. *Ibid.,* p. 2.

16. *Ibid.,* p. 3.

Mexican-American Values and Attitudes Toward Education

By Hector Farias, Jr.

What the Mexican-American student learns in school frequently comes into conflict with what he has learned from his parents. This situation creates severe personality problems and inhibits intellectual performance. The following case studies, taken from my work with Mexican-American students in Northwestern University's Upward Bound Project, illustrate the problem. I also had the opportunity to talk to their parents and teachers. I have not used the students' real names; all attended Marshall, Harrison, or Waller High School in Chicago. Each case reflects a particular aspect of the Mexican-American culture.

Loyalty to the Family

Jesus is very unhappy because his father has just lost his job; he is worrying about what will happen to his family. He is doing well in school and doesn't want to leave, but he knows that he must help his family. Jesus will drop out of school and get a job.

There is great emphasis on loyalty to the family and maintenance of strong family ties. The Mexican-American youth in this case feels that the most important thing for him to do is to concentrate on the immediate problem and leave the future in the hands of God. In the dominant society, however, greater emphasis is placed on the individual than is placed on family ties, in order to facilitate both physical and social mobility, and achievement of material wealth and related status and prestige is considered important.

According to the 1960 U.S. census, the median number of school years completed by all Mexican-American males and females 14 years of age and over is 8.1 and 8.2 respectively.[1] Limited education severely handicaps not only Mexican-American youth but the entire ethnic group. Extensive formal education is generally not considered necessary or highly valuable by the adult population. In- effect, Mexican-American youths are initially handicapped by their own cultural value system with regard to making an adjustment to the environment of the educational institution. Preparation and orientation in the home are generally unrelated to the types of experi-

PHI DELTA KAPPAN, June 1971, pp. 602-604.

ence on which school life is based.

Loyalty to the Ethnic Group

Mario was scolded by the teacher for speaking a language that wasn't English on the school grounds. He didn't know what to do. He didn't want to make the teacher angry, but he knew his friends were watching him and if he didn't stand up for his rights and for his people they would call him a traitor. The teacher told him not to do it again, or she would send him to the principal. Mario continued to do it and was suspended for three days.

This teacher has caused deep psychological problems for Mario and his Spanish-speaking friends. They all live in humble homes and neighborhoods where Spanish is the only language spoken. Now, Mario is supposed to discard this language which the teacher feels is inferior and unworthy to be spoken at school. He is confused because the value that the school expects him to place on the English language is in direct conflict with the values he has learned at home. The teacher has failed to understand, as Salvador Ramirez states, that "speech is a reflection of culture and represents the set of common understandings. It is the means by which we symbolize all culture for purposes of communication."[2]

Mrs. Kendall is a dedicated teacher who regularly visits the homes of Mexican-American students to encourage the parents to use English at home. Such visits are seldom welcome because the average teacher unwittingly violates every rule of Mexican etiquette, leaving behind a feeling of hostility. Mr. Martinez recalls a visit from his child's teacher:

"She burst in here without even waiting for an invitation. Then she started telling me what to do. This is my home and I will decide what is to be done here. She tried to tell me not to speak the language of my forefathers. She does not understand, nor does she want to. My children go to school to learn, but they are merely taught not to respect their parents. It is an evil thing. I no longer blame my children for not liking school."

For the Mexican child from a lower-class family, school is often a bewildering and hostile environment. He hears the teaching of his parents contradicted, and he is urged to behave in ways that are uncomfortable for him. Mexican-American students especially dread being forced to recite in class. They know that their mistakes in English will be criticized in class and ridiculed after class by the Anglo students. The push to excel and compete for grades violates their noncompetitive values. A Mexican-American student who conspicuously outshines his schoolmates in academic endeavors is mocked or shunned.[3]

The Father's Role

Marta's father gets angry when he arrives home from work and she is not yet home from school. He wants to find his family at home when he comes home. When she tried to explain he said, "I don't want any excuses; you forget I am the boss of the house."

The authoritative role of the father in relation to the child becomes very clear with the onset of puberty, when the Mexican father withdraws from his position of doting father to become dignified master of the home. He avoids demonstrations of affection and demands that the child show him respect. Younger-generation Mexicans who are more anglicized than their

140

parents often resent this absolutism of the traditional father.[4]

Folk Medicine

Reymundo has a ruptured eardrum, and the teacher has told him time and time again to see a doctor. He does not want to appear disrespectful, but he persists in using folk medicine even though his teacher has threatened to take him to the school nurse.

Many Mexican-Americans are caught in the conflict between scientific theories of modern medicine and supernatural theories of folk medicine. Even the sophisticated Mexican relies on folk medicine, although he may be ashamed to admit it to the outside world.

Margarita is also caught in this conflict. She became very upset when her Anglo classmates teased her for taking folk medicine every time she was ill. She has refused to go to school and endure their insulting remarks because she feels that they are wrong and that doctors take advantage of their patients.

Opposition to modern medicine stems largely from rejection of the germ theory of disease. Mexican-Americans of the lower class are aware of the germ concept, but many of them refuse to recognize the existence of microbes. They dismiss germs as an invention dreamed up by Anglo doctors to dupe the people. The majority of uneducated Mexicans have never looked through a microscope. Their view of microscopic life comes from cartoons shown in TV advertising and public health clinics, and they do not find this evidence very convincing. Even though classroom education has changed some beliefs, many parents refuse to accept the ideas their children bring home from school.[5]

Problems of Acculturated Mexicans

Eduardo is the son of anglicized parents who fought their way up the economic ladder and now completely identify with the Anglo world. His parents look back with contempt at the conservative Mexican world they left behind. Eduardo has always been urged to earn high grades in school and eventually to qualify for a profession. He has alienated all of his classmates who are Mexican, and this has caused him many unpleasant experiences in school.

The value conflicts of Mexican-Americans are multiplied with the acceleration of acculturation. Eduardo attends school where the majority of the Mexican students come from lower-class families. In these families, parents see little value in the academic success of their children. Parental indifference toward formal education is reflected in their children's academic performance. Moreover, these students scorn competitive scholastic endeavor as an attempt to outdo and demean other students.[6]

Lack of Goal Orientation

Rodrigo is the son of middle-class parents who financed his four years of college. While in college, he changed his major several times and graduated as a "C" student in history. Today he is a clerk in his father's small store. Sometimes he talks about going back to school to study engineering. His biggest doubt is whether he will be able to get a job as an engineer due to his ethnic background. He knows that his father wants him to take over the store some day. "My parents are sure proud of my degree," he says, "but I didn't learn a darn thing in college that is going to help me be a better storekeeper. I guess I'll keep the old man happy and stay on with him. I'll let my kids be the engineers."

A good many of the Mexican-Americans who go on to college don't seem to know what they want from an education. This lack of purpose is particularly characteristic of Mexicans who are seeking a higher education than their parents received.[7]

What Should Be Done

The problem of educating the Mexican is rather complex and needs study and research. It is time the federal government took a serious look at this ethnic group which has been short-changed educationally for so long. As more and more Mexican-Americans move into urban centers, they face the problems that characterize urban school districts. The federal government must encourage educators to find ways to spread the base we use to support public education in urban centers. Interstate migrations to cities like Chicago place impossible burdens on local tax sources.

Mexican-Americans and their schools must be drawn closer together. Priorities must be established for programs that will bring more teachers and parents together in a learning situation. Parents and community leaders must be taught how to deal with school administrators to get what they want. If necessary, the federal government should pay Mexican-American parents to attend sessions where they become involved with schools.

Mexican-Americans need a crash program in higher education. This level of education plays a unique role that merits close attention. Mexican-American leaders will increasingly come from college-graduate ranks, because a college degree has replaced the high school diploma as the badge of acceptance or professional union card. Present programs in higher education do little for the Mexican-American because too few of these young people can meet ever higher and more formal standards. As a group, the Mexican-American is out of the running for admissions and scholarships because he must compete with the best. There are no million-dollar foundations to help him, nor several score of special schools, like Negro colleges, to favor him. Guidelines for existing and future programs could include priorities or quotas to meet Mexican-American needs in areas such as research, institutes, conferences, scholarships, and loans, to cite but a few.

As long as Mexico and the United States share a border, the Mexican-American will be in a unique situation when compared to other minority groups in our country. With no vast ocean to separate him from the "old country," he faces powerful forces which pull him in two directions. Yet his loyalty to the Stars and Stripes is unquestionable. Although Mexican-Americans make up only 11% of the U.S. population, they represent 25% of the casualties in Vietnam.[8]

The Mexican-American is important because he is here. Assistance to him should be no less obvious, no less pointed, and no less generous than that to agriculture, railroads, or oil interests that feel it is their right to claim and receive assistance from public revenues. The ultimate justification for such subsidies must be the general welfare. Help for the Mexican-American will benefit all other Americans as well.

[1] Salvador Ramirez, "Employment Problems of Mexican American Youth," in *The Mexican American*. Washington, D.C.: Inter-Agency Committee on Mexican American Affairs, 1967, p. 76.

[2] *Ibid.*, p. 93.

[3] George Sanchez, *Forgotten People*. Albuquerque: University of New Mexico Press, 1940, p. 109.

[4] Munro Edmundson, *Los Manitos*. New Orleans: Middle American Research Institute, 1957, p. 96.

[5] Lyle Saunders, *Cultural Differences and Medical Care*. New York: Russell Sage Foundation, 1954, p. 44.

[6] Carey McWilliams, *The Spanish Speaking People of the United States*. Philadelphia: J. B. Lippincott, 1948, p. 130.

[7] *Ibid.*, p. 158.

[8] Julian Nava, "Educational Problems of Mexican Americans," in *The Mexican American, op. cit.*, p. 100.

143

Seymour Fersh

ORIENTALS AND ORIENTATION

There is a Chinese saying that when there is a horse and cart, there are three things: a horse, a cart, and a horse-and-cart. This wise observation shows an awareness of the dynamic relatedness which emerges and changes when individuals, items, aspects, or events are combined. An examination of "education for and about Orientals in the United States" centers on "Orientals," but our considerations must include many mixtures: Orientals in the United States (past and present), the U.S. (past and present), and the international as well as domestic contexts. One more dimension should be added: We are mainly concerned here with the implications of our observations for educators. The messenger is the message when the carrier is a teacher – how we feel internally influences the ways in which we create and communicate our attitudes and opinions. The major purpose of this article, therefore, is not to provide prescriptive answers but hopefully to identify the kinds of information and understandings which we need in the overall consideration of our Oriental population.

The word "orient" itself is a good starting place. With a capital "O" it refers to the "Eastern" part of the globe – if you accept the Latin (*oriens*) version of where the East is. In a similar way, the Orient is referred to as the "Far East" – by those who accept the notion that the Prime Meridian is the center of the earth. Consequently, people who live in the Orient are "Orientals" – but this term conceals more differences than it reveals affinities. We do not place as much confidence in the word "European" to indicate similarities, because our national experience with Italians, French, Germans, Swedes, Englishmen, etc., have demonstrated that there is no typical European. But the term "Oriental" has often been used indiscriminately – for purposes of discrimination – to describe all people whose ancestry is Asian. This definition has denied the so-called Oriental peoples their right to be appreciated as separate ethnic groups; and the connotation has encouraged the belief that Orientals, being different, are also deficient.

The verb "orient" provides another clue: It means "to adjust with relation to, or bring into due relation with surrounding circumstances; to *orient* one's ideas to new conditions." Our concern then is to consider Orientals and orientation – within and without the United States, through time and in changing combinations with special reference to education.

PHI DELTA KAPPAN, January 1972.

144

Who Are the U.S. Orientals?

The U.S. Census Bureau does not define "Oriental" except by deduction. It starts out by saying that "nonwhite" consists of such races as the Negro, American Indian, Japanese, Chinese, Filipino, Korean, Asian Indian, and Malayan. But a warning is added: "Racial categories such as Chinese, Japanese, Filipino are based largely on country of origin, and not necessarily on biological stock." Using these guidelines, we can determine overall statistics for Orientals in this country.

1. Of the total U.S. population, nonwhite is about 12.5%. Of these, Negroes are about 11%, American Indians are about .4%, and the total of Chinese, Japanese, and Filipinos is about .7%. The remaining "all other" nonwhites (Koreans, Hawaiians, Aleuts, Eskimos, Malayans, Polynesians, among others) is about .4%. No individual figures are available for groups in the "all other" category.

(Subsequent references to Orientals in this article will be concerned mainly with the three largest American groups of Asian ancestry – the Japanese, Chinese, and Filipinos.)

. 2. The total population of Orientals in the U.S. is probably about 1.5 million in an overall national total of 204 million. Among the Orientals, the Japanese total about 600,000, the Chinese about 435,000, and the Filipinos about 345,000; thus, the Japanese are almost two-fifths of the total, the Chinese almost one-third, and the Filipinos almost one-fourth.

3. The distribution of American Orientals is concentrated rather than widespread:

—Of the Japanese, more than 80% are in Hawaii and California, equally divided; the next largest populations are in Washington, Illinois, and New York, with 3% each.

—Of the Chinese, about 40% are in California, about 20% in New York, about 12% in Hawaii, and the next highest numbers are in Illinois and Massachusetts, with 3% each.

—Of the Filipinos, about 40% are in California and about 30% in Hawaii. The next highest concentrations are in New York, Illinois, and Washington, with about 3% each.

4. Another important characteristic of the American Oriental population is that the great majority live in urban areas: about 95% of the Chinese, about 80% of the Japanese, and about 75% of the Filipinos. The Chinese, moreover, have established major "Chinatowns" in San Francisco, New York, and Los Angeles.

Statistics aren't always interesting reading, but any attempt to consider questions related to American Orientals must include a clear understanding of their relative numbers in the U.S. Overall, between 1820 and 1967 immigrants from Asia were 1.3% of a total of more than 42 million immigrants. The relative percentages for Orientals increased after the Immigration Reform Act of 1965 revised the prior "national origins" quota system which had discriminated against Asians. In the decade of 1960-70, while the white American population increased by about 12%, Filipinos increased by about 95%, Chinese by about 85%, and the Japanese by almost 30%.

Despite these percentage increases, the American Oriental population is still well below 1% of the U.S. total. Therefore our concern with Americans of Asian ancestry results not from their numbers but from a consideration of their rightful place as Americans in a country where more than 99% of the people are descended from post-Columbian immigrants.

Historical Perspective

Before we consider American Orientals today we need historical perspective to accompany our statistical generalizations. All of us have studied some American history, but the treatment of American Orientals (and other ethnic minorities) was often passed over with slight and sanitized references. The memory of those offended is usually longer than those who give offense. What kind of welcome have Orientals received in the U.S.?

The Chinese were the first to come. The gold rush of the 1850's attracted them to California; later their numbers increased rapidly when labor was needed to complete the transcontinental railway. By 1870 there were about 65,000 Chinese in the United States; only a few hundred were women. In the next ten years, 250,000 more Chinese came; about 80% lived in California.

American attitudes toward the Chinese changed when immigrants of European ancestry reached the West Coast and competed for jobs. The Chinese, who at first were described as orderly, industrious, thrifty, sober, and inoffensive, had by the 1880's become — in the minds of most civic and industrial leaders — clannish, secretive, dangerous, criminal, and deceitful. Obviously, the Chinese themselves could not have changed their nature so extremely; the change was more in the viewer than in the viewed.

The growing discrimination against the Chinese led to the Chinese Exclusion Act of 1882, which denied immigration for 10 years to Chinese laborers. The act was renewed in 1892, and Chinese immigration was suspended indefinitely in 1902. Many Chinese returned home. About 250,000 lived here in 1882, but the number shrank to 90,000 in 1900 and 60,000 in 1920. The Chinese who remained suffered from continued physical and legal abuse. "To have a Chinaman's chance" came to mean to have no chance at all. The Exclusion Act also denied citizenship to Chinese who were not born in America, a discriminatory act which later included other Orientals and continued until shortly after World War II.

Japanese immigration to the U.S. occurred almost entirely within the first 25 years of this century. Discrimination against the Japanese followed the same pattern of prejudice encountered by other "yellow men," even though the Japanese tended to follow the European-type immigration pattern, bringing their wives and settling in integrated communities. The U.S. government, in the "Gentlemen's Agreement" of 1908, persuaded the Japanese government to restrict the immigration of Japanese laborers and farmers to the U.S., so that friendship between the two countries would not be disrupted. The crisis had been precipitated when the San Francisco Board of Education ordered all Japanese pupils, native- and foreign-born, to attend the segregated Oriental school in Chinatown.

Special and drastic discrimination against the Japanese came during World War II, when, by Presidential decree, the total Japanese population — alien and citizen, old and young — of more than 110,000 people in Oregon, Washington, and California were evacuated to 10 "relocation centers" in sparsely populated, isolated parts of the U.S. interior. The barrack-type communities were surrounded by barbed wire and were under armed guard. The relatively small Japanese populations in other parts of the U.S. were not moved; in Hawaii, where a third of the population was Japanese, no internment was attempted. The loss of labor there would have crippled the islands' effective functioning; also, the logistics of shipping more than 100,000 people to the mainland during wartime

146

alism where each contributes what
ique, where each knows and honors
own roots and can, therefore, be
re enough to honor what is differ-
n his neighbor."[4]

uoted in New York Post, September 22, 1971, p. 11.

2. Pierre Teilhard de Chardin, *The Future of Man.* New York: Harper and Brothers, 1962, p. 132.

3. Marshall McLuhan, *The Gutenburg Galaxy.* Toronto: University of Toronto Press, 1962, p. 31.

4. 1971 commencement address delivered at Jersey City State College.

was overwhelming.

The Filipinos, the third largest American Oriental group, came to Hawaii and California in the 1920's. Like other Orientals, they were ineligible for naturalization but because the U.S. ruled the Philippines, the Filipinos carried U.S. passports and could not be excluded as aliens. The announcement in 1935 that the government promised to free the Philippines ended mass immigration immediately; a quota of 50 per year was substituted. Thus ended, until after World War II, any significant immigration of Orientals into the United States.

Present Patterns

Since World War II, attitudes and actions toward Orientals in the U.S. have been changing. Alien Asians became eligible for citizenship. The basic immigration law was changed in 1965 so that the national origin quota system is no longer used. Now, immigration from the Eastern Hemisphere and dependent areas is limited to an annual total of 170,000 (for the Western Hemisphere the total is 120,000), of which not more than 20,000 may come from any one country. The significant criterion for immigration – aside from family relationships such as spouses and children – is whether the applicant will compete with Americans who are able, willing, and qualified to do the same work.

Other significant current changes relate more directly to the American school system and its effect on ethnic groups. There are at least four major considerations: the role assigned to schools in the "Americanization" of students; the new emphasis on learning about cultural regions of the world; the accompanying change in attitudes toward ethnic groups within the U.S.; and the changing self-image which ethnic minorities are developing. All of these events are related. We cannot examine each in detail, but we can consider some outstanding aspects so that we are more aware of their individual nature and of the ways in which they affect each other.

The Changing School Role

When the first public schools were established in the 1830's, their major goal was to help create students who would become similar in aspirations and attitudes. Educators were expected to help impose a single standard of behavior. This Americanization process – the notion of a "melting pot" where many ethnic ingredients would be blended to produce one nationality – was specifically designed for a nation of immigrants. But from the start, English as a language and Western Europe as a culture were the basic stock; minority ethnic groups added seasoning but were to be absorbed. By the end of the nineteenth century, says historian John Hope Franklin, "America's standards of ethnicity accepted Anglo-Saxons as the norm, placed other whites on what may be called 'ethnic probation,' and excluded from serious consideration the Japanese, Chinese, and Negroes."[1]

Now there is growing support for American schools where multi-ethnic standards are recognized – where there is a sharing of generalized ideals and goals of American culture which include respect for rather than rejection of differences in racial, religious, and ethnic heritage. On a global basis, Americans are beginning to realize that we represent a national-ethnic minority. On a national basis, we are trying to combine the positive features of integration and of ethnic identification in harmony with our special nature as a nation of immigrant ancestry. This innovation can be especially beneficial for American Orientals and other nonwhite groups, because racial characteristics could cease to be a basis of discrimination.

Changing Attitudes

Another change which affects American Orientals – and all ethnic groups within the U.S. – is the way in which American students are beginning to gain a different perspective of foreign cultures. How one feels about Chinese-Americans (or Mexican-Americans or African-Americans or European-Americans) depends greatly upon one's understanding and appreciation of the culture from which a person is originally descended.

Until recently the pattern of foreign studies in American schools was clear. In a course inappropriately called "world history" students learned that man's most significant development occurred in Europe and later in the U.S. The study of areas beyond Europe entered this version of world history only peripherally, mainly when these areas were "discovered" by Europeans. References to China were usually limited to three or four: when it was a "cradle of civilization," when it was "discovered" by Marco Polo, when it came under European domination, and when it became an "emerging nation." In this version, Japan's "history" begins when it is "opened" by Commodore Perry.

A dramatic change is occurring in the curriculum. Almost to the same degree that Americans have become involved in the real world beyond our shores, the representation of that world has moved into the American classroom. As the United States became a world political power and also extended its global economic investments, its educational system was expected to prepare students for a future in which Americans would increasingly be involved throughout the world. The end of American cultural isolation was also hastened by another development, the communications revolution. The mass expansion of television, materials in print and in other media, travel, and reportage of global events in which Americans were deeply involved began to bring the rest of the world into American consciousness.

The attempts to understand with empathy the cultures in Asia, among others, have helped to change the attitudes of American students toward the descendents of those cultures *within* the U.S. When we begin to comprehend and appreciate differences among global cultures, we are also preparing ourselves to perceive positively the ethnic variations which exist inside national borders. There is, for example, a connection between our feelings toward the Chinese civilization and Chinese everywhere. Because most Americans have usually thought of themselves as being superior among all global cultures, the majority of Americans have also felt superior to those ethnic representatives within the U.S. who favored customs which were considered outside "the mainstream of American life." These groups are often described as being "culturally disadvantaged" in the same ways that cultures outside of the United States are considered "backward" to the degree that their achievements and values have low scores when measured by our standards.

Few members of the so-called culturally disadvantaged groups in this country would deny that they receive lower wages or have fewer educational opportunities, but does this condition also mean that their *cultural values* are inferior? Should we be surprised that people who are labeled as culturally disadvantaged may develop a low self-image which itself interferes with educational attempts to provide assistance? For some American Orientals, prejudice works the other way; teachers may believe that Chinese, for example, have superior intelligence and work harder than other students. Consequently, more is expected from them and this "compliment" increases pressures on the learner. Many studies have demonstrated that teacher attitudes permeate the classroom and that students "catch" the spirit of prejudice and preference.

A crucial element of self-image is the mirror held up for reflection. Recently, Asian-American students founded the *Amerasia Journal* because, "At one time we were perceived as a 'heathen' race to be dealt with forcibly, while at other times as a successful minority that should be emulated by others. Our purpose in initiating this journal resulted from these seemingly contradictory perceptions and self-images." The editors have an important insight: They realize that the American view of Orientals depends less upon the Orientals themselves and more upon the conditions of our own viewing.

The most dramatic example of one current Chinese-American self-image is in San Francisco, where the Chinese community has been protesting a federal court order to bus its children to schools outside Chinatown. Parental objection to the busing has been almost unanimous. Chinese leaders say that the transfer of the students will destroy the cultural and educational life of Chinatown. Their first appeal to the Supreme Court was denied by Justice William O. Douglas, who cited an 1875 Supreme Court decision on the rights of a San Francisco Chinese laundryman who had been wrongfully deprived of a license because he was Chinese. In Douglas's ruling, he said that the present court order applies to all San Francisco children, regardless of racial or ethnic background, and that rights and laws — and

court integration
to all races. Furth

'The Planetizatio

Our concern w
the U.S., regardl
increasingly be
context. Teilharc
"the planetizatio
will make us "m
alized and huma
similar vision:

We can no
phibiously in
guished world:
in many wo
simultaneously
committed to
single ratio a
senses – any
book or to one
technology…
ing of human
cultures will sc
specialism in s
has become.[3]

One of our pr
ceiving American
"problem." We h
ate – literally, "tc
enrichment and s
ethnic differences
an Americanized c
other country, the
sents in its people
ing of diverse cult
begin to welcome
opportunity rathe
the realities of A
experienced differ
liberated consciou
quently voiced by
ark, Kenneth Gibs
"achieving an Ame
and hope of the w
this country a "nai
and religious div

plur
is u
his
secu
ent

1.

GOOD DAY AT ROUGH ROCK

Paul Conklin

On the northern flank of Arizona's Black Mountain, an experiment has been started that could change the entire structure and philosophy of Indian education in America. Here, in a bleak setting of desert, rock and sagebrush, near the center of the country's largest reservation—25,000 square miles—that is home to 105,000 Navajos, Robert A. Roessel, Jr., director of the Rough Rock Demonstration School, is applying a community control approach that could hold promise for poor, uneducated people everywhere. His method—to work with the Indians, not on them. His thesis—that Indians ought to be able to be Americans and Indians, too. "Education as the Indian knows it on the reservation can best be characterized as the Either-Or type," says Dr. Roessel, a vigorous man with an unruly, greying thatch of hair. "One is either an Indian or a white man, and the way we have traditionally weighted things, the good way is always the non-Indian way and the bad is always the Indian. We tell Indian children they are superstitious and primitive and that their hogans are dirty. We try to impose our values and tell them they should eat green, leafy vegetables and sleep on a bed and brush their teeth. In short, we try to make white men out of Indians. The Indian child listens and looks at himself and sees that he doesn't measure up. In his own eyes he is a failure. Education can be a shattering experience when one is taught nothing but negative things about himself for 12 years."

As he talks, Roessel occasionally squints through the window of his comfortable living room which, in keeping with his educational beliefs, is furnished in modern and Navajo. Outside, the wind blows incessantly, swirling sand against the panes and wearing away at the light-colored buildings that blend with the monochromatic landscape. In the far distance can be seen the looming red sandstone monoliths of Monument Valley. "Now Indians have begun to question whether it is necessary for them to lose their heritage in order to become citizens of the United States," he continues. "And so the Both-And—both white and Indian—approach to Indian education was born."

Rough Rock Demonstration School is a self-contained community within a scattered population of about 600. It has to be. The nearest paved road is 16 miles away and the nearest sizable town, Gallup, N. Mex., 120 miles. The school has its own water system and fire engine, a spacious classroom-office building with a gymnasium, a separate kitchen-dining room, and a boys' dormitory and a girls' dormitory, each with a capacity of 165 children. The staff are quartered in 36 houses and 8 apartments. Roessel's expectations and hopes for the experiment come through clearly as he speaks of the school.

"Rough Rock is the first school to have the tools and resources to see whether this new approach can be effective. We want to instill in our youngsters a sense of pride in being Indian. We want to show them that they can be Indian and American at the same time, that they can take the best from each way of life and combine it into something viable. When I first came on the reservation as a teacher, I told children they had two legs, one being their Navajo heritage and the other the best part of the white world. They couldn't get along with just one leg, but needed both to be secure and whole."

AMERICAN EDUCATION, February 1967, pp. 4-9.

151

The Rough Rock staff includes ten full-time classroom teachers, a remedial reading specialist, a speech therapist, an art teacher, a librarian, two TESL (Teaching English as a Second Language) specialists, and two recreation leaders. Fifteen members of the Volunteers in Service to America (VISTA) also work at the school. Of the 91 full-time people on the payroll, 46 are Indian, 35 of them from Rough Rock, a fact that illustrates a vital part of the Roessel philosophy — involving the local community in school life as much as possible.

The school laundry is a good example. Bureau of Indian Affairs schools typically contract their laundry out to private firms, which are usually located in towns many miles away. In the Rough Rock budget $5,000 was set aside for this purpose. Roessel spent $2,000 on washing machines and used the rest to hire two local women to operate them.

No opportunities are missed at the school to help the children **understand themselves as Indians. Navajo motifs are freely mixed in with other classroom decorations. The library has a Navajo corner. Recordings of the Navajo music and rituals are played during the school day.**

In the evening old men, the historians and medicine men of the tribe, come to the dormitories and tell Navajo folk tales and legends. The staff is preparing biographies of successful Navajos to give the students something on which to pattern their own lives.

Each day, 35 minutes of class time are set aside in the pre-school sections and lower three grades, and 45 minutes in grades three through six for "cultural identification" lessons. During the first six weeks the lessons cover the Navajo hogan — its history, how it is built, the ceremonies that surround it, and how life is conducted in it. The second six weeks cover farming and caring for livestock. The third period deals with reservation facilities, **the land and climate, Navajo history and tribal government.**

A crucial part of "cultural identification" at Rough Rock is the adult arts and crafts program, which has a twofold purpose: to revive dying Navajo handicrafts so that the children of the school can observe the process, and to produce more local wage-earners.

This is the domain of Dr. Roessel's wife, Ruth, who is Navajo. A graduate of Arizona State University and a member of the Governor's Advisory Committee on Indian Education, Ruth is one of the reservation's most skilled weavers. She has also proved herself an able recruiter. Ambrose Roanhorse, renowned as the reservation's most skillful silversmith, came to Rough Rock at her invitation. His first apprentices have already reached the stage where they are ready to market their jewelry.

Sharing the school's arts and crafts center with the silversmiths are a weaver and a moccasin maker. They will soon be joined **by basketmakers, potters, leather craftsmen, and rawhide workers.**

"This is not art for art's sake, although the Navajo puts great store in creating beautiful things. These skills are extremely marketable and we are training people who otherwise would have no income," Roessel explains. The Indians now eke out a precarious existence herding sheep.

At one time in most Indian schools the children were punished if they spoke Navajo. At Rough Rock they are encouraged and even forced to use their own language. Navajo is taught in the fourth, fifth, and sixth grades for one hour three days a week. Also, for the first time on the reservation, portions of regular classes, such as arithmetic and social studies, are held in Navajo. The purpose is to see whether students find it easier to retain subject matter when taught in their native language, as research has suggested may be the case.

Roessel provides evening tutoring lessons in Navajo for his staff **members who do not speak the language. They find it tough going, since Navajo—a harsh, guttural tongue—is classified by linguists as the world's second most difficult language.**

Because of the importance the Both-And philosophy places on mastery of both English and Navajo, Rough Rock's TESL department is highly active at the school. English is taught formally twice a day, informally at all times. For example, as the children pass through the cafeteria line at noon they must ask for their food in English.

A teaching aid which TESL director Virginia Hoffman has found invaluable is the school's closed-circuit TV system. Once a month she writes a simple play, using staff members and VISTA personnel in the cast. A recent drama, "The Zegafferelebra," took place in a painted jungle. The message, spoken by animals with papier mache heads, dealt with correct intonation and the lengthening of vowels. Future produc- **tions will be concerned with gender, number, tense, "to be," and "is going to."**

The idea for the **Rough Rock** experiment began to take shape at **Arizona State University** in 1959 and 1960 while Roessel studied for a doctor's degree. To gather raw material for his thesis, he visited over 100 Indian communities, talking to the elders about their needs and aspirations.

Much of what Roessel learned during that period was incorporated in a proposal which he and a number of Indian leaders later presented to the Office of Economic Opportunity (OEO) for the establishment of a different kind of Indian school. The result, in 1965, was the Lukachukai Navajo Demonstration School, which foundered after only one year, primarily because of an awkward administrative set-up. The school was funded by OEO, which superimposed a staff of academic and community development specialists on the existing staff of the **Bureau of Indian Affairs (BIA) boarding school at Lukachukai, a hamlet not far from Rough Rock.** The administrative dichotomy proved too much, and OEO reluctantly withdrew its support.

BIA and OEO, still mindful of the need for a new approach to Indian education and wary of repeating their mistakes at Lukachukai, put up money for another demonstration school that would be independent of them both. The funds, $335,000 from OEO and $307,000 from BIA, were awarded to a private, nonprofit corporation called Demonstration in Navajo Education, Inc.—whose Navajo acronym DINE means the Navajos, or "the people." Roessel was recruited as director and BIA turned over a brand new $3.5 million school which it had just built in Rough Rock.

At the time, Roessel was director of Arizona State University's Indian Community Action Center, one of three such centers established by OEO to provide technical assistance and training to reservation Indians under its Community Action Program.

His decision to go to Rough Rock was not easily made. "I was happy at Tempe, and felt important. I had real influence in the OEO Indian program and went to Washington every week. It wasn't easy to come out here where the roads are terrible and the phones never work. But I had been writing articles too long saying what was wrong with Indian education and Indian programs. Here was a chance to put into practice what I believed, or shut up."

Soon after Roessel's arrival, the people of Rough Rock elected one woman and four men to the school board. All were middle-aged Navajos and only one had ever had as much as a day of formal education. In a move that must have raised eyebrows in many quarters, control of the demonstration school was immediately passed over to the board.

"At least 50 schools on the res-ervation have their own boards, so in this respect Rough Rock is not unique," Roessel points out. "But the traditional Indian board has a housekeeping function: it builds roads, maintains buildings, and acts as a truant officer. It has no authority or decision-making power, and the superintendent really calls the shots. What we have here is local control in the true sense for the first time.

"The greatest need of Indian education today," he continues, "is to involve Indians. The belief persists that Indians have neither the desire nor the ability to manage their own affairs. It's the old 'father-knows-best' approach that says it's up to me, an expert sitting behind my desk, to make policy for them. But the Both-And philosophy says that Indians are eager for responsibility and, if given a chance, they'll act creatively and assume leadership."

Roessel takes the principle of local control seriously. Once a week he and a few of his senior staff discuss a part of the master program with the school board, explaining the reasons the staff consider it important. In each instance the board has accepted the proposal, modifying it, however, and adding a Navajo cast to it. Roessel sees the modifications as strengthening the demonstration program. So strong is his faith in the board members that he is willing to scrap completely any part that they oppose.

It is not simply rhetoric when Roessel says of Rough Rock, "This is a community-oriented school, rather than child-oriented. In the past, Indian schools have taken little interest in their communities, but here we want to involve adults and teenagers, dropouts, people who have never been to school."

Rough Rock's school facilities—gym, kitchen, dormitories, shower rooms, library—are open to anybody who wants to use them. School fairs, movies, basketball games, talent nights have drawn crowds that increase steadily.

Rough Rock parents are encouraged to come to the school for board meetings, to spend time in the classrooms, to eat in the cafeteria, and to stay overnight in the dormitories. They sometimes come in team-drawn wagons, the men with stiff-brimmed hats and, if they are of the old generation, their hair drawn into tight knots at the back. The women wear long velveteen skirts, silver jewelry, and strings of turquoise and coral. Quiet and grave, they flit shyly about the school like old-fashioned ghosts.

"Our school board has told the parents of this district that they can't use the school as a dumping ground where they can leave their children and forget them. We believe the kids belong to their parents and not to the school. Instead of limiting the child to two or three visits home a year, as is the case in most schools, we let parents take their children home any weekend they want," Roessel says.

To make the dormitories more homelike and to avoid the usual ratio in dormitory staffing of one adult for every 60 children, Roessel employs eight parents to mend clothes, tell stories, help with the twice-a-week shower, and do a variety of other chores that parents know how to do best. For this they receive a dollar an hour. The parents change every six weeks; the school board handles recruiting. With help from instructional aides, parents, and VISTA workers, the Rough Rock adult-child ratio has dropped to 1 to 15.

Just as most Navajo parents know virtually nothing about the way reservation schools are operated, so, too, is it rare to find a teacher in the system who has any first-hand knowledge about how life is lived in the Navajo hogan. In a study conducted in 1963, the Indian Education Center at Arizona State University found that only 15 of 100 reservation teachers had ever visited an Indian home.

One of the reasons for this failure was that the heavy daily routine makes escape from the classroom almost impossible for the teacher. And often the teacher is afraid he will be unwelcome in the hogan. Rough Rock teachers visit the homes of all their students at least twice a year. They are accompanied by the child, and an interpreter when necessary, and tell the parents about their children's progress.

Roessel would also like each of his non-Indian teachers to live in a Navajo hogan for a week. "I want them to see what it means to haul water five miles, to chop wood for heat, to go to bed at dark because there is no light, to eat bread and coffee for a meal," he says.

By giving his staff an awareness of the peculiar texture of Navajo life, Roessel hopes to avert a repetition of the small-scale tragedy that resulted from a teacher's inexperience at another reservation school. The teacher was from the East. Her credentials were excellent, but she had never taught Navajo children before. She noticed one morning that the face and arms of one of her third grade boys were covered by something that looked like soot. In his hair was a substance that resembled grease. With a normal respect for cleanliness, the teacher asked the boy to wash himself. When he refused she took him to the bathroom and washed him.

The boy never returned to school. It turned out that his family had conducted an important healing ceremony on his sick sister, the "soot" and "grease" being part of the ceremonial painting. With her soap and water the teacher destroyed the healing powers of the ceremony. The girl died and the parents could not be shaken in their belief that it was the teacher's fault. No member of the family has set foot in a school since.

Programs for adults have claimed only the peripheral attention of Indian education officials in the past. **Through a canvass of the 600 Navajos who live in the area of Rough Rock, it was** learned that the men are most interested in auto mechanics instruction. Women want classes in cooking and nutrition. Both are interested in classes in basic literacy. They want to gain a rudimentary knowledge of money and how to make change so they will

not be cheated when they buy at the store. They want to acquire a basic English vocabulary of about 50 words that can carry them through their trips to the local trading post and to the outside world.

"It is here in our work with adults that the most significant thrust is being made at Rough Rock. It is an area to which other demonstrations have not been directed, an area of little prior activity," Roessel says. "At Rough Rock the BIA and OEO have said to the Indians in effect, 'This is your school. Make of it what you want. Develop a curriculum that will reflect what you think is important.' This is an isolated, illiterate community where 95 percent of the people are unedu**cated, but I am convinced that they have the necessary vision and concern for their future."

It would be hard to find a more disadvantaged community than Rough Rock, where the average family of six makes $500 a year and where cultural life is utterly threadbare. Roessel believes that if Rough Rock can succeed—if these uneducated people can determine the educational needs of their children and their community, then it cannot be said that impoverished, uneducated people any place are unable to provide self-leadership.

"This is why Rough Rock is the most exciting thing going on in Indian education anywhere in the country," says Roessel. "This is why our program has ramifications far outside the Indian world."

CHAPTER IV : TEACHING THE URBAN CHILD

Teaching in the slum or ghetto school containing culturally different children is no easy job by any means. The absolutely overwhelming feeling of frustration that first happens to the beginning teacher is something which cannot be really understood until one has experienced it. All at once, the new teacher is faced with situations not covered in any of his courses in the teacher education institution. He is all alone with perhaps as many as 40 children with few books and other materials. In some ways it is a sink-or-swim type of situation, where the mentally and physically strong survive and the weak sink. Unfortunately, there are few resources that a new teacher can grasp hold of in the first several years of inner-city teaching. Many new inner city teachers mean well and have an earnest desire to help the children but lack the understanding and skills to do so. In this chapter, the articles attempt to give the new or prospective inner-city teacher a few tips on how to operate with the kinds of problems that exist.

The all-important problem of inner-city education is that of reading. Reading is definitely the name of the game and each teacher from the kindergarten to the senior level in high school must in essence be a reading

teacher. For many reasons culturally different children do not learn to read at the precise intervals the
K-12 lockstep system demands and thus are left behind
when the teacher moves on into the next unit of instruction.
The sequential and group type learning experience is
perhaps one of the greatest handicaps faced by inner-
city school children.

Many students in teacher education institutions
are afraid of teaching in the inner city for various
reasons. Many times they ask if they really possess
the skills to handle the inner-city children in a learning
situation. Many have read the educational "pop" literature and see every inner-city school as a blackboard
jungle, full of pimps, prostitutes, pushers, con artists,
and rip-off men. Actually, most inner-city schools have
an adequate amount of order and procedure and many times
over-structured schools are found where the students are
extremely regimented and ordered. Thus, inner-city schools
vary in terms of control and discipline just as suburban
schools do. The problems might be somewhat different in
the inner city as life is more real and more earnest and
often more deadly than in the suburbs.

A great help to new teachers in inner-city schools
is a knowledge of how the school really operates. Such

things as what types of regulations exist, how does a
teacher get paper, pencils and duplicating supplies,
need to be learned. These are all things which if known
beforehand can make the transitional process of the
first several months much easier. A young or inexperienced teacher has his hands full in working with the
class of children, let alone about having to worry about
the administrative problems of the school and classroom.

Whether or not inner-city teachers are made or
born is not really a question. The important aspect of
inner-city teaching is adaptability and creativity. If
a teacher can adapt to the situation and then remain
constantly creative a positive learning situation can
occur. Money does not buy learning and no huge inputs
of monies into materials and teaching staffs will automatically produce quality education. Unfortunately, the
production of creative teachers who really care about
the children do not have price tags and cannot be
bought from an educational supply house.

Unfortunately, there is no teachers' manual for
teaching in the inner-city school that is going to give
a step-by-step direction on how to get the job done.

FRANK RIESSMAN

The strategy of style

I WOULD LIKE TO DISCUSS a concept which I think has been ignored a good deal in teaching and guidance. It is the concept of style—in particular, the style of learning. I believe a crucial element in the development of the individual's learning relates to a careful understanding of the idiosyncratic style elements in the learning process. Students of learning have focused a good deal on rather abstract, molecular concepts of learning derived from pigeons and rats via B. F. Skinner and Clark L. Hull. I am not suggesting that these concepts of learning are not useful, but I think that we have missed the possible value of a more wholistic (molar) or global dimension of learning, operative at the phenomenal level, which I am referring to as style.

An Illustrative Model

One index of style relates to whether you learn things most easily through reading or through hearing or whether you learn through doing things physically, whether you learn things slowly or quickly, whether you learn things in a one-track way or whether you are very flexible in your learning. These examples are not to be conceived as separate from one another. There can be such combinations as a visual-physical learner who learns in a slow, one-track fashion. As a matter of fact, this last pattern is quite characteristic of the disadvantaged child. He learns more slowly; he learns through the physical (that is, by doing things, touching things); he learns visually, and he functions in a rather one-track way in that he doesn't shift easily and is not highly flexible in his learning. This is, of course, an ideal statement—a model.

Let me cite just a few other dimensions of style so that different aspects of it can be seen. For example, some people like to work under pressure; they like a deadline, and they like tests. (Low-income youngsters do not like such conditions.) Some people like to leave a lot of time for their work, enjoying a slow tempo. Some people like to think or even read while walking. Some people like to work in a cold room, some in a warm one. Some people like to work for long periods of time without a break; some people like to shift and take frequent breaks. Some people take a long time to warm up, whereas others get into their work very

TEACHERS COLLEGE RECORD, March 1964, pp. 484-489.

quickly. Some people like to have all of the facts in front of them before they can do any generalizing, and others prefer to have a few facts. Some people like "props," some people do not.

Typically, people do not know their own style nearly well enough. What I am really concerned about is how one can use this concept to improve one's manner of work—whether it be teaching or guidance, social work or psychiatry. Although I am mainly concerned with working with lower socioeconomic groups, I do not mean to imply that the concept of style must be limited to these social strata.

Cognition vs. Emotion

Guidance workers have focused far too much on the categories of emotion, motivation, and personality rather than on the cognitive categories of learning and thinking. There has been much too much emphasis on the emotional approach in attempting to understand why a child doesn't learn. Little careful analysis is given to how the child's learning might improve simply by concentrating on the way that he works and learns, rather than on his affective reasons for not learning. This thesis is almost directly counter to the current view. Today if a child doesn't learn (and if he has intellectual ability), it is quickly assumed that his difficulties must be due to some emotional block or conflict. I am trying to suggest a different way of looking at the problem. He may not be learning because his methods of learning are not suited to his style, and hence he cannot best utilize his power. I would be willing to argue that even where his troubles are, in part, emotional or due to conflict, it still may be possible to ignore this particular focus and concentrate profitably on the specific expression of the difficulty itself—his learning pattern. Even if one rejects my premise that the emotional causes have been overemphasized, one may still give a willing ear to the possibility of dealing with crucial problems of learning in nonemotional, nonpsychodynamic terms. Unfortunately, teachers too often have behaved like psychologists and social workers. It seems to me that they do not sufficiently stress learning processes and styles of learning, apparently preferring motivational categories. One way to build up appropriate prestige in the teaching profession is *not* simply to borrow from psychologists and sociologists, but to concentrate on the development of what education is most concerned with, learning and teaching. When one does borrow from psychology, it may be better to concentrate on learning and cognition rather than personality and motivation.

Animals and Men

If we examine the outcomes of teacher-education courses in learning, educational psychology, and the like, we typically are forced to the suspicion that they amount to very little. Borrowing heavily from animal learning experiments (which by itself is not necessarily bad), such courses are victimized by the fact that the particular concepts and formulations developed in the animal literature have not been easily applicable to human learning problems—whether a child learns slowly, whether he is a physical learner, or whether it takes him a long time to warm up. Although these problems are nearer to our subjective experience, the psychological literature and animal experiments have not really helped us very much to deal effectively with them. When educational psychology courses have actually studied human learning, the focus has not been on the significant problems that I think are related to style. When they attempt, for example, to deal with study habits, they are entirely too general. There is a great deal more to study habits than meets the eye of the introductory psychology textbook. The typical suggestions in the chapter on study habits are based upon various experiments which seem to indicate that distributive learning is better, that one should survey material first, etc. But very little is directed toward the *idiosyncratic* factors that are involved.

For example, some people simply can't tolerate surveying a chapter first. They become so anxious, so disturbed, by being asked to look at the over-all view of the chapter that they can't function. These people want very much to read a chapter atomistically. This is their style. It won't help simply to tell such a person that he is not proceeding in the right way and that he really ought to read the chapter as a whole first. The same is true in terms of the general recommendation that one should have a quiet place to study. Strangely enough, some people study quite well in a noisy place, or with certain kinds of noise, and completely quiet places are not best for them. Some people take a long time to warm up; consequently, a great deal of spacing (or distribution) of learning would not be useful for them. This is their style. But the textbook does not tell you this because, in general, over a large number of cases, spaced learning is best.

The same argument applies to examinations or tests. For some people, a test operates as just the right mild anxiety to stimulate the integration of a great deal of material that needs to be learned. On the other hand, there are large numbers of people for whom tests are terrible because they disorganize them, make them too anxious, and thus prevent them from working. Tests are not conducive to the style of these individuals. When it is argued that tests are educationally undesirable because they produce too much anxiety for learning, the arguments refer to such people. When others argue that tests are marvelous because they aid pupils by providing corrections and criticism, they are referring to persons with a different style. Undoubtedly, tests work happily for some pupils, but there are others who forget their wrong answers on tests because it disturbs them so much to remember them.

As a matter of fact, there is a great deal of controversy in the traditional literature on the very question of whether repression of wrong answers occurs or whether "punishment" for giving the wrong answers on tests helps to produce better recall. I am suggesting that two different kinds of styles are involved here. For some people, the information that they gave wrong answers is extremely useful and challenging. If this information is called to their attention in a definite and stimulating way, it makes the wrong answer the figure in the ground. It draws the incorrect responses productively to their attention. For other people, knowing that they have made a mistake is extremely disturbing, distructive of their morale, and leads to a repressing of this material. Therefore, depending upon one's style and one's way of dealing with these problems, tests may be useful or not useful.

Strategies of Modification

My main task is to try to formulate the possible ways in which the strengths of the individual's style can be utilized and its weaknesses reduced or controlled. At this stage in our discussion, I mean the more fundamental, underlying characteristics—for example, the physical style already discussed. This style is laid down early in life and is not subject to fundamental change, although it is possible to *bend* it and to *develop* it. Another aspect of style may be much more malleable and may be more related to habit or set; that is, it may be a derivative or secondary expression of style.

Let us take as an example, what I call the "games" focus of low income youngsters. They like to learn things through games rather than through tests. To put something in the forms of games is an excellent transitional technique for winning their interest. But I do not know how basic a habit this is. It may be much more changeable than the underlying physical style. Such questions are obviously open to further investigation and research. I am simply trying to provide a general framework by means of which to deal with the issue. I am not sure which elements are more or less changeable, but I do believe that some are quite unchangeable and quite basic, whereas some are more susceptible to intervention. A person who likes to learn by listening and speaking (aural style) is unlikely to change completely and become, say, a reader. I am not suggesting that such a pupil will not learn to read and write fluently, but his best learning, the long-lasting, deep learning that gets into his muscles, is more likely to derive from speaking and hearing.

Now let me return to the problem I am essentially trying to deal with—the strategy of style, the strategy of producing basic changes in people through understanding and utilizing their styles. I want to develop the idiosyncratic strengths, find ways of employing the unorthodox, the specific, the unique, and in some ways limit the weaknesses in the person's style. Under certain conditions, one can overcome some of the weak elements of the style pattern through compensatory efforts and through special techniques. I think, however, that weaknesses in learning are more likely to be alleviated when they are at the level of sets and habits.

Awareness and Utilization

In approaching our problem, the first aim is to have the person become aware of the strengths and potentials in his style—because this is going to be the source of his power. Thus, if an individual has a physical style, he has to learn the special attributes of this style and how to use them. The guidance counselor or teacher will have to help him overcome the invidious interpretations of this style that are prevalent in our society.

Let us take an illustration of a different type. A youngster tells us that he sits down to work but cannot concentrate. It is extremely important at this point (and this is crucial in the diagnosis of style) to ascertain as precisely as possible exactly what takes place in this youngster's routine. For example, when does he study? What time does he come home from school? What does he do first when he comes into the house? He may say,

> I come home, throw down my books, and then I start to remember that I have to do some work. So I get out my books. I try to work. I take out the book, but my mind wanders. I look at the book; I look away. I can't get into the work, and after a few minutes of trying this, I begin to feel discouraged; I begin to feel bad. I feel I can't work. I'm not interested. I'm no good. I get very worried, panic builds up, and then I run away from the work.

There are many possibilities operating in this pattern. One possibility is that this youngster has a slow period of warm up. He does not easily get into something new; he does not shift from whatever he's been doing before (whether he's been outside playing ball or inside listening to the radio). This may be due to a number of reasons. He may be a physical learner. If one is a physical learner, one generally must be involved physically in the work process. One has to get one's muscles into it, and this takes time. If this is our student's pattern, then he must come to understand that although he is slow to warm up, this is not necessarily a negative quality; it is simply a different way of approaching work.

As a matter of fact, it may very often be connected to perseverance, once he gets involved! Once he is immersed, he may go deeper and deeper and not be able to shift away from the work easily. The inability to shift doesn't then operate as a negative feature but as a positive element in his style. But the youngster I described here rarely gets to this point. It's not that he doesn't persevere somewhere, in baseball or somewhere else. But in his school work, he's never gotten past the point of the slow warm up. In order to use his pattern effectively, he has to schedule work accordingly. He cannot schedule his time so that he works for one hour. That's no good because it takes him a half hour to warm up. Even if he were to be successful and stick with it for the half hour as a result of a teacher's or guidance worker's support and stimulation, the problem would remain at the end of the half hour of only having a short time left to work. Consequently, he has to plan a larger time period of work and recognize in advance that it will take him about a half hour to warm up. In other words, the person who would help him must give him a definition of his work pattern in order to realize the positive potentialities in it.

Strength over Weakness

When this new definition is provided, it is probable that a number of consequences will follow if I'm right about the diagnosis. Over a period of time, the warm-up period will shorten because part of the difficulty in the long warm up is the anxiety that emerges as he tries to get into the work and fails. Thus, by getting into the work, his anxiety decreases, and his interest has a chance, concomitantly, to increase.

Now let us take another example, one in which the person's strengths can be used to deal with his weaknesses. How do you teach a person how to read when reading is not his basic style? Everyone is going to need reading ability and writing ability regardless of his style. In order to teach reading to youngsters for whom it is stylistically uncongenial, one may want to use role-playing, which is more related to the physical style of the individual. He can read about something that he just role-played, or he can read about a trip he has recently taken. While teaching reading under these conditions, the teacher must remember that he is not developing a reading style; he is developing a skill, a *balance* in the pupil's style. He is developing minimal efficiency in an area which is not rooted in the learner's style. In a sense, the teacher is going after his Achilles heel, his weakness, the reading difficulty, by developing it through his strength, whether it be visual, physical, or whatever. This is a basic tactic for defeating or limiting the weakness by connecting it and subjecting it to the strengths.

Minimal Goals

There are some other things one can do in employing the strategy of style. Various transitional techniques can be used, for example, for overcoming some of a pupil's educational weaknesses. Illustratively, low-income youngsters come to the school situation ordinarily with a very poor auditory set. They're not accustomed to listening to people read stories to them. I suggest that this kind of pattern can be limited quite a bit and can be overcome up to a point. I don't think that the school can develop a basic aural style in such children, but effective teachers can teach them to learn through listening even though this isn't their *best* mode of learning. One of the techniques for doing this was developed by a man who worked with schizophrenic children. The technique was simply to make a game out of the auditory problem. He would say, for example, What is six and five? Everybody in the class would have to answer many different times. The pupil cannot fall asleep in such a class. Answering once doesn't leave him free because he may be asked the same question (or somewhat different ones) often. This is an excellent technique for waking up youngsters, and it has been effective with low-income students who are not used to listening. The objective is to bring them up to minimal listening ability, up to grade level. I want to bring low-income youngsters far beyond grade level in most areas, because I think they have considerable creative ability; but in their areas of weakness, I would be happy to bring them simply up to grade level. In areas of weakness, our primary aim should be functioning on a minimal level of adequacy so that weaknesses will not destroy strengths. Techniques of the kind described may be useful in reversing habits and sets which have grown out of the negative aspects of the person's style.

To sum up: In everybody's style, there are certain strengths, and each of us has his own Achilles heel. The issue in developing a powerful change in a person is related to how one gets to the Achilles heel and how one utilizes the strengths. This is the central problem of the strategy of style, especially in its application to the low-income pupils of our urban schools.

MATERIALS THE DISADVANTAGED NEED

—AND DON'T NEED

MARTIN HABERMAN

WHAT makes a book, a film or a live fireman instructional material? What makes particular material of special use to the disadvantaged?

The disadvantaged are often defined operationally as those less predisposed, than some equally vague group of "others," to benefit from school programs. The causes of this condition are usually attributed to inadequacies at home—e.g., few material goods, sensory deprivation, a lack of basic information about the world, an absence of successful adult models, and inadequate amounts of loving care. For older children, the school program, with its overemphasis on reading and on abstract content, is often cited as the source and perpetuator of its own problems.

Given such assumptions, it is easy to understand the present search for preschool materials to replace what youngsters have missed. If they lack commodities—things, pictures, noises, smells and even body warmth—then these materials are sought out and provided. For those already in school the causes of disadvantagement become subsumed under the rubric "under-achievement" and the search for materials becomes a grasping at systems —i.e., approaches guaranteed to teach basic skills, notably reading, to all but the most severely disturbed or retarded. Once we have exposed our assumptions about what puts certain youngsters at a disadvantage in school, the materials, media and methods we seek are predictable.

A cohesive view of the disadvantaged should include theoretical underpinnings from which to derive action programs.

Actually, experts in human development hunch that lower-class children are likely to be exposed to even *more* stimulation than middle-class children.[1]

Researchers also have suggested that there is no evidence of real differences in rate of development during the first two years, when such differences in stimulation would have to occur to have a lasting impact on development.[2]

[1] J. McV. Hunt. "How Children Develop Intellectually." *Merrill-Palmer Quarterly* 10: 209-48; 1964.

[2] Hilda Knobloch and B. Pasamanick. "Environmental Factors Affecting Human Development, Before and After Birth." *Pediatrics* 26:210-18; 1960.

EDUCATIONAL LEADERSHIP, 1967, Vol. 24, pp. 611-61 /.

The source of much of the impetus for the sensory deprivation approach comes from those who emphasize superficialities—e.g., the inability of many youngsters to attend to the teacher's voice. But whether couched in terms of scholarly research efforts to explain the neurological development of infants, or programmed into tape recorders to help four-year-olds pick out the teacher's voice in a noisy classroom, sensory deprivation is an insufficient explanation.

Perceiving disadvantagement as an absence of concrete and life experiences can result in a shallow emphasis on field trips, color cards and geometric blocks. But just as scholars offer little, beyond their conflicting opinions, regarding which concepts are "keys" to their disciplines, psychologists can suggest little regarding which concrete and life experiences are critical to normal development. When is lack of knowledge or experience merely ignorance and when is it the cause of subsequent and cumulative retardation in the ability to form concepts? Teachers indicate more pervasive and lasting benefits for children who learn to use "or, but, how, if and when"—in any content area—than any information gained from scurrying-around on field trips.

Bereiter makes the most cogent argument for deemphasizing the lack of concrete experiences as *the* causal explanation.

Blind children, on the average, show little or no intellectual and academic deficiency, whereas deaf children are typically about ten points below normal in I.Q. and show gross inadequacies in academic achievement. . . . this finding may be interpreted as meaning that deaf children are culturally deprived in much the way that lower-class children are deprived, regardless of their home backgrounds. It would appear from this that social class opportunities for concrete experiences either do not exist or are not important, whereas lack of opportunity for language experience has serious effects that closely correspond to those found in cultural deprivation.[*]

My basic assumption is that those who are less able to move from the social uses of language to the levels of conceptualization and transmission will be disadvantaged in schools and in American society generally. Bernstein's formulation of how linguistic codes can trap children into self-perpetuating restrictions, or propel them into lifelong elaborations, provides a basis for both understanding and planning programs for the disadvantaged.[*] The suggestions for materials which follow derive from this belief that adding to children's language codes should be the critical purpose of special programs.

An Approach to Materials and Experiences

I recently had two opportunities of working with six-year-olds. On an individual basis, I took children who had not yet spoken in school or who were speaking in very restricted, limited ways to do the following:

—feel carpets
—taste fruits and vegetables

[*] Carl Bereiter and Siegfried Englemann. *Teaching Disadvantaged Children in the Preschool.* Englewood Cliffs: Prentice-Hall, Inc., 1966. p. 30-31. © 1966. Reprinted by permission of the publisher.

[*] Basil Bernstein. "Elaborated and Restricted Codes: Their Social Origins and Some Consequences." *American Anthropologist* Vol. 66, No. 6, Part 2, 1964.

visit a motel swimming pool
—throw rocks into Lake Michigan
—steer my automobile around a vacant field.

As a group, using private cars, we took a whole class of almost nonverbal six-year-olds to visit a suburban school. The children observed classroom activities, displays of children's work and physical facilities.

While there is much to criticize in these activities, I found that using these materials and experiences stimulated the youngsters to talk more than ever before. They were encouraged to describe and react, and even more, to compare, contrast, explain and summarize. We began with no commitment to any material or subject matter but with a behavioral objective—to get youngsters to express and to share ideas.

Once children reach the age when teachers feel pressured to teach reading, the search for materials often deteriorates into a search for a systematized reading program. While no reasonable person is against the teaching of reading, the critical question is the degree to which each child will have a hand in expressing his need, his readiness, his way of learning. Those who understand the nature of development and the struggles of the disadvantaged, recognize that language development is broader than reading and that intellectual development is more pervasive than the ability to call the written word at the earliest possible age.

Representatives of private industry, foundations, publishers and funding offices of government, have introduced the concept of "teacher-proof packaging of systems," to indicate their search for materials which will guarantee the teaching of reading by even the least able teachers. Field tests report the notable success of using S.R.A., Lubach, i/t/a, Sullivan, Words in Color, The Detroit Series, The Bank Street Readers, pocket books and local ethnic newspapers.

It is difficult to deny this "evidence" on the basis of feelings and hunches of classroom teachers. Yet it seems to me and to those who make detailed analyses of all materials for teaching the disadvantaged, that *there is no ultimate system* for teaching reading or anything else; that what is needed is a variety of approaches and materials in each class.[5]

The interests, predispositions and learning styles of youngsters can help them to select materials. While there is no best material for all, there are better materials for individual pupils —and the "better" materials are those which pupils and teachers help to select and control.

Although the availability of certain kinds of materials in the classroom is a necessary part of a program for intellectual development, neither the existence of certain pieces of equipment in the room, nor the development of specific kinds of experiences will guarantee maximum intellectual growth in the children. This can only be accomplished by the teacher's synthesis of a variety of experiences and the use of many kinds of materials concentrating on specific learning.[6]

[5] Conversation with Rose D. Risikoff. Curriculum Consultation Service, Bank Street College of Education, N.Y.C.

[6] Helen F. Robison and Bernard Spodek. *New Directions in the Kindergarten.* New York: Teachers College Press, 1965. p. 145. Copyright © 1965 by Teachers College, Columbia University. Reprinted with the permission of the publisher.

The School Learning Center

One effective approach to developing and using materials with the disadvantaged is the creation of a learning center.[7] Since this approach involves three full-time teachers using three classrooms to cover only two teaching loads, it may very well be that the significant factors that have been added are teacher time and attention. But the addition of a listening center, films, pictures, filmstrips, records, transparencies, science materials, language kits and a wide variety of additional materials seems to be part of what is making the difference.

Youngsters are not plugged into systems with "no-exit do-loops" but work with materials in small groups and on an individual basis. Materials are prescribed for and chosen by youngsters. This may sound like a mushy, poorly controlled approach but recent research is supporting many of our experiential beliefs. A recent study of over 600,000 youngsters indicates that the disadvantaged feel helpless—and that this perception of powerlessness is not removed by innovations which *others* initiate.

It appears that variations in facilities and curriculums of schools account for relatively little variation in pupil achievement as measured by standardized tests. . . . A pupil attitude factor, which appears to have a stronger relationship to achievement than do all the "school" factors together, is the extent to which an individual feels he has control over his destiny. . . . Minority pupils, except for Orientals, have far less conviction than whites that they can affect their own environments and futures. When they do, however, their achievement is higher than whites who lack that conviction.[8]

If feeling powerful is central to what the disadvantaged learn, then what better means for building in feelings of control over their environment could they have than participation in the selection of materials?

Real vs. Fake Materials

As part of the learning center described here, we tried two experiences that have implications for determining what causes certain materials to be effective. First, we tried to involve some fifth graders in a unit that would tell us about their interests and self-perceptions by asking them to fill a non-existent time capsule. We told them that people would dig this capsule up in the future and learn all about them—provided they stocked it with pictures, songs, stories, tapes and whatever they wanted to use in order to preserve themselves for posterity. There are many good reasons why the children did not become involved in this unit, but one of the better explanations is that there was not really a capsule being sunk into the school yard.

The second attempt at getting the pupils to describe themselves, was to have each youngster write something on a card, place it into his own special balloon and allow it to float away. The balloons went for hundreds of miles and came down in eastern U.S. and

---

[7] The Howell Elementary School, Racine, Wisconsin, is a good demonstration of the learning center approach. J. Sullivan, A. Hovgaard and J. Ban, are the teachers involved.

[8] James S. Coleman *et al. Equality of Educational Opportunity.* Washington, D.C.: U.S. Department of Health, Education, and Welfare, 1966. p. 22-23. Supt. of Documents Catalog No. FS5.238:38001.

Canada. As a result, the pupils received real letters asking for more information about themselves, their activities and their community.

This example supports what we all know; that 10-year-old youngsters deal more easily with the real than with the imaginary and prefer to be in the present rather than in the future. It also suggests that materials which are authentic will involve pupils. It is the need for honesty rather than merely concreteness that is the critical element. The time capsule was a contrived experience but the balloons were real.

A Centralized but Teacher Controlled Materials Center

Another materials program that seems to work effectively is a centralized materials center which caters to the needs of particular teachers and classes. Individual teachers can literally receive crates of materials containing books, pictures, films, filmstrips, objects, transparencies and other materials organized around some unit of study.

This means that available material has been organized around some topic and drawn together, rather than separated on the basis of whether the material is a film, a book, etc. The real values of such a program are that each teacher can receive several crates of materials each week and keep the material for a full week to use at the most opportune time. But even more, individual teachers can and do request the purchase of new materials and the discarding of outdated materials—and have their advice acted upon.

The most efficient such materials center I have visited is in Racine, Wisconsin. Here an interview revealed:

—Teachers of the disadvantaged have markedly increased their requests for materials in the past few years.

—Materials used by teachers of the disadvantaged are soon requested by all other teachers.

—Whereas the main source of new materials for the system used to be the needs and recommendations of teachers in suburban-type schools, the teachers of the disadvantaged have become the source of introducing materials into the district.

—The drive for new materials is greatest among classroom teachers and more common among consultant supervisors than building principals.

—The teachers of the intermediate grades make the most requests, but primary level requests are catching up.

—Secondary teachers make few if any requests for materials and seem to rely on an occasional film and texts.

—Film ordering and use have leveled off and requests for a wider variety of materials have become more usual.

—The multi-media approach, including tapes, strips, transparencies and slides, has replaced the overdependence on films.[*]

The director of this center indicates some outstanding strengths of this approach to be: the on-going ordering which enables teachers to make requests for new purchases at any time in the school year; the multi-media materials included in the crates; and the fact that while social studies, language arts and science are the most popular content areas, art and music materials are being requested more frequently. It is also noteworthy that since teachers explain their problems when they call

[*] Conversation with William D. Grindland, Director, Instructional Materials Center, Racine Public Schools, Racine, Wisconsin, December 1966.

170

up to place orders for materials, they are revealing decreasing amounts of prejudice and an increased understanding of the disadvantaged. It may seem like hairsplitting but when teachers change from seeking materials that will force or guarantee learning for all, to the requesting of materials for eliciting individual development, this would, I believe, indicate a change in their influence on pupils.

The key organizational point in this example is that in a system covering 40 schools and more than 1200 teachers, centralization is used as a force for individualizing teacher requests. Some believe it would be better for each school to duplicate miniature centers. Actually the economies effected by one main but efficient depot enable the center to have the means to be responsive to individual teacher requests. Finally, this approach has resulted in a large urban system's not having to rely on packaged systems or "teacher-proof" materials. Rather, this approach has created a situation in which individual teachers are requesting ever increasing amounts of more varied materials.

And So . . .

We now, I believe, have had sufficient experiences with gadgeterial seduction, with packaged teacher-proof systems and programs of step-by-step control of materials, as means for involving and teaching the disadvantaged. We seem to be entering a more professional phase in which the differentiation of pupil activities is once again becoming accepted as the critical criterion of teacher effectiveness. In order to execute such differentiation, each teacher needs a variety of materials which he can help the pupils to mediate and control on the classroom level.

Computers have been proposed as the ultimate media for reaching all youngsters. Yet while computers may individualize instruction in the sense of differentiating tasks, they cannot personalize. If our assumptions that a variety of language forms and the power to help shape one's situation are the most critical needs of the disadvantaged, then plugging people into walls may be a cure-all for a nonexistent disease.

Living and learning are synonyms and all the "stuff" of life is instructional material. The development of thinking processes neither precedes nor follows language development but occurs as an oscillation; new terms trigger new relationships which lead to other words for handling new concepts. All youngsters need to develop a language that will go beyond immediate social and material needs to usages that will help them to share ideas, control their own behavior and engage in the processes of thinking.

Materials which foster growth of multiple language forms—in a variety of content areas—are of particular benefit to the disadvantaged. But language is not merely a tool and improving the language of the disadvantaged is not simply to facilitate learning in the rest of the curriculum. Quite the contrary, the curriculum, its materials and experiences, is the instrumentality for teaching a variety of subject matter languages in their several forms.

THE COMPELLING CASE FOR BILINGUAL EDUCATION

BY JEFFREY W. KOBRICK

In 1968 a Spanish-speaking community worker named Sister Francis Georgia, observing certain children "visibly roaming the streets" of Boston, conducted a door-to-door survey in a Puerto Rican section of the city. Of the 350 Spanish-speaking school-aged children she found, 65 per cent had never registered in school; many others rarely attended or had dropped out. Armed with these facts, Sister went to the Boston School Department to seek help in locating and providing meaningful programs for Spanish-speaking children who were out of school. Skeptical, Boston school officials told her to produce the "warm bodies"; if she did, they said, "seats" would then be found.

At about the same time, leaders from Boston's poverty communities formed a "Task Force on Children out of School" to investigate the way the school system dealt with poor children generally. Among other things, the task force found that as many as half of Boston's estimated 10,000 Spanish-speaking school children were not in

Jeffrey W. Kobrick is an attorney at the Harvard Center for Law and Education.

school. Between 1965 and 1969 only four Puerto Rican students graduated from Boston high schools.

Three years later, through the efforts of Sister Francis Georgia, community leader Alex Rodriguez, the Boston task force, and two key legislators, Education Committee Chairman Michael Daly and House Speaker David Bartley, Massachusetts passed the nation's first comprehensive state bilingual education law.

The law declares that classes conducted exclusively in English are "inadequate" for the education of children whose native tongue is another language and that bilingual education programs are necessary "to ensure equal educational opportunity to every child." Massachusetts thus became the first state to *require* school districts to provide bilingual programs for children whose first language is not English. (Other states including New York, California, Illinois, and Texas have laws *permitting* local school districts to provide bilingual programs.) The law calls for the use of both a child's native language and English as mediums of instruction and for the teaching of history and culture associated with a child's native language. It authorizes state expenditures of up to $4-million a year to help districts meet any extra costs of bilingual programs.

The Massachusetts law is a carefully constructed and innovative piece of legislation that hopefully will stimulate legislative efforts elsewhere. Indeed, because the federal Bilingual Education Act has been so underfunded—"Congress has been appropriating drops," notes Senator Walter Mondale, "when showers or even downpours are needed"—there is a critical need for state legislation and funding in areas where there are substantial numbers of Puerto Rican, Chicano, Indian, and other non-English-speaking children. The U. S. Office of Education estimates that five million children attending public schools "speak a language other than English in their homes and neighborhoods." And increasing evidence reveals the almost total failure of our monolingual, monocultural school systems to provide for these children's educational needs.

In New York City alone, 250,000 Puerto Rican children attend the public schools. The estimated dropout (or "pushout") rate for these students has been put as high as 85 per cent. Of those who survive to the eighth grade, 60 per cent are three to five years below reading level. Nor is the plight of thousands of Puerto Rican children any better in the schools of Bridgeport, Chicago, Philadelphia, Newark, Hoboken, or Paterson. In "The Losers," a report on Puerto Rican education in those cities, Richard Margolis writes: "Relatively speaking, the longer a Puerto Rican child attends public school, the less he learns."

Between two and three million Spanish-speaking children attend school in five Southwestern states where, as Stan Steiner shows in *La Raza: The Mexican Americans*, the schools serve only to "de-educate" any child who happens not to be middle class. More than a third of the Spanish-speaking children in New Mexico's schools are in the first grade, and over half of those in grades above the first are two years or more overage for their grade level. One Texas school board required "Spanish-surname" children to spend three years in the first grade until a federal court

stopped the practice. Chicanos are still put into classes for the mentally retarded on the basis of intelligence tests administered only in English; again, federal courts are in the process of abolishing this form of discrimination. The average number of school years completed by the Chicano in the Southwest is 7.1 years.

Statistics relating to the education of the more than 200,000 Indian children in public or Bureau of Indian Affairs schools are equally dismal. In 1960, 60 per cent of adult Indians had less than an eighth-grade education. Today the Indian dropout rate is more than twice the national average and in some school districts is 80 or 90 per cent. In an all-Indian public elementary school near Ponca City, Oklahoma, 87 per cent of the children have dropped out by the sixth grade. In Minneapolis, where some 10,000 Indians live, the Indian dropout rate is more than 60 per cent. In Washington, Muckleshoot children are automatically retained an extra year in first grade; and the Nook-Sack Indians automatically are placed in slow-learner classes.

One reason schools are failing in their responsibility to these children is that they offer only one curriculum, only one way of doing things, designed to meet the needs of only one group of children. If a child does not fit the mold, so much the worse for him. It is the child who is different, hence deficient; it is the child who must change to meet the needs of the school.

During the first four years of life, a child acquires the sounds, the grammar, and the basic vocabulary of whatever language he hears around him. For many children this language is Spanish or Cree or Chinese or Greek. Seventy-three per cent of all Navajo children entering the first grade speak Navajo but little or no English. Yet when they arrive at school, they find not only that English is the language in which all subjects are taught but that English dominates the entire school life. Children cannot understand or make themselves understood even in the most basic situations. There are schools where a child cannot go to the bathroom without asking in English. One little boy, after being rebuffed repeatedly for failure to speak in Eng-

173

lish, finally said in Spanish: "If you don't let me go to the bathroom, maybe I piss on your feet."

The effects of this treatment on a child are immediate and deep. Language, and the culture it carries, is at the core of a youngster's concept of himself. For a young child especially, as Theodore Andersson and Mildred Boyer point out, "Language carries all the meanings and overtones of home, family, and love; it is the instrument of his thinking and feeling, his gateway to the world." We all love to be addressed, as George Sánchez says, *en la lengua que mamamos* ("in the language we suckled"). And so when a child enters a school that appears to reject the only words he can use, "He is adversely affected in every aspect of his being."

With English the sole medium of instruction, the child is asked to carry an impossible burden at a time when he can barely understand or speak, let alone read or write, the language. Children are immediately retarded in their schoolwork. For many the situation becomes hopeless, and they drop out of school. In other cases, believing the school system offers no meaningful program, parents may fail to send their children to school at all.

Schools seem unmoved by these results. At any rate, the possibility of hiring some teachers who share a child's culture and could teach him in a language he can understand does not occur to them. Since the curriculum is in English, the child must sink or swim in English.

The injustice goes further: Having insisted that a child learn English, schools make little or no constructive effort to help the child do so. Instead schools assume, or expect, that any child in America will "pick it up" without any help from the school. Alma Bagu tells this story about a little Puerto Rican girl's day in school in New York:

Sitting in a classroom and staring at words on a blackboard that were to me as foreign as Egyptian hieroglyphics is one of my early recollections of school. The teacher had come up to my desk and bent over, putting her face close to mine. "My name is Mrs. Newman," she said, as if the exaggerated mouthing of her words

would make me understand their meaning. I nodded "yes" because I felt that was what she wanted me to do. But she just threw up her hands in despair and touched her fingers to her head to signify to the class I was dense. From that day on school became an ordeal I was forced to endure.

Like most of the people teaching Spanish-speaking or Indian children, Mrs. Newman presumably did not know the child's language. Yet she treated a five- or six-year-old as "dense" for the crime of not knowing hers.

The variety and perversity of the abuses committed against children are unending. In New York it is not unknown for teachers to lecture Puerto Rican students on how rude it is to speak a "strange" language in the presence of those who do not understand it. In the Southwest, where it is widely believed that a child's native language itself "holds him back," children are threatened, shamed, and punished for speaking the only language they know. Stan Steiner tells of children forced to kneel in the playground and beg forgiveness for speaking a Spanish word or having to write "I will not speak Spanish in school" 500 times on the blackboard. One teacher makes her children drop a penny in a bowl for every Spanish word they use. "It works!" she says. "They come from poor families, you know."

These are not the isolated acts of a few callous teachers. America's intolerance of diversity is reflected in an ethnocentric educational system designed to "Americanize" foreigners or those who are seen as culturally different. America is the great melting pot, and, as one writer recently stated it, "If you don't want to melt, you had better get out of the pot." The ill-disguised contempt for a child's language is part of a broader distaste for the child himself and the culture he represents. Children who are culturally different are said to be culturally "deprived." Their language and culture are seen as "disadvantages." The children must be "reoriented," "remodeled," "retooled" if they are to succeed in school.

Messages are sent home insisting that parents speak English in the home or warning of the perils of "all-starch diets" (which means rice and beans).

174

THE MASSACHUSETTS STATUTE

Every school district is required to take an annual census of all school-aged children of "limited English-speaking ability" and to classify them according to their dominant language. Whenever there are twenty or more children who share the same native language, the district must provide a bilingual program. A separate program must be provided for each language group.

The statute calls for the teaching of academic subjects both in a child's native language and in English; for instruction in reading and writing the native language, and in understanding, speaking, reading, and writing English; and for inclusion of the history and culture associated with a child's native language as an integral part of the program.

Although the school district's obligation to provide a bilingual program is mandatory, participation by the children and their parents is voluntary. Any parent whose child has been enrolled in a program has a right to prompt notice of such enrollment (in two languages), a right to visit his child's classes and to confer with school officials, and, finally, a right to *withdraw* his child from the program.

Parent Involvement:

Parents are afforded the right to "maximum practical involvement" in the "planning, development, and evaluation" of the programs serving their children. Parents, along with bilingual teachers, bilingual teachers' aides, and representatives of community groups, also have the right to participate in policy-making and implementation of the law at the state level.

Bilingual Teachers:

The statute creates a new state certification procedure for bilingual teachers that softens some of the previous rigidities and repeals a former U. S. citizenship requirement (which still exists in thirty states). It also allows bilingual teachers who have met some, but not all, of the certification requirements for teachers to serve provisionally and to count two years of provisional service toward a three-year tenure requirement.

State Reimbursement:

The bilingual statute provides for state reimbursement to local school districts for that portion of the cost of a bilingual education program that "exceeds" the district's average per pupil cost. Additional costs not covered under the bilingual statute are eligible for reimbursement under the general aid to education statute. Although the program is "transitional"—a student's *right* to participate lasts only three years—any individual school district is allowed to go beyond this minimum, and programs that are "permitted" by the statute are reimbursed on the same basis as those that are "required." If a program gains support in a particular community, it is entirely possible that it could be extended into a full bilingual program.

The English-speaking:

The major weakness of the statute is that it is *silent* on whether English-speaking children may be enrolled in bilingual programs and thus does not contain adequate safeguards against the isolation of minority children in such programs. Bilingual education can be of great benefit to English- as well as non-English-speaking children, and provision for the enrollment of English speakers should be made. The *Harvard Journal on Legislation* has recently published a revised version of this statute, which provides for the enrollment of English-speaking children in the bilingual program. ☐

Children are preached middle-class maxims about health and cleanliness. The master curriculum for California's migrant schools prescribes "English cultural games," "English culture, music, and song," "English concept of arithmetic"; nowhere is there mention of the Indo-Hispanic contributions to the history and culture of the Southwest. When Robert Kennedy visited an Indian school, the only book available on Indian history was about the rape of a white woman by Delawares. Even a child's *name* is not his own: Carlos becomes Charles; María, Mary.

Humiliated for their language and values, forced to endure the teaching of a culture that is unrelated to the realities of their lives, it is no wonder that children withdraw mentally, then physically, from school. "School is the enemy," said a Ponca Indian testifying before Congress. "It strikes at the roots of existence of an Indian student."

Far from accomplishing its professed aim of integrating minorities into the "mainstream," the monolingual, monocultural school system has succeeded only in denying whole generations of children an education and condemning them to lives of poverty and despair. There is no more tragic example of the fruits of such policies than that of the Cherokees.

In the nineteenth century, before they were "detribalized," the Cherokees had their own highly regarded bilingual school system and bilingual newspaper. Ninety per cent were literate in their own language, and Oklahoma Cherokees had a higher English literacy level than native English-speakers in either Texas or Arkansas. Today, after seventy years of white control, the Cherokee dropout rate in the public schools runs as high as 75 per cent. The median number of school years completed by the adult Cherokee is 5.5. Ninety per cent of the Cherokee families in Adair County, Oklahoma, are on welfare.

Obviously, no particular "program," not even a bilingual one, can be expected to cure all this. The remark of the 1928 Meriam Report on Indian education holds true today: "The most fundamental need in Indian education is a change in point of view."

Bilingual-bicultural education is perhaps the greatest educational priority today in bilingual communities. Its aim is to include children, not exclude them. It is neither a "remedial" program, nor does it seek to "compensate" children for their supposed "deficiencies." It views such children as *advantaged*, not disadvantaged, and seeks to develop bilingualism as a precious asset rather than to stigmatize it as a defect. The very fact of the adoption of a program recognizing a child's language and culture may help to change the way the school views the child. It may help to teach us that diversity is to be enjoyed and valued rather than feared or suspected.

There are also strong arguments supporting the pedagogical soundness of bilingual education. Experts the world over stress the importance of allowing a child to begin his schooling in the language he understands best. Such a policy makes it more likely that a child's first experience with school will be a positive rather than a negative one. Moreover, as John Dewey and others have said, language is one of the principal tools through which children learn problem-solving skills in crucial early years. Policies that frustrate a child's native language development can cause permanent harm by literally jamming the only intellectual channel available to him when he arrives at school. Those who would concentrate on teaching a child English overlook the fact that it takes time for a child unfamiliar with the language to achieve a proficiency in it even approaching that of a child raised in an English-speaking home. In the meantime, struggling to understand other academic subjects, children fall hopelessly behind. In a bilingual program, by contrast, two languages are used as mediums of instruction; a child is thus enabled to study academic subjects in his own language at the same time he is learning English. Bilingual programs teach children to read their own language and to understand, speak, read, and write English (in that order). Language is oral. It is "*speech* before it is reading or writing." When a child enters school already speaking and understanding a language, he is ready to learn to read and write it. A program that prematurely forces English on a child can guarantee his eventual illiteracy in that language.

The "English-only" approach also misses the prime opportunity to teach a child to read his own language. Recent experience indicates that development of literacy in one's native language actually enhances the ability to learn English. When the Navajos evaluated their own bilingual school at Rough Rock, Arizona, they found that the children were more proficient in both languages than they would have been "if you tried to stuff English down the throat of a child who can't understand what you're talking about." Nancy Modiano reports similar results in a highly controlled experiment with Indian children in Chiapas, Mexico. The children who had read first in their native language showed greater proficiency in reading *Spanish* (the national language) than their control peers who had been instructed solely in Spanish. Modiano explains that the children were much more confident about learning to read in a language they already knew; having learned the mechanics of the reading act, they could apply their skill in learning to read another language.

In addition to facilitating the learning of English, bilingual education has other benefits. It helps to correct what Bruce Gaarder, former chief of the U. S. Office of Education's modern language section, has called "an absurdity which passeth understanding." More than $1-billion a year is spent on foreign language instruction. "Yet virtually no part of it, no cent, ever goes to maintain the native language competence which already exists in American children." Bilingual education also allows English-speakers to learn a second language far more effectively than they could in a foreign language program, because their classmates are native speakers. And it develops and enhances children's intellectual capabilities. Bertha Treviño found that in the Nye School, outside Laredo, Texas, both Spanish- and English-speaking children learned mathematics better bilingually than they did when taught in English alone. In Montreal, children who were educated bilingually scored higher on both verbal and nonverbal intelligence tests and "appeared to have a more diversified set of mental abilities" than their monolingual peers.

Despite the promise of bilingual education, however, only a handful of programs were in operation in the United States during the 1950s and 60s. In fact, prior to 1968, twenty-one states, including California, New York, Pennsylvania, and Texas, had laws requiring that all public school instruction be in English. In seven states, including Texas, a teacher risked criminal penalties or the revocation of his license if he taught bilingually.

In the late 1960s the Chicanos in the Southwest and other groups mounted a widespread campaign for bilingual, bicultural education. In 1967 Senator Ralph Yarborough of Texas introduced a bilingual education bill in Congress, which finally passed, in modified form, as an amendment to Title VII of the Elementary and Secondary Education Act of 1965.

The psychological impact of the federal Bilingual Education Act, a landmark in our history, cannot be overestimated. It reversed a fifty-year-old "one-language" policy and committed the moral force of the national government to meeting "the . . . educational needs of the large numbers of children of limited English-speaking ability in the United States." The act provided financial assistance to local educational agencies for, among other things: "1) bilingual educational programs; 2) programs designed to impart to students a knowledge of the history and culture associated with their languages; 3) efforts to establish closer cooperation between the school and the home."

This commitment by the federal government has slowly influenced states and local communities. Since 1968 eleven states have passed laws permitting local school districts to provide bilingual instruction and, as stated earlier, one state, Massachusetts, has required school districts to provide bilingual education programs (although participation by the children is voluntary).

Nevertheless, even today very few children enjoy the "luxury" of bilingual education. Title VII has become a highly selective program presently serving only 88,000 of an estimated five million non-English-speaking children.

The problem rests primarily with the funding structure of Title VII, which has proved singularly unable to stimulate comparable state and local efforts. The federal act, for example, pays the entire cost of the programs it supports. But since Title VII is grossly underfunded, the federal programs necessarily remain limited. If a local government wishes to institute additional bilingual programs, it must appropriate money from local funds. There is no provision for sharing costs across levels. Thus each level of government becomes reluctant to support a comprehensive bilingual program because it fears it alone will bear the possibly large costs of the program. If, however, costs were shared among the different levels of government—federal, state, and local—each agency might be willing to contribute more.

The Massachusetts legislation provides a needed innovation in this respect. The law requires school districts to offer bilingual programs but provides for state reimbursement of that portion of the cost that *exceeds* the district's average per pupil cost. For example, if a district's annual expenditure per child is $800 and the cost to offer bilingual education is $1,000, the district will be reimbursed $200. The philosophy of the Massachusetts law is that a local school district has an obligation to spend at least as much for the education of a bilingual child as it does for the education of any other child. The funding formula thus allows state money to go much further than if the state alone bore the cost. By redirecting money from the regular program to a program that better serves the needs of the non-English-speaking child, scarce resources are put to much more productive use.

The appeal here, however, is not to expediency. Many children in this affluent land are being denied their fundamental right to equal educational opportunity. To the needs of these children society must respond, and now.

BLACK CHILDREN AND READING:
WHAT TEACHERS NEED TO KNOW

Kenneth R. Johnson
Herbert D. Simons

"If I could get my hands on my first-grade teacher now, I'd break her chalk."

A commerical education institute which promises to teach reading to people who failed to learn how in school is running an ad with this caption. In the ad a forlorn young girl peers at a pile of books she is not able to read. The girl in the picture is white. If she had been black her statement about her first-grade teacher might have suggested a broken neck, because of the greater failure of black students in learning to read.

Why is the failure of black students greater? Teachers are both ill-prepared and perhaps unwilling to move in directions which could make the difference between the success and failure of their black students. In this article three suggestions are made both for initial teacher training and for in-service training for teachers presently in the schools. First, they must study black culture with an eye toward sympathetic recognition of it as a legitimate minority culture; second, if they are to teach reading, especially to poor black children, they must understand black dialect; third, once they understand black culture and black dialect, they must adapt their teaching strategies accordingly.

Understanding Black Culture

"Change the child or change the curriculum" is at once a basic tenet and a cliché of American education. Most educators agree on the latter alternative and feel that they follow it. But this is not the case in the education of black children. How can a curriculum be tailored to the needs of these children when the teachers and curriculum writers know little about or simply disdain black culture? Educators who view black culture as a sick white culture are hardly qualified to make useful curriculum changes.

In their failure to recognize that black children are different, not inferior, American teachers have not been alone. It is a societal problem, but how can it be rectified? Toward this end we suggest a thorough steeping in black culture. Consider for a moment the value to a white teacher of this knowledge. In the black culture the relationship between a child and an adult differs from that in the dominant culture. The black child is not expected to carry on a discussion with an adult as if he or she were an equal, or an almost equal, with the adult. A teacher from the dominant culture whose criteria have been set by her experience with children from the dominant culture expects a conversational skill from the black child that is

PHI DELTA KAPPAN, January 1972, pp. 288-290.

179

simply outside of his life-style. The teacher then often judges the child dull purely because he lacks a knowledge of the child's culture.

Another important difference is that many black children, particularly poor ones, are members of extended families. Often grandmothers, aunts, uncles, and cousins live under one roof. The small nuclear family characteristic of the white middle class is not their concept of a family. In addition, many reports have pointed out the disproportionate number of black families headed by females. This is partially a result of economic racism but, whatever its cause, it has produced a matriarchal cultural pattern which means that many black children think of a family as a mother, a grandmother, and children. Incidentally, if the family is economically sound, it can be a good family; a male head does not automatically mean that a family is as good as the literature would have one believe.

A black child from such an extended family will have difficulty identifying with the nuclear white family of the basal reader. He would be better served by beginning reading literature which honored and reflected his history rather than patently rejecting it.

One of the stereotypes many whites have of black people is that blacks have more so-called natural rhythm. Black people as a group do have more rhythm and the reason for this is not genetic but cultural. Dancing and participating in musical activities is an integral part and much more emphasized in the black culture (compare a black church service with a white one). Again, knowledge of the culture could aid the student and the teacher. More rhythmic activities should be incorporated in teaching black children – for instance, putting multiplication tables to music and dance patterns.

Another cultural pattern that is somewhat different in black culture is nonverbal behavior. In many ways, black people communicate differently with their body movements. For example, black children can communicate anger, hostility, and rejection with their eyes. The movement – shifting the eyes away from another person in a quick low arc with the eyes partly closed – is called "rolling the eyes." The most aggressive stance a black female can take is to place one hand on the hip with one foot in back of the other and the weight shifted to the back foot. A slow fluid walk with the head slightly raised and one hand either hanging limply or tucked partly in a pocket is a sure sign that a black male is defiantly walking away from an authority figure after a conflict situation. This kind of information can be extremely valuable to teachers who work with black children.

These are but a few characteristics of the black culture, but they clearly make the point. Teachers of black children must understand the culture of these children if they expect success. Perhaps the reading readiness of the black children should be determined by criteria from his own culture.

Understanding Black Dialect

Many teachers believe that one variety of English is correct, hence best. This variety is the one that teachers think they speak and is the one taught in school. Linguists have labeled it standard English.

Many black children, however, speak a variety of English linguists have labeled black dialect, black English, or nonstandard Negro dialect. Black dialect differs somewhat from standard English in its phonology and grammar. If teachers are to work effectively with black children who speak this dialect, they must understand: 1) that black dialect is a legitimate linguistic system; 2) that standard English is not "better" than black dialect; and 3) that black dialect is systematic.

Black dialect is a legitimate linguistic system. Many black people use it exclusively, while others use both standard English and black dialect. The social situation and audience determine which dialect or variety of English is used. Therefore correctness is a relative term. Standard English is not correct if the audience has more difficulty in understanding it than in understanding black dialect. Furthermore, language, in this case black dialect, is an identity label; it is an index or reflection of the speaker's culture. When teachers reject black dialect or look on it as an illegitimate or inferior variety of English, they reject part of the identity of the person who speaks it.

Black dialect is systematic. That is, it is not a collection of sloppy, random erroneous sounds and grammatical structures which the speaker carelessly utters. Instead, when the phonological and grammatical deviations from standard English heard in the speech of many blacks are contrasted with the points in standard English, it is clear that these deviations are consistent and systematic. Black people are not making just any noises, but particular noises.

For example, there are certain phonological rules in black dialect and particular sounds that are systematically substituted where particular standard English sounds occur.[1] One of the phonological rules can be summarized as follows: If a word ends in two consonant sounds and both of them are either voiced or voiceless, and the last consonant sound is /b/, /d/, /k/, /p/, or /t/, then the last consonant is reduced or omitted. Some words ending in two consonant sounds conforming to the above rule are *test, desk, lift,* and *expect.* These end in voiceless pairs of consonants, and black children will pro-

nounce them *tes, des, lif,* and *expec.* The words *told, mind, killed,* and *lived* end in voiced pairs of consonants; black children will consistently pronounce them *tol, mine, kill,* and *live.* Teachers often note that black children leave off the endings of words. They'd be able to better instruct black children if they knew which endings and the linguistic environments where the leaving-off occurs.

There are other examples of phonological deviations from standard English that really comprise the system of black dialect, and teachers can discover these when they quit looking at black dialect as a collection of mispronunciations and note the system, consistency, and frequency of these deviations in the speech of black children.

The same phenomenon of system occurs in grammar. The grammatical deviations black children make are not random. For example, the copula (*is, am, are*) is systematically omitted in present progressive tense (He looking at me); the plural ending is often omitted if another word in the sentence indicates pluralization (She have two brother); the verb *been* is used to indicate distant past action (He been left for home); this agreement-sound on the end of third person, present tense verbs is omitted (He walk home). Linguists have pointed out, by the way, that the verb system of black dialect in some cases can indicate duration or time of action more precisely than standard English.

Black Dialect and Teaching Reading

In recent years heated debate has raged about the relationship between black dialect and learning to read. Teachers should be aware of and keep up with the findings and suggestions coming from the research generated by the debate.

First, it is important for teachers to

understand the nature of the conflict that arises when a child's language is rejected either explicitly or implicitly by his teachers. They must understand the devastating emotional and social consequences of such an act, which the child views as a rejection of himself and his culture. The negative impact upon motivation and progress in learning to read is serious.[2]

The frustration of having one's language rejected would be clear to teachers if they themselves experienced the rejection the black child goes through in school. Imagine a teacher training class conducted by a black teacher who will only tolerate black dialect. Every time the "students" lapse into standard English, the black teacher admonishes and corrects them for errors or stupidity. The teachers would soon experience the torture of rejection and the difficulty of changing one's dialect.

Second, teachers must become aware of specific conflict points between black dialect and standard English. This knowledge will enable them to make the very important distinction between reading errors which must be corrected **and pronunciation differences which are dialectic, hence are not errors and can therefore in many cases be safely ignored.** For example, teachers can stop confusing and frustrating black children by telling them that pin and pen have different vowel sounds. In black dialect they both have the same vowel sound. And when a black child reads "tol" for "told" the teacher should not correct him, since he has not made a reading error. On the other hand when the child reads "pass" for "passed" or "like" for "liked," he may or may not know that the past tense has been signaled.[3] Here the teacher must determine from the larger sentence or paragraph context or from diagnostic tests whether or not the child needs to learn that the "ed" is a past tense marker.

Again, these are just a few examples; but they serve to give the teacher a sense of the significance for teaching of a knowledge of the phonological conflict points. Teachers should further be aware that synthetic or blending phonics methods also may create problems, because they exaggerate the conflict points and therefore must be tailored to ghetto teaching. This is not a suggestion to abandon phonics – just a reminder that it must be adjusted to avoid conflict points, as many teachers now do to compensate for regional dialect difference. As a general rule children should be allowed to impose their phonological systems on standard English spellings.

Grammatical conflict points must be clear in the minds of teachers also. The deletion of the copula in black dialect mentioned earlier is a good example of this. Teachers' sensitivity to this area of conflict will prevent many comprehension difficulties.

At present there are three major curriculum proposals for handling grammatical conflict points. The first is to delay reading until the child learns to speak standard English grammar or to teach standard English concurrently with reading. The second is to allow dialect reading of standard English texts. The third and most radical suggestion is to translate beginning reading texts into black dialect.[4]

Teachers are already aware of the problems inherent in the first approach. Until now they have tried to change the dialect of these children and have failed. It is almost impossible to change dialect in school, since children get their dialect from peer groups. Only massive integration would make this a feasible alternative and massive integration is not imminent.

The second proposal, allowing dialect reading of standard English texts, seems a sensible first step in line with current knowledge. Essentially, the child would be translating standard English into his own dialect. Using this method, for example, the teacher would allow the child to read "He going" for "He is going" as long as it didn't interfere with his comprehension. In order to implement this proposal teachers must have, as mentioned previously, a working knowledge of black dialect and where it conflicts with standard English.

The third proposal, which involves writing at least the beginning readers in dialect, is based on two assumptions. First, children will learn to read better from materials written in their own language. Second, books written in dialect will eliminate the need for the child to translate into his own dialect. This extra translating, it is suggested, interferes with comprehension. Whether or not these assumptions are correct and thus justify the use of dialect readers is not yet known.

Much more research needs to be done on these alternatives before there can be any definitive answers. In the meantime it is important for teachers to remain flexible and to be willing to try these new ideas. What is quite clear is that we are now failing miserably to teach black children to read, and there is no justification for maintaining the status quo.

To summarize, teachers need much more knowledge of black culture. They need to know black dialect, its conflict points with standard English, and how to handle these conflicts in teaching reading. This knowledge and its application in the classroom will provide a first step in improving the reading skills of black children. There is no excuse for allowing a teacher's ignorance of his student's culture and language to stand in the way of a child's learning to read.

1. Ralph W. Fasold and Walt Wolfram, "Some Linguistic Features of Negro Dialect," *Teaching Standard English in the Inner City.* Washington, D.C.: Center for Applied Linguistics, 1970, pp. 41-86.

2. W. Labov and C. Robins, "A Note on the Relation of Reading Failure to Peer Group Status, *Teacher's College Record,* 1969, pp. 395-406.

3. W. Labov, "The Reading of the -ed Suffix," in H. Levin and J. Williams (eds.), *Basic Studies on Reading.* New York: Basic Books, 1970.

4. W. Stewart, "On the Use of Negro Dialect in the Teaching of Reading," in J. Baratz and R. Shuy (eds.), *Teaching Black Children to Read.* Washington, D.C.: Center for Applied Linguistics, 1969.

CHAPTER V: INNOVATIONS FOR URBAN SCHOOLS

The gross academic underachievement of culturally different children attending urban or rural schools has become a problem of study for many educators in the past few years. And, each time a new educational program, package, gadget, or idea from Europe appears on the horizon many educators grab hold of the new concept and attempt to apply it to this group of children. However, if the truth be known, many of these new alternatives or concepts in education are not really new but merely rebirths of those written about long ago by such people as John Dewey. One of the most modern educational books available today is SCHOOLS OF TOMORROW written in 1903 by John Dewey. In this book the open classroom is masterfully presented, perhaps better than by any current author.

Most students in teacher education institutions read the current educational "pop" literature such as that written by John Holt and Jonathan Kozol, two of the current educational reformers. The ridiculousness of modern day education and the tragedy of slum schools are the highlights of the current "pop" literature. The "pop" literature's shortcoming is that it says all is wrong and should be done away with; however, what is to replace it is left unanswered. Critics are plentiful but designers of the schools of tomorrow are not so numerous in the current educational literature.

It is not to say that young educators should not read the current "pop" literature but many times the impressions left by these books are not truly representative of the conditions that really exist in urban teaching assignments.

What is important is that young teachers in urban schools be aware of the current innovations in education and be able to make decisions for themselves whether or not these innovations might be of use to them in their classrooms. The article dealing with "Teacher Centers" is extremely important as this might be the most viable way in which to get information about innovations to all teachers in a building and also about how to spread new programs in a meaningful way.

It must be remembered that many innovations in education are good; however, what constantly happens is that innovations are put into a demonstration project or school which demonstrate and then die when they cannot be funded adequately for wider distribution. In-service programs are sometimes of the same type: the trainers come into the school, train and then leave without any adequate follow-up. The new methods are dispensed almost in a wholesale manner but little customer service is provided at a later date when the teacher tries to use the product.

The article by Robert Blume concerning the humanizing of teacher education is also of importance as it deals with the problem of making teacher education institutions less like factories and more responsive to the human needs of the future teacher. Most teacher education students, especially those in large colleges and universities, will see much merit in this article. The question must be asked how can humanism and dealing with children in a humane way be implemented by teachers trained in impersonal educational factories where students exist to meet the needs of the higher educational institution rather than having the institution exist to meet the needs of the students. This idea might also be carried over into the urban schools where slum school teaching staffs rarely live in the slum neighborhoods but merely travel into the ghetto each day to teach and leave. Thus, inner-city schools especially have temporary teaching staffs and permanent communities. It might be said that many teachers in inner-city schools teach there to have a job, not necessarily to help the children of the community. Humanism in the urban schools

is definitely needed as this would be a giant step toward
accepting the culturally different children and making
them feel a part of the school and the type of education
being dispensed by it.

There are many other types of innovative ideas
being expressed in educational circles today; however,
the several contained in this short chapter are important
and possible within the context of urban school systems.

Stephen K. Bailey

TEACHERS' CENTERS: A BRITISH FIRST

Effective change comes from teachers, not from their critics or superiors.

Ever since DeWitt Clinton called America's attention a century and a half ago to the British infant schools as worthy of emulation, this country has derived policy nourishment from educational experimentation in the United Kingdom. In the 1960's the British open school received particular attention, serving as a basis for many of the reforms featured in the writings of distinguished American educators – including especially Charles Silberman's *Crisis in the Classroom.*

Perhaps the most significant potential British contribution to American education, however, is only now being identified and discussed: the development of teachers' centers. British experience with these centers, at least in their present form, is a matter of three or four years only. But the idea is so simple, so obvious, so psychologically sound, as to make one wonder why teachers' centers have not dotted the educational landscape for decades.

Teachers' centers are just what the term implies: local physical facilities and self-improvement programs organized and run by the teachers themselves for purposes of upgrading educational performance. Their primary function is to make possible a review of existing curricula and other educational practices by groups of teachers and to encourage teacher attempts to bring about changes.

Stimulated by a working paper on school-leaving age prepared by Britain's Schools Council* in 1965, and by a variety of *ad hoc* study groups and curriculum-development committees in the middle sixties, teachers' centers have mushroomed in the past half decade. Today there are approximately 500 centers located throughout England and Wales, over half with full-time leaders. The centers vary greatly in size, governance, scope of work, and the

*The Schools Council is an independent body with a majority of teacher members. Its purpose is to undertake in England and Wales research and development work in curricula, teaching methods, and examination in schools, and in other ways to help teachers decide what to teach and how. The council is financed by equal contributions from the local educational authorities on the one hand and the Department of Education and Science of the national government on the other.

PHI DELTA KAPPAN, November 1971, pp. 146-149.

quality of tea and biscuits, but most of them are engaged in exciting and profoundly significant educational activities.

The underlying rationale for teachers' centers may be stated succinctly in terms of three interlocking propositions: 1) Fundamental educational reform will come only through those charged with the basic educational responsibility: to wit, the teachers; 2) teachers are unlikely to change their ways of doing things just because imperious, theoretical reformers – whether successions of Rickovers or Illiches or high-powered R & D missionaries from central educational systems – tell them to shape up; 3) teachers will take reform seriously only when they are responsible for defining their own educational problems, delineating their own needs, and receiving help on their own terms and turf.

The more these intertwining propositions buzz around the brain, the more apparent their validity becomes. In the United States, for example, we have developed in the past several years a slew of educational R & D centers, Title III supplementary centers, and educational laboratories, each in its own way designed to discover and disseminate new educational truths. Most of these centers and laboratories have done important work. But the impact of this work upon continuing teacher performance (and pupil performance) in the classroom has been miniscule. And well before federal largess was directed toward inducing educational reform through a trickle-down theory, many state and local education departments and teachers colleges had developed curriculum-improvement supervisors charged with being "change agents" through workshops and in-service training. But the initiative was almost always from the bureaucrat or the educrat, rather than from the teachers themselves.

Few professionals have suffered more painfully or seriously from "being done good to at" than teachers. In spite of the fact that they are the ones who work day in and day out on the firing line, the definition of their problems, of their roles, of their goals, always seems to be someone else's responsibility: supervisors, parents, college professors, text book publishers, self-styled reformers, boards of education, state and national education officials.

What the teachers' center idea does is to put the monkey of educational reform on the teacher's own back.

And they love it!

When teachers find out that they have their own facility where they can exchange ideas, learn from each other, receive help as they see fit, munch bread and jam and drink tea without the interruption of a bell or buzzer, they come alive. New ideas come from old heads, and the new tends to be sounder because the heads are experienced.

How does a teachers' center work?

Let us look at an example.

One British teachers' center in a county borough of roughly 60,000 population emerged from a "new math" project sponsored in 1966 by the Nuffield Foundation. The deputy headmaster, a mathematician, provided "crash courses" for teachers from both primary and secondary schools. From a very successful crash course experience, participating teachers urged continuation and extension of the general activity. The deputy headmaster agreed to serve as secretary of a committee of elected teachers and each school in the area was asked to nominate members. The cooperation of the chief education officer in the district was sought and he sent a representative from his staff.

The Schools Council report on this prototypic development (SC Pamphlet No. 1, 1969) says: "It was clear that the local teachers felt a need to come together to widen their experience and share ideas, not only in 'in-service' training, but in the wider area of curriculum reform. It was clear also that, such was the interest, they would be prepared to spend some of their own time on this."

Adequate physical facilities for the new teachers' center were found in the form of an empty old primary school. The local education authority allocated 750 pounds for improvements. The facilities finally included a curriculum workshop for mathematics and science, a lounge, a small library, and the beginnings of a film collection. A part-time assistant acts as keeper of the schedule and as building superintendent. The program itself, however, is entirely teacher-initiated and controlled.

The Schools Council report on this particular center is studded with illuminating phrases:

—"The center's first task will always be to stimulate and draw together local initiative."

—"[Policy remains] . . . firmly in the hands of the teacher committee."

—"The whole concept of a teacher's job is getting more complex . . . and the more complex it gets, the more necessary it will be to mobilize the expertise of the teachers."

—"The teachers are asked to suggest the program of activities ['The committee is anxious to know the type of course you desire. Suggestions should be forwarded to the secretary. . . .']."

—"Any group of teachers may use the building in and out of school time, for projects and meetings. All you have to do is book ahead."

—". . . making locally relevant any innovation, from whatever source, which commends itself to teachers in the area."

—"It is important that the center reflect local teacher opinion about the curriculum and test ideas locally generated. . . ."

These give the spirit and flavor of the entire teachers' center movement. But the fact that initiative is local and is from the teachers themselves does not preclude valuable relationships with local educa-

Photos: Central Information Office, London

The burgeoning of teachers' centers is one more sign of British educational renaissance. The open primary, illustrated above, is better known in America. This is the Evangeline Lowe Primary in London, with not a desk in sight and no clanging of the school bell.

tional authorities, with representatives of the national Schools Council, with nearby teachers colleges and universities. The centers' committees facilitate such relationships, but on a basis far healthier than has often obtained in the past. Gone are the traditional deferential attitudes and the superciliousness that have so frequently marked "workshops-organized-for-teachers" by educational reformers in official or academic-status positions.

What are the activities? In the teachers' center noted above, programs have included, during school time: Nuffield Junior Maths (six meetings), junior science (six meetings), decimalization and the school (one day), infant environment (six lectures), maladjusted children (four lectures), and athletic coaching for schools (three days).

Typical after-school programs were: lecture/demonstration on understanding numbers, nine weekly meetings and discussions on how children learn, three lectures and workshops on visual aids, gymnastics and dance display, and devising a humanities course for leavers (those not planning further academic work beyond school-leaving age).

The teachers' center also promotes and provides exhibits of new textbooks, programmed instruction, audio-visual aids, homecrafts and handicrafts, and student art. Promotional and informational activities (bulletins, newsletters, posters, etc.) are disseminated to keep all teachers and other interested people in the area informed about programs and exhibits. After-school experimental classes on family life, adolescent identity crises, and community problems are undertaken with selected students.

But reports on the activities of a single center should not suggest a rigid format for all such centers. The key to the success and the enthusiasm associated with the teachers' center notion is control by *local* teachers. In consequence, center facilities and programs vary widely, depending upon the definition of need constructed by the local teacher-controlled center committees working intimately with local center leaders or "wardens." Some centers limit their curriculum investigations to a particular field like math or science; others attempt a wholesale review of the adequacy of an entire curriculum by grade or age; others have a strong social emphasis; still others feature outside lecturers and exhibits of new materials. Many centers feature formal in-service training courses; others stress informal workshops; still others provide facilities for self-study. Some centers are primary school oriented; others draw heavily from secondary schools. Some attempt to draw in students, parents, supervisors, professors of education, and others directly related to the educational process; others keep such types at arm's length and relish the sense of teacher autonomy and the sense of dignity that come from self-directed accomplishments.

Tactfully, in the background, are the supporting services of the Schools Council: studies, reports, curriculum R & D, conferences, etc. The council

leaders, including their distinguished staff of field officers, are exquisitely sensitive to the importance of teachers' centers being locally operated and defined. The field officers of the Schools Council are themselves teachers loaned for short periods of time only to the itinerant functions of the Schools Council.

For the first time, local teachers are not low on the totem pole. They are prime movers in reforming an inevitably sluggish system. The reforms are not imposed by the arrogance of ministries, authorities, supervisors, or academicians. The reforms emerge from the teachers' own experiences and creative impulses. Through the field officers of the Schools Council and through the outreach of the local leadership of the teachers' centers, important educational innovations from whatever sources can be scrutinized and tested; but, once again, this is done on the teachers' own terms and turf.

Who pays? Local education authorities and, through contributions of time and materials, the teachers themselves. Capital improvements, major equipment and facilities, and basic operating costs come from the education committees of local authorities. But without significant inputs of time and talent (as well as marginal voluntary donations to help defray the costs of social food and beverages), teachers' centers could not exist — at least in their present form.

Depending on the size of the center, annual budgets may run from a few to thousands of pounds. In some cases, where teachers' centers agree to serve as area distribution headquarters for educational A-V materials, their local-authority budget may be sweetened substantially.

Experience with the center idea is still meager. But their stunning proliferation is testament to their meeting a felt need among teachers and among those who understand the futility of attempts to reform British education without the teachers' being directly and importantly involved.

In 1970, the Schools Council sponsored three national conferences on teachers' centers in the United Kingdom. A total of 300 people attended. The liveliness of discussions and debates was indicative of the variety of opinions, experiences, and goals that inform the teachers' center idea. The conference spectrum ranged from the total enthusiast to the cynic.

Among the most insistent questions raised at the conferences were the following:

—How many of the center activities should be on an "in-school" as against an "after-school" basis?

—Should the "wardens" or "leaders" of the centers be part-time or full-time? And how should they be selected and trained? Is a new kind of profession emerging (i.e., teachers' center wardens?

—Should teachers' centers encourage membership from those who are nonteachers?

—Should teachers' centers concentrate special attention upon the evaluation of, and experimentation with, new educational technology?

—How can more teachers be induced to use the centers — especially the apathetic who need the centers the most?

—What are the best methods for spreading the word of experts or even of "Charlie Jones's" good ideas?

The greatest problem seen by all members was the demand of development work on the time and energy of teachers. Although some of the work is presently done during school hours, much of it takes place after 4 p.m. The financial and logistical problems associated with this central issue are at the heart of the possibilities for long-range success and survival of teachers' centers in Britain.

Even at their best and most creative, teachers' centers are still tentative. New regional linkages and national information networks will surely be needed to supplement local insights and resources. At the moment, there is an inadequate flow of information about what is going on in other centers and areas; and extant knowledge and research directly related to locally defined problems is inadequately collected and disseminated. The Schools Council is sponsoring a series of regional conferences this coming year in order to address many of these issues.

But the basic concept remains structurally and psychologically sound, and our British cousins have good reason for being enthusiastic.

Fortunately, the idea is beginning to catch on in the United States. Don Davies, acting deputy commissioner for development in the U.S. Office of Education, is actively promoting the notion of a major network of local teachers' centers. Leaders in both the National Education Association and the American Federation of Teachers have shown considerable interest in the teachers' centers concept.

Would it not be wonderful if, after years of telling teachers what to do and where to go, American educational savants and officials suddenly discovered that the only real and lasting reforms in education in fact come about when teachers themselves are given facilities and released time "to do their own thing"? Perhaps in the not too distant future, following the pioneering experiment voted by the Unity, Maine, School District for the fall of 1971, a four-day week for teachers in the classroom will be standard. On the fifth day, the teachers will be in their teachers' centers, rapping about their common problems, studying new ways to teach and to understand students, imbibing a Coke or Pepsi, talking shop over billiards, and cheerfully allowing management to check off dues, parts of which will be assigned to defray the operating costs of the federally or state-funded teachers' center facilities. Linked through regional associations, informed by the R.& D activities of a National Institute of Education, teachers' centers could form the essential but presently missing link between innovative ideas and pupil performance in the classroom.

191

Humanizing Teacher Education

By Robert Blume

There is no single method of teaching which can be demonstrated to be superior for all teachers. Nor will knowledge about good teaching insure superior performance. These findings from research conducted over the past 10 years have thrown teacher education into a dilemma. If not knowledge and methods, what shall we have our prospective teachers learn in college?

A study published in 1961 by the National Education Association, in which all of the research available on good and poor teaching was reviewed, failed to find any method of teaching which was clearly superior to all others.

At about the same time, Combs and Soper conducted research with good and poor teachers to determine if the good ones knew better than the poor ones the characteristics of a good helping relationship.[1] They found no significant difference between the knowledge of the two categories of teachers.

What does distinguish between good and poor teachers? Certainly we all think we can tell the difference, but does research bear out our beliefs?

Twenty years ago a startling finding came out of a study of various styles of psychotherapy. At that time the psychoanalysts and the Rogerians were debating whether it was more effective for the therapist to be direct and forceful in dealing with his client, or whether the client should be encouraged to think out his own solutions to problems while the therapist assumes a client-centered role.

Fiedler found that expert therapists, no matter what school of thought they belonged to, tended to advocate the same kind of relationship with their clients. In fact, these experts were more alike in their beliefs about the therapeutic relationship than were the beginners and experts in the same school. This relationship has come to be called "the helping relationship."

Combs and Soper modified the questions Fiedler used with the therapists, in order to make them appropriate for educators, and administered the instrument to a group of expert classroom teachers. They found that these teachers agreed with the expert therapists about the relationship which was most desirable and productive for

PHI DELTA KAPPAN, March 1971, pp. 411-415.

192

helpers and helpees.

As mentioned above, when they asked poor teachers the same questions, they found that they, too, knew the answers. They concluded that a good helping relationship is something most people know about, but not all are capable of practicing.

With these questions in mind — "What does make a difference in the ability of teachers to practice the good helping relationship?" and "What shall we have future teachers learn in college?" — let us turn to some of the recent criticism of the schools.

The new critics (as opposed to the all testify to the failure of the school to educate people in a way that gives them a feeling of dignity and an understanding of their world.

Some consider this indictment too harsh. They hold that the school can't be blamed for all of society's ills. Whether or not the school is responsible for causing our problems, it is the institution responsible for producing educated people, who will in turn make the wise decisions, both large and small, that will gradually improve life. Unfortunately, we are not moving in this direction now; on the contrary, life is becoming more grim and joyless all the time, and therefore the school *is* vulnerable to the above charge.

Education must include more than the acquisition of a few more facts and a faster reading rate. It must be the instrument through which people release the tremendous creative potential that was born into all of us. Whatever methods and materials are needed to do the job — that is education.

But this isn't enough. We must also help our young to develop compassion, concern for others, faith in themselves, the ability to think critically, the ability to love, the ability to cooperate with others, the ability to maintain good health, and, above all, the ability to remain open to other people and new experiences. This is *humanistic* education.

In order to achieve this kind of school we must abandon the old patterns along with the old assumptions, and search together for a concept of education that will in Jourard's words "turn on and awaken more people to expanded perspectives of the world, new challenges, possible ways to experience the world and our own embodied being." We *can* create educational patterns that are much more exciting than anything we adults have experienced in our elementary or secondary schooling. The University of Florida has begun a program of elementary teacher education which is a radical departure from those of the past. This program has abolished courses and regularly scheduled classes, replacing them with individual study and small discussion groups. Each student becomes a member of a seminar led by the same faculty member for the two years he is enrolled in the program. Students have the opportunity to work with children every week, and almost every day, from the beginning of their teacher education to the end.

This program is based on principles which have emerged in educational literature over the past two decades, and more specifically on extensive research which Arthur Combs and his associates have conducted at the University of Florida. These principles are:

O People do only what they would rather do (from Freud). That is, people behave according to choices they make from among alternatives they see available to them at the moment.

O Learning has two aspects: 1) acquiring new information, and 2) discovering the *personal meaning* of that information. Information itself is useless. Only when individuals find the link between specific information and their own lives are they able to put it to use. This principle is not well understood by educators. Most of our efforts to improve education involve new ways to deliver information to people. Very few innovations involve helping learners to discover the personal meaning of that information.

○ It is more appropriate for people to learn a few concepts rather than many facts.

○ Learning is much more efficient if the learner first feels a need to know that which is to be learned. This principle has been known for a long time, but the response of educators to it has been to artificially "motivate" students with letter grades and other rewards. None of these schemes works as well as the genuine desire to learn, and in fact they frequently get in the way of that desire by substituting artificial for real motivation.

○ No one specific item of information, and no specific skill, is essential for effective teaching. Any one fact or skill that could be mentioned might be missing in a very effective teacher. Furthermore, it would be presumptuous for teacher educators in the 1970's, drawing on their experience in the 40's, 50's, and 60's, to declare certain teaching skills or knowledge essential for teachers in the 80's, and 90's, and beyond. We just don't know what the job of the teacher will be in 20 years, or even 10. Hopefully it will be quite different from what it is today.

○ People learn more easily and rapidly if they help make the important decisions about their learning.

○ People learn and grow more quickly if they aren't afraid to make mistakes. They can be creative only if they can risk making errors.

○ Objectivity is a valuable asset for a researcher, but it is not very useful for workers in the helping professions, such as teaching. What is needed instead is the opposite of objectivity — concern and caring. As Jack Frymier has said, we want students not only to know about cold, hard facts, but to have some "hot feelings about hard facts." We must produce teachers who have developed strong values about teaching.

○ Teachers teach the way they have been taught — not the way they have been taught to teach. If we want elementary and secondary teachers to be warm, friendly people who relate positively and openly with their students, then we must treat them that way in our college programs. We must respect our teacher education students if we expect them to respect their pupils.

○ Pressure on students produces negative behaviors, such as cheating, avoidance, fearfulness, and psychosomatic illness. Students tend to become more closed in their interpersonal relationships when they are pressured.

○ Our teachers would be more effective if they were self-actualizers. Teachers ideally should be more healthy than "normal" people. They should be creative, self-motivated, well-liked persons.

In his book, *The Professional Education of Teachers*, Arthur Combs reviews "third force psychology," the alternative to the Freudian and stimulus-response theories which have dominated our educational thought for the past half century. Three basic principles of perceptual psychology are significant for humanistic education:

1. All behavior of an individual is the direct result of his field of perceptions at the moment of his behaving.

2. The most important perceptions an individual has are those he has about himself. The self-concept is the most important single influence affecting an individual's behavior.

3. All individuals have a basic need for personal adequacy. We all behave in ways which will, according to our view of the situation, lead to our self enhancement. Once aware of this fundamental drive toward growth and improvement, we can see that it is unnecessary to reward a child to encourage him to learn. If he already wants to learn, we need only help him, by giving him the environment which makes it easy and the materials which are appropriate for the kind of learning toward which he is motivated. We need to become aware of his motivation and plan learning experiences which will fit into it. The role of the teacher, then, is that of facilitator, encourager, helper, assister, colleague, and friend of his students.

Teaching is therefore a helping relationship rather than a command relationship. It is similar to counseling, psychotherapy, nursing, human relations work, social work, and many other helping professions.

A number of studies have been conducted at the University of Florida which have investigated the nature of the helping relationship. Combs and others have studied counselors, teachers, Episcopal priests, nurses, and college teachers to see if the more effective practitioners in these fields have different ways of perceiving than do the ineffective ones. The perceptual organizations of these professionals were examined in great detail in the following four categories:

Category 1: *The general perceptual organization.* Is he more interested in people or things? Does he look at people from the outside, or does he try to see the world as they see it? Does he look for the reasons people behave as they do in the here and now, or does he try to find historical reasons for behavior?

Category 2: *Perceptions of other people.* Does he see people generally as able to do things or unable? As friendly or unfriendly? As worthy or unworthy? As dependable or undependable?

Category 3: *Perceptions of self.* Does he see himself as with people or apart from them? As able or unable? As dependable or undependable? As worthy or unworthy? As wanted or unwanted?

Category 4: *Perceptions of the professional task.* Does he see his job as one of freeing people or controlling them? Does he see his role as one of revealing or concealing? As being involved or uninvolved? As encouraging process or achieving goals?

The results of these studies consistently indicated that the effective helpers saw people from the inside rather than the outside. They were more sensitive to the feelings of students. They were more concerned with people than things. They saw behavior as caused by the here-and-now perceptions, rather than by historical events. They saw others and themselves as able, worthy, and dependable; they saw their task as freeing rather than controlling, and as involved, revealing, and encouraging process.

As mentioned above, one significant finding of these studies was that objectivity had a *negative* correlation with effectiveness as a helper. For example, the teacher who observes two boys fighting and tries to "get to the bottom of the problem" by asking how it started, what led up to the first blow being struck, etc., is not helping as effectively as the teacher in a similar situation who says, "Mike, I can see you are very angry with David and you want to hurt him, but I can't let you do that. How do you feel, David? Are you mad too?" The latter teacher is not being so objective; he isn't trying to place the blame logically on one boy or the other. Instead he is trying to show the two boys that he recognizes the way they feel *at this moment,* and he wants them to know that he is a friend of each of them and will help them to express their feelings. Violence is usually an attempt to express strong feelings. The best helpers are those who help people to express these feelings without violence.

The implications of this research are important for the Florida New Elementary Program. For example, if good teachers are more sensitive to the feelings of students, we should provide more opportunities for teacher education students to enter into more personal, meaningful relationships with other students, faculty, and children. If effective teachers see others as able, well-intentioned, and dependable, they need a warm, friendly, cooperative atmosphere in which to interact with children and in-service teachers during their teacher education. If the effective teacher sees himself as able, likable, and dependable, he must be treated as a person of worth, dignity, and integrity from the very beginning of his professional program. Finally, if effective teachers see the teaching task as one of freeing and assisting, rather than controlling or coercing, we must provide teacher education which does not insist on particular methods, but which encourages students to seek their own best methods. These programs themselves should encompass a wide variety of approaches. The instructors will need to be concerned with the attitudes and perceptions of teachers, not merely with subject matter and methods.

Various members of the College of Education saw a challenge in this research and in the book Combs published in 1965. They decided to build a new program for the preparation of elementary teachers. This program consists of three parts: the seminar, the substantive panel, and field experience.

The seminar is the heart of the program. It is here most of all that the student develops a close relationship with a faculty member, one who knows him well over the entire period of his professional program. He also becomes a member of a small group of students. Thirty students are assigned to each of the three seminar leaders. They range from beginners, who have just come into the program, to seniors, who have completed all but the final phases of their work. When a student graduates, a new one is taken in to replace him. The 30 students are divided into two groups of 15 for discussion purposes, and each small group meets for two hours per week. These meetings are for the purpose of discussing everything which comes to the minds of the students and their leader relative to education. More specifically, the purpose is the discovery of the personal meaning of the information and experiences which the students are encountering in the other aspects of the program.

The seminar leader serves as advisor to each of the 30 students in his group. He is responsible for helping them schedule outside course work and for keeping the records of their work within the program. He also conducts evaluation activities for his group in the form of weekly activity sheets and the midpoint and final review conferences.

The second aspect is the substantive panel. It includes faculty members who normally teach methods, foundations, and curriculum courses. Included are math, reading, language arts, social studies, science, art, social foundations, psychological foundations, curriculum, black studies, and testing and research. In each of these areas the faculty member distributes lists of competencies for students to complete and hand in, or to discuss in faculty-student conferences. The competencies range over the entire area of didactic learnings within each of the fields mentioned. Certain competencies are required, while others are optional. In the area of curriculum, for example, there are four required competencies, and each student must do three more from a list of seven optional ones. Even the required competencies may be done in two different ways, thus carrying through the idea of giving students wide latitude for choice making. Some of the competencies involve working with a small group of children and writing a critique. The students do these while they are involved in their field experience. Others include reading in the library and writing papers summarizing the literature, or reacting to it. Students are encouraged to design their own competencies as alternatives to some of the optional ones. They write out a contract form for this purpose. The faculty member signs the contract when he has approved the design, and again when the competency has been completed. Substantive panel members conduct some small-group sessions each week to help students develop the understanding needed to complete the competencies. Students are free to sign up for these meetings or not as they choose, but if they sign up they are expected to attend. These meetings are usually offered as a series of three or four. Some competencies consist of passing a test over material which has been presented in these small-group meetings.

Obviously, the student can't work in all substantive areas at once. He must choose which three or four he will work on each quarter, depending on his schedule of field experiences and outside classes. With this much freedom and responsibility, there is danger that students who have been spoon-fed all of their lives will goof off and get behind in their completion of the competencies. We feel this is a calculated risk worth taking, in order to gain the advantages of having students feel free to explore and probe in directions dictated by their growing interest in becoming teachers.

The field experience aspect of the program begins with level one, which consists of tutoring an individual child and observing classrooms in the Gainesville area. The student and his advisor decide when he has had enough observation experience — usually about 10 one-hour observations. The tutoring continues for an entire quarter. In level two, the student is designated "teacher assistant." He does whatever needs to be done — work with individual children or small groups, or even record keeping. Teacher assistants spend a minimum of six hours per week in the classroom. In level three, the student is designated "teacher associate." He now accepts more responsibility for planning and teaching certain groups of children within the class, or certain aspects of the curriculum for the whole class. As teacher associate he teaches two hours every day. Eventually he must do an intensive period of teaching, level four, which requires full time in the classroom for five weeks.

One of the unique aspects of this program is the flexibility of time requirements. The program is expected to take six quarters to complete, but a student who wants to push harder can complete it in as little as four quarters. The student who needs more time to finish, or to develop confidence or maturity, might take a longer period of time. This is as it should be, we feel. If we seriously believe in individual differences in learners, we must make provision for people to go through our program at different rates.

The evaluation of each student's work within the program is handled by the seminar leader, the student himself, and the members of the substantive panel. The student completes competencies in each substantive area, and they are evaluated by the panel member. He rates them on a pass-fail basis and checks them off as the student completes his list for his area. He sends a list of the competencies completed to the seminar leader who keeps the student's records.

Approximately half-way through the program each student has a mid-point evaluation, during which he goes over his progress with the seminar leader and one member of the substantive panel. The number of competencies completed in each area, the number yet to be done, and the field experiences to date are all discussed, and a proposed timetable for completion of the program is written down in his folder. When the student has completed all of the requirements he sits for a final review in the same way, and it is determined if he is ready to teach. The seminar leader is aware of each student's progress each quarter, because he keeps all of the records, and

he receives feedback from other faculty members who have observations about particular students.

One of the strongest features of the program is the participation of students in every phase of decision making. The students feel ownership in the program as a result of being on various faculty-student committees, such as a committee to write a handbook for new students, a committee to evaluate the competencies in the various substantive areas, or a committee to plan next term's schedule. Each seminar sends a representative to the bi-weekly staff meetings, not only to observe and report back, but to participate in the discussions as a full-fledged member of the group.

Within one year, two very significant, student-initiated changes were made in the program. The group petitioned the dean of the College of Education to place the entire program on a pass-fail basis rather than the letter-grading system then in use. Their logic was persuasive and the change was made.

In another case, a small group of students asked for some academic preparation for teaching in integrated schools. They were all having some teaching experience in schools that were predominantly black, and they recognized their own lack of background for teaching in those classrooms. This suggestion was followed by the creation of a faculty-student committee, which eventually planned a black-studies program and received some limited funding for its operation.

Whether students learn as much about teaching here as they would in a more standard program will have to be determined by the research which is under way at the present time, but several perceptions are generally shared by the staff members who work most closely with these future teachers. One perception is that the students leave our campus with a solid feeling of confidence about their ability to teach.

A fact which pleases the staff is that *many* of our students ask for an intensive teaching assignment in a school which has large numbers of disadvantaged children. It isn't clear just why this is happening, but it reflects the kind of attitudes we hope to see students developing.

One coed who was having her final review conference said, "It took me almost a year in this program before I felt like these ideas were mine — and then it was easy after that." That statement summarizes what this program is trying to do: not merely to have students *learn about* principles of humanistic education, but to have them feel that they are *their* ideas.

The specific elements of the Florida New Elementary Program are still evolving, and will continue to evolve. What is more important, we believe, are the ideas on which they are based. These principles are valid for humanistic education at any level. We hope to introduce them into elementary classrooms by preparing teachers in ways that are consistent with those principles, because teachers teach the way they were taught.

---

[1]More information concerning this study and others cited here can be found in A. W. Combs, *et al., Florida Studies in the Helping Professions*, Social Science Monograph No. 37. Gainesville, Fla.: University of Florida Press, 1969.

SO YOU WANT TO CHANGE
TO AN OPEN CLASSROOM*

Roland S. Barth

Another educational wave is breaking on American shores. Whether termed "integrated day," "Leicestershire Plan," "informal classroom," or "open education," it promises new and radical methods of teaching, learning, and organizing the schools.[1] Many American educators who do not shy from promises of new solutions to old problems are preparing to ride the crest of the wave. In New York State, for instance, the commissioner of education, the chancellor of New York City schools, and the president of the state branch of the American Federation of Teachers have all expressed their intent to make the state's classrooms open classrooms. Schools of education in such varied places as North Dakota, Connecticut, Massachusetts, New York, and Ohio are tooling up to prepare the masses of teachers for these masses of anticipated open classrooms.

Some educators are disposed to search for the new, the different, the flashy, the radical, or the revolutionary. Once an idea or a practice, such as "team teaching," "nongrading," and (more recently) "differentiated staffing" and "performance contracting," has been so labeled by the

*For a further discussion of these assumptions, practices associated with them, and the difficulties of implementation, see Roland S. Barth, OPEN EDUCATION AND THE AMERICAN SCHOOL, Agathon Press, Inc., 1972

PHI DELTA KAPPAN, October 1971, pp. 97-99.

Establishment, many teachers and administrators are quick to adopt it. More precisely, these educators are quick to assimilate new ideas into their cognitive and operational framework. But in so doing they often distort the original conception without recognizing either the distortion or the assumptions violated by the distortion. This seems to happen partly because the educator has taken on the verbal, superficial abstraction of a new idea without going through a concomitant personal reorientation of attitude and behavior. Vocabulary and rhetoric are easily changed; basic beliefs and institutions all too often remain little affected. If open education is to have a fundamental and positive effect on American education, and if changes are to be consciously made, rhetoric and good intentions will not suffice.

There is no doubt that a climate potentially hospitable to fresh alternatives to our floundering educational system exists in this country. It is even possible that, in this brief moment in time, open education may have the opportunity to prove itself. However, a crash program is dangerous. Implementing foreign ideas and practices is a precarious business, and I fear the present opportunity will be abused or misused. Indeed, many attempts to implement open classrooms in America have already been buried with the epitaphs "sloppy permissivism," "neo-progressive," "Communist," "anarchical," or "laissez-faire." An even more discouraging although not surprising consequence has been to push educational practice further away from open education than was the case prior to the attempt at implementation.

Most educators who say they want open education are ready to change *appearances*. They install printing presses, tables in place of desks, classes in corridors, nature study. They adopt the *vocabulary*: "integrated day," "interest areas," "free choice," and "student initiated learning." However, few have understanding of, let alone commitment to, the philosophical, personal, and professional roots from which these practices and phrases have sprung, and upon which they depend so completely for their success.

It is my belief that changing appearances to more closely resemble some British classrooms without understanding and accepting the rationale underlying these changes will lead inevitably to failure and conflict among children, teachers, administrators, and parents. American education can withstand no more failure, even in the name of reform or revolution.

I would like to suggest that before you jump on the open classroom surfboard, a precarious vehicle appropriate neither for all people nor for all situations, you pause long enough to consider the following statements and to examine your own reactions to them. Your reactions may reveal salient attitudes about children, learning, and knowledge. I have found that successful open educators in both England and America tend to take similar positions on these statements. Where do you stand?

201

Assumptions about Learning and Knowledge[2]

INSTRUCTIONS: Make a mark some- where along each line which best represents your own feelings about each statement.

Example: School serves the wishes and needs of adults better than it does the wishes and needs of children.

| strongly agree | agree | no strong feeling | disagree | strongly disagree |

I. ASSUMPTIONS ABOUT CHILDREN'S LEARNING

Motivation

Assumption 1: Children are innately curious and will explore their environment without adult intervention.

| strongly agree | agree | no strong feeling | disagree | strongly disagree |

Assumption 2: Exploratory behavior is self-perpetuating.

| strongly agree | agree | no strong feeling | disagree | strongly disagree |

Conditions for Learning

Assumption 3: The child will display natural exploratory behavior if he is not threatened.

| strongly agree | agree | no strong feeling | disagree | strongly disagree |

Assumption 4: Confidence in self is highly related to capacity for learning and for making important choices affecting one's learning.

| strongly agree | agree | no strong feeling | disagree | strongly disagree |

Assumption 5: Active exploration in a rich environment, offering a wide array of manipulative materials, will facilitate children's learning.

| strongly agree | agree | no strong feeling | disagree | strongly disagree |

Assumption 6: Play is not distinguished from work as the predominant mode of learning in early childhood.

| strongly agree | agree | no strong feeling | disagree | strongly disagree |

Assumption 7: Children have both the competence and the right to make significant decisions concerning their own learning.

| strongly agree | agree | no strong feeling | disagree | strongly disagree |

Assumption 8: Children will be likely to learn if they are given considerable choice in the selection of the materials they wish to work with and in the choice of questions they wish to pursue with respect to those materials.

| strongly agree | agree | no strong feeling | disagree | strongly disagree |

Assumption 9: Given the opportunity, children will choose to engage in activities which will be of high interest to them.

| strongly agree | agree | no strong feeling | disagree | strongly disagree |

202

Assumption 10: If a child is fully involved in and is having fun with an activity, learning is taking place.

strongly agree | agree | no strong feeling | disagree | strongly disagree

Social Learning

Assumption 11: When two or more children are interested in exploring the same problem or the same materials, they will often choose to collaborate in some way.

strongly agree | agree | no strong feeling | disagree | strongly disagree

Assumption 12: When a child learns something which is important to him, he will wish to share it with others.

strongly agree | agree | no strong feeling | disagree | strongly disagree

Intellectual Development

Assumption 13: Concept formation proceeds very slowly.

strongly agree | agree | no strong feeling | disagree | strongly disagree

Assumption 14: Children learn and develop intellectually not only at their own rate but in their own style.

strongly agree | agree | no strong feeling | disagree | strongly disagree

Assumption 15: Children pass through similar stages of intellectual development, each in his own way and at his own rate and in his own time.

strongly agree | agree | no strong feeling | disagree | strongly disagree

Assumption 16: Intellectual growth and development take place through a sequence of concrete experiences followed by abstractions.

strongly agree | agree | no strong feeling | disagree | strongly disagree

Assumption 17: Verbal abstractions should follow direct experience with objects and ideas, not precede them or substitute for them.

strongly agree | agree | no strong feeling | disagree | strongly disagree

Evaluation

Assumption 18: The preferred source of verification for a child's solution to a problem comes through the materials he is working with.

strongly agree | agree | no strong feeling | disagree | strongly disagree

Assumption 19: Errors are necessarily a part of the learning process; they are to be expected and even desired, for they contain information essential for further learning.

strongly agree | agree | no strong feeling | disagree | strongly disagree

Assumption 20: Those qualities of a person's learning which can be carefully measured are not necessarily the most important.

strongly agree | agree | no strong feeling | disagree | strongly disagree

Assumption 21: Objective measures of performance may have a negative effect upon learning.

strongly agree | agree | no strong feeling | disagree | strongly disagree

Assumption 22: Learning is best assessed intuitively, by direct observation.

strongly agree | agree | no strong feeling | disagree | strongly disagree

203

Assumption 23: The best way of evaluating the effect of the school experience on the child is to observe him over a long period of time.

strongly agree	agree	no strong feeling	disagree	strongly disagree

Assumption 24: The best measure of a child's work is his work.

strongly agree	agree	no strong feeling	disagree	strongly disagree

II. ASSUMPTIONS ABOUT KNOWLEDGE

Assumption 25: The quality of being is more important than the quality of knowing; knowledge is a means of education, not its end. The final test of an education is what a man *is*, not what he *knows*.

strongly agree	agree	no strong feeling	disagree	strongly disagree

Assumption 26: Knowledge is a function of one's personal integration of experience and therefore does not fall into neatly separate categories or "disciplines."

strongly agree	agree	no strong feeling	disagree	strongly disagree

Assumption 27: The structure of knowledge is personal and idiosyncratic; it is a function of the synthesis of each individual's experience with the world.

strongly agree	agree	no strong feeling	disagree	strongly disagree

Assumption 28: Little or no knowledge exists which it is essential for everyone to acquire.

strongly agree	agree	no strong feeling	disagree	strongly disagree

Assumption 29: It is possible, even likely, that an individual may learn and possess knowledge of a phenomenon and yet be unable to display it publicly. Knowledge resides with the knower, not in its public expression.

strongly agree	agree	no strong feeling	disagree	strongly disagree

Most open educators, British and American, "strongly agree" with most of these statements.[3] I think it is possible to learn a great deal both about open education and about oneself by taking a position with respect to these different statements. While it would be folly to argue that strong agreement assures success in developing an open classroom, or, on the other hand, that strong disagreement predicts failure, the assumptions are, I believe, closely related to open education practices. Consequently, I feel that for those sympathetic to the assumptions, success at a difficult job will be more likely. For the educator to attempt to adopt practices which depend for their success upon general adherence to these beliefs without actually adhering to them is, at the very least, dangerous.

At the same time, we must be careful not to assume that an "official" British or U.S. government-inspected type of open classroom or set of beliefs exists which is the standard for all others. Indeed, what is exciting about British open classrooms is the *diversity* in thinking and behavior for children and adults — from person to person, class to class, and school to school. The important point here is that the likelihood of successfully developing an open classroom increases as those concerned agree with the basic assumptions underlying open education practices. It is impossible to "role play" such a fundamental-

204

ly distinct teaching responsibility.

For some people, then, drawing attention to these assumptions may terminate interest in open education. All to the good; a well-organized, consistent, teacher-directed classroom probably has a far less harmful influence upon children than a well-intentioned but sloppy, permissive, and chaotic attempt at an open classroom in which teacher and child must live with contradiction and conflict. For other people, awareness of these assumptions may stimulate confidence and competence in their attempts to change what happens to children in school.

In the final analysis, the success of a widespread movement toward open education in this country rests not upon agreement with any philosophical position but with satisfactory answers to several important questions: For what kinds of people — teachers, administrators, parents, children — is the open classroom appropriate and valuable? What happens to children in open classrooms? Can teachers be *trained* for open classrooms? How can the resistance from children, teachers, administrators, and parents — inevitable among those not committed to open education's assumptions and practices — be surmounted? And finally, should participation in an open classroom be *required* of teachers, children, parents, and administrators?

---

1. For a fuller description of this movement, see Roland S. Barth and Charles H. Rathbone, annotated bibliographies: "The Open School: A Way of Thinking About Children, Learning and Knowledge," *The Center Forum,* Vol. 3, No. 7, July, 1969, a publication of the Center for Urban Education, New York City; and "A Bibliography of Open Education, Early Childhood Education Study," jointly published by the Advisory for Open Education and the Education Development Center, Newton, Mass., 1971.

2. From Roland S. Barth, *"Open Education,"* unpublished doctoral dissertation, Harvard Graduate School of Education, 1970.

3. Since these assumptions were assembled, I have "tested" them with several British primary teachers, headmasters, and inspectors and with an equal number of American proponents of open education. To date, although many qualifications in language have been suggested, there has not been a case where an individual has said of one of the assumptions, "No, that is contrary to what I believe about children, learning, or knowledge."

Practices that Improved Academic Performance in An Inner-City School

By Seymour Fliegel

I t has become fashionable to dismiss money as a prerequisite for quality education in low-income areas. This line of reasoning is pure pap and detrimental to educational change.

Additional funds represent commitment — a commitment which must begin at the top. Before education in the inner city can be improved, top decision makers must indicate that they really want to do something about education in low-income areas. It was out of such a commitment that P.S. 146 in the East Harlem section of Manhattan was organized in September of 1964 as part of the More Effective Schools (MES) program. That commitment, demonstrated in joint planning of the UFT, the Council of Supervisory Associations, and representatives from the office of Superintendent of Schools Calvin E. Gross, added up to $500,000 per year in additional personnel, materials, and equipment for P.S. 146.

The next key factor in the chain of commitment is leadership at the building level. This leadership is supplied by Principal Matthew Schwartz, who has provided a structure for successful operation of P.S. 146. Commitment at the classroom level does not blossom in a vacuum. It is unrealistic to expect successful performance on the part of many inner-city teachers as long as they are overburdened with large classes, provided little practical help from supervisors, given inadequate materials and equipment, treated as objects of blanket community distrust, and experiencing repeated failure in the classroom. On the contrary, such conditions can create only expectations of further failure.

Accordingly, teachers at P.S. 146 have small classes (a maximum of 22 in grades one through six — equivalent to a "good" suburban school), supportive supervision (four assistant principals and one administrative assistant), and sufficient materials and equipment, all provided in a context stressing expectations of success rather than failure.

Teacher Participation in Decisions

Teachers are involved in establishing school policy. Two teachers are

PHI DELTA KAPPAN, February 1971, pp. 341-343.

members of the principal's cabinet, which includes the principal, his four assistants, and two parents. (At present, representatives from the student council may appear before the cabinet to communicate students' requests and points of view.) Changes brought about at P.S. 146 as a direct result of teacher participation in the cabinet include the following:

1. A system of supplies that allows teachers to pick up supplies immediately upon making a simple verbal request.

2. **Voluntary meetings before school and during lunch periods.**

3. Establishment of an Afro-American and Pan-Hispanic culture committee.

4. Formation of an orientation committee for new teachers.

5. Regulations allowing students to come directly to their classes in the morning instead of lining up in the indoor yard.

6. Video-taping of classroom lectures for teacher training.

The Cluster Concept

MES schools are organized into "clusters" of about 66 pupils taught by three classroom teachers and an additional cluster teacher. Teachers at P.S. 146 are involved in curriculum planning through weekly cluster meetings. Participants include the three classroom teachers, the cluster teacher, and the assistant principal in charge of the grade. A major purpose of these meetings is to carve out areas of responsibility for the cluster team. For example, at the beginning of the school year the team determines the exact role the cluster teacher will be expected to perform. In some clusters, she may be responsible for a specific subject matter area; in others, she may

be integrated into the individualized instructional program now receiving special emphasis at P.S. 146. In the upper grades, the responsibilities of the cluster teacher are to relieve each classroom teacher in the cluster for a daily preparation period, provide instruction in a particular subject matter field, teach a reading group twice a day, work with children in small groups, and in some cases share periods of instruction with a classroom teacher.

An example of a successful program is the image-building project carried out by one sixth-grade cluster. The teachers wanted to do something to help raise their students' aspiration levels. The program started when a black teacher invited several friends and acquaintances to visit the cluster classes. Subsequently, once-a-week guests included an author, a chemist, a politician, an educator, an editor, a probation officer, and a football player. Visitors, most of them black or Puerto Rican, were treated as heroes: Students demanded autographs and an opportunity to shake hands with each guest.

Parent Involvement

Parent involvement is crucial to the success of the program. As noted above, two representatives from the parents' association are engaged in decision making as members of the school cabinet. In addition, a parents' room has been set up on the first floor, and coffee is always available for parents who may wish to sit and talk. A community coordinator and a bilingual teacher have offices adjacent to the parents' room.

Throughout the year activities are conducted to bring parents and teachers together. A recent workshop for parents of first graders drew 40 participants, who learned about the reading program and were given instruction in how to make and use reading games and puzzles. Last year parents sponsored two luncheons for teachers, one to celebrate Puerto Rican discovery week and the other on teacher recognition day. The faculty, in turn, prepared a luncheon for over 100 parents.

Parents can be a great force for change in a school, by exerting pressure on public officials, local politicians, and the board of education. When P.S. 146 opened, there was no play area for the children, and the block adjacent to the school was used as a refuse dump. Supervisors, teachers, children, and parents organized a picket line and notified the news media. In less than one year, a beautiful playground was built for use by the school and the community. Events like this help us remember that the school can no longer exist as an island in the community.

At the first PTA meeting this year, parents organized a More Effective Schools Publicity Campaign Committee. They are planning an MES open house week. They want to organize support to make certain that the new decentralization arrangements in New York City will not result in cuts in personnel and funds at P.S. 146. At this meeting, parents told how the school had become an important force for community stabilization: Families were not moving away because they did not want their children to change schools.

Orientation Toward Students

In most of the schools in New York City, classes are grouped homogeneously according to reading level, but no matter how cleverly level designations are disguised, after one week every child can tell you which classes are "smart" and which are "dumb." At P.S. 146, classes are organized on a heterogeneous basis. I once asked a child who was sent to our school because he was a serious behavior problem what, if anything, he liked about P.S. 146. "No dumb classes in this school, Mr. Fliegel," he replied, "no dumb classes."

Children are citizens. What happens to their rights when they enter school? Generally they must get permission to go to the bathroom or to get a drink of water. When they eat lunch, they are told where they must sit and when they may talk.

We are looking at children in a different manner now. One way to treat children as citizens is to deal with them as individuals. When P.S. 146 first opened, we thought that with small classes and additional personnel all we had to do was teach as we were taught. Teachers stood in front of the class dispensing wisdom. We were criticized for this in the Fox evaluation, and it was a valid criticism.[1] We have done much to correct this since 1967. Now, our office bulletin board reminds us that the teachers' main responsibility is more to ensure that students learn than that subjects get "taught": "I taught that, but the children didn't learn it," a sign proclaims, and then asks the reader to "define taught as it is used in this sentence." We are beginning to realize that children's learning is more important than teachers' "teaching."[2]

Training and Supervision

It is easy for supervisors to say that teachers must individualize instruction and then ask teachers to take red pencils and indicate in their planbooks what they are doing to individualize. But it is unlikely that teachers will succeed unless a specific structure and

208

continuous support are provided to show the way. Teachers need help in selecting and using materials, in determining levels and sequences of instruction, in grouping, and in utilizing new techniques. Above all, they need encouragement and recognition for their efforts. This is one reason why P.S. 146 has four assistant principals whose primary assignment is to work with teachers in the classroom.

In recent years, individualization has become the "in" word in education. Last year, when we moved intensively into individualization, many teachers felt threatened and insecure. Today, teachers are successfully individualizing instruction in almost every class. Much of the credit must go to Mrs. Hortense Jones, director of the MES project, and her staff. For years Mrs. Jones had been pleading the case for individualized instruction, but had met resistance and token acceptance. In the past year there has been a dramatic change. What happened? After five months of haggling, permission was obtained to modify the federal funds budget to establish a training program for teachers, supervisors, and paraprofessionals. With selected teachers doing the training, approximately 900 participants were paid to attend training sessions during the school year and through the summer, at a cost of $200,000. Eight teachers from P.S. 146 were selected to serve as trainers. Of the eight, four originally were not firmly committed to an individualized approach. Today, they provide a strong nucleus of leadership for winning support and enthusiasm from other teachers.

Achievement Results

Staff and parents are enthusiastic about the accomplishments at P.S. 146 brought about through the committed

use of resources expended according to the approaches and policies outlined above. We were particularly proud when Charles E. Silberman's recent study for the Carnegie Corporation cited P.S. 146 as one of "at least three public schools in New York's Harlem" in which:

... academic achievement approximates or even surpasses the city-wide and national norms, and where students are having a full, rich, varied, happy school experience.... P.S. 146 in East Harlem is 45 percent black and 50 percent Puerto Rican. Achievement is high in all three schools, but without the grim, almost martial environment sometimes associated with academic achievement. On the contrary, all three schools have a relaxed, warm atmosphere.... The children are visibly happy and engaged; disruptive behavior, if evident at all ... is at a minimum — comparable to the best middle-class suburban schools. In all three schools, moreover, parents come and go freely and are visible everywhere.[3]

Our most urgent goal and major emphasis at P.S. 146 has been to improve reading performance. Students have reading two periods a day, one of which is grouped homogeneously and the other heterogeneously. The period of grouping according to reading level is used to concentrate on helping poorer readers. For example, the sixth grade presently has seven classes, but utilizing two cluster teachers and two reading specialists allows us to divide our 134 sixth graders into 10 reading groups. The high-achieving groups have 22 or more children; the low-achieving groups, which frequently are taught by the reading specialists, have as few as five or six. At the present time (December, 1970), students in the fifth and sixth grades are distributed in the homogeneous reading groups as follows:

Numbers of students at each reading level in grade five (five classes, eight reading groups):

6.1 and above	 23
5.5 to 6.0	 21
5.1 to 5.5	 17
4.5 to 5.0	 14
4.1 to 4.5	9
3.5 to 4.0	6
2.5 to 3.0	7
2.5 and below	 10

Numbers of students at each reading level in grade six (seven classes, 10 reading groups):

6.5 and above	 24
6.1 to 6.4	 23
6.0	 20
5.5 to 6.0	 10
4.5 to 5.0	 14
4.1 to 4.5	 10
3.5 to 4.0	7
3.1 to 3.5	6
2.5 to 3.0	6
2.0 and below	5

Students are placed in reading groups according to their functional reading levels. Every child is given an informal textbook test administered by a reading specialist. When P.S. 146 opened in September, 1964, most of our fifth and sixth graders were two or more years behind in reading; today, 50% are at or above their grade level.

Have we done our job once we have taught a child to read? Our answer is a resounding *no!* We once had a boy who came to us an illiterate young gangster. He left P.S. 146 reading on a sixth-grade level — he had become a literate gangster. We don't consider that a great accomplishment. Improving academic achievement is only a part — though an indispensable part — of what must be done to provide adequate education for youngsters in urban schools. At P.S. 146 and other schools like it in the big cities, our task has just begun.

---

[1]David Fox, "Expansion of the More Effective Schools Program," Center for Urban Education, New York, 1967.

[2]We are indebted for this reminder to Neil Postman, who stressed it in a course on communications in the school.

[3]Charles E. Silberman, *Crisis in the Classroom: The Remaking of American Education.* New York: Random House, 1970, pp. 98-99.

A school without walls:
A city for a classroom

Donald W. Cox
Liza Lazorko

Less than two years ago, Philadelphia's unique Parkway program — the "school without walls" — was little more than an amorphous alternative to a multimillion dollar high school the system couldn't afford to build. Today, looking at the program's heady plans for expansion, its threefold increase in enrollment, and its write-up in *Life* magazine, one's initial reaction is that the Parkway experiment may well turn into an educational empire.

The Parkway program has an obvious jumping off point that makes it different from other high schools. It has no central school building and no fixed site for class sessions — except a rented loft where students keep their belongings and hold weekly meetings with the faculty.

The city is the school, and in tapping its resources, some 400 students this fall will attend classes at a wide variety of cultural, scientific and business institutions, the majority of which are located along a two mile stretch of the famous Benjamin Franklin Parkway in the heart of Philadelphia.

Perhaps best equipped to articulate the philosophy that props up the program is its director, John Bremer, a 42-year-old educational import from England and former superintendent of the Two Bridges decentralized school district in New York City.

"Our schools today imagine that students learn best in a special building or 'box' separated from the larger community," explains Bremer. "This has created a refuge in which students do not need to explore but only to accept."

The student's learning is evaluated within the "boxes" and it is never tested against the realities of life, Bremer continues. "It is a common feeling that what is learned in school is learned only for the purposes of the school and this is the well known irrelevance of education."

It is not possible, Bremer believes, to improve the high school

NATION'S SCHOOLS, 1969, Vol. 84, pp. 51-54.

211

as we now know it. "What is needed," he concludes, "is a new kind of education institution. In the Parkway program, we study the city in the city. Since our lives are inseparable from the city, it is our campus and our curriculum."

On foot or on specially provided shuttle buses, Parkway students roam their city, choosing from some 90 different courses offered at the participating institutions. English and literature, for example, are taught at the Free Public Library that houses nearly a million volumes; zoology and anthropology at the Philadelphia Zoo; biology at the Academy of Natural Sciences; statistics and business management at the Insurance Company of North America.

Students may also find themselves at such institutions as the city's newspapers, radio and TV stations, city hall, the police station or the county court building (where a special course in law enforcement is taught by a young law graduate working as an assistant district attorney).

While the high schoolers must satisfy state requirements in basic subjects such as English, mathematics and social studies, these are offered in a variety of different courses geared to the needs and interests of the students. Mathematics, for example, is taught at the Franklin Institute where students can choose from offerings like mathematics for science or mathematics for computers.

The Parkway program is unusual not only in the physical facilities provided for the youngsters, but also in the extent of student involvement in the program's overall management.

Students make their own decisions about the subjects they want to study, designing their curriculum to add courses, like photography and filmmaking, as they go along. They also have an equal voice with the program's administrators in selecting their teachers and regularly attend Friday morning faculty meetings.

The ungraded classes combine youngsters at all four high school levels — drawing from an extremely heterogeneous collection of academic and cultural backgrounds across the city. No behavioral or academic standards are used for admission — more than 2,000 applied for the 143 places available in the program last February and selection was made by dividing the applicants into eight district categories and then drawing names from a hat.

In keeping with the casual air that surrounds the school, students call teachers by their first names. There are no formal discipline codes and no dress or hair regulations.

But in spite of the Parkway's apparent free-wheeling atmosphere, Bremer insists, the program is actually tightly structured. Students, he feels, spend more time studying than their counterparts from regular high school. The school day lasts from nine to five for many of the program's youngsters, with special Saturday classes.

Although future plans call for

boosting student enrollment from the original figure of 143 to 400 this fall (reaching a projected peak of 2,400 by 1972), the basic structure of the program is expected to remain the same — with enrollment siphoned into units of approximately 150 students each.

Staff for the first unit of the program numbers nine full-time certified teachers and 13 university interns. Teachers contributed by business and industry help reduce the faculty-student ratio.

Students are randomly divided into nine groups called tutorials with about 16 students in each. The tutorial is the group in which the student works on basic skills required for a diploma and is given remedial or advanced work. Theoretically, it is also the place where he receives personal support and counsel from his teachers and in which he and the teachers undertake an evaluation of the program as a whole. The program also has student "management groups" to run the school. Management groups have been formed around areas like self government, public relations, athletics, fund raising, and extracurricular activities.

In addition to the institutional offerings and the basic skills, the academic curriculum also includes elective offerings in the humanities, physical sciences, and social studies taught by the Parkway faculty. Students are encouraged to participate in individual study programs with one or two other students and also are given the opportunity to enter the work pro-

grams which can lead to vacation jobs or career possibilities.

Students receive only pass or fail grades, but evaluation of their performance is, nonetheless an important part of the process. At the end of each semester, students and teachers are involved in a two-week evaluation which takes place in the tutorial groups. The faculty **evaluates the student's progress and each student evaluates his own progress and that of the faculty. A form is sent home to parents asking them also to evaluate their child's growth in the program.**

Although a number of parents were doubtful at first, Bremer recalls, reactions up to now have been "enormously favorable."

Most of the students and teachers also appear to be enthusiastic. Students, for example, call the program a "school for kids," an epithet the staff evaluates as the highest form of flattery. An informal survey indicates that roughly one-third had plans to drop out of their original high schools; since last February only one youngster has left the Parkway program.

Teachers praise the "flexibility" and freedom the program offers to utilize experimental methods and a variety of places to meet, but admit that the Parkway could use some "stabilizing." A definite weak point, as far as teachers are concerned, is the poor intra-staff communication that the flexibility often leads to.

"Teachers just don't know what's going on all the time because of so many changes in plans or schedules," said one staff member. "For example, one time we weren't even aware of a news conference being held about the program."

Teachers also are concerned about what one faculty member calls a "lack of genuine, across-the-board interaction between black and white students after class. Parkway students come from very different areas of the city and socially they seem to feel that it's safer to go with people they already know."

Apart from these criticisms, however, the Philadelphia Board of Education, for one, has been sufficiently impressed by the program to take over its funding next year from the Ford Foundation. (Cost per student is $680 — the same amount now being spent by the board for regular instruction.)

And numbered among the Parkway's most vigorous supporters is Philadelphia Superintendent of Schools, Dr. Mark Shedd, who sees the "potential high quality program" resulting in the "richness of an offering that no single school can afford."

However, one veteran education administrator, who served as a consultant in the planning phase of the program, cautions that the success or failure of the Parkway concept will depend largely on the evaluation system used to test students' academic competencies and learning skills.

How can independent study be properly evaluated? Can the tutors offer effective remediation? Is there enough self-motivation in the average student so that he can extend himself on his own — as the program assumes that he will?

Some observers have called the Parkway approach an overly simplistic, naive or "Utopian" solution to the urban educational bind. First of all, they argue that the program doesn't begin to provide a solution to the more complex problems urban schools are confronting — like teachers who are inadequately trained and students burdened by the physical and psychological effects of poverty. They question, too, the educational validity of the courses offered at the city's institutions, and wonder whether institutional personnel are really equipped to be teachers — or just competent public relations men and tour guides.

These are some of the questions still to be answered in the young Parkway experiment. The final report card will not be in for several years. But the school's supporters are confident that when it does come out it will, at the very least, credit the Philadelphia program with an innovative attempt to gear education to needs of youngsters who will be living the bulk of their lives in the 21st Century.

CONFESSIONS OF A GHETTO ADMINISTRATOR

Sidney Trubowitz

I am stereotyped. I am the unsympathetic automaton programmed by a white bureaucracy to maintain Establishment rule over a black community, the represser of teacher creativity blind to the hopes and emotions of black children, the symbol of punishment and fear for pupils and teachers alike. I am the man described by Herndon in *The Way It 'Spozed' To Be*:

> All of a sudden there stood Grissum, looking in as he had said he would. He stood there in the door, erect, unsmiling, while the readers faltered and stopped. He took a quick look around the room and then, when everything was silent, glared straight into the room. Glared; there was no question that he didn't like very much what he saw. We all knew it; we suddenly all felt pretty guilty. We wished we had been sitting up straight in our desks, all in rows, silent, diagramming sentences or writing out our spelling words. After perhaps 20 seconds he stepped back, closed the door, and was gone without saying a word.*

And so rarely am I seen as someone who knows hope and frustration, love and fear, anger and intimacy. Rarely am I seen as someone who relies on feeling as well as logical analysis to make administrative decisions. Rather, I am seen as a cold, ineffective machine who follows rules, who lives by

---

*James Herndon, *The Way It 'Spozed' To Be*. New York: Simon and Schuster, 1968, p. 168.

PHI DELTA KAPPAN, December 1971, pp. 210-213.

the book, and who in the words of a child is "like a giant policeman who sits behind a desk far away and makes all the rules, good or bad, and he expects us to obey them."

My day is one of action. I visit classes, respond to telephone calls, coordinate staff conferences, meet with individual teachers, work with committees, handle children's problems, check reports, talk with visitors, supervise school activities. To describe my role by presenting a detailed picture of what I do is to give only a partial view of how I function. For underlying much of what I do as a ghetto school principal is intense emotion, emotion which arises as I deal with the results of educational and social conflict. An analysis of my internal reactions to daily situations can give a more complete picture of my role and may also help to counteract the notion that all ghetto school leaders operate as uncaring robots. In addition, it may have the value of encouraging other administrators to look to themselves for guides to action, for if they are to affect people and events positively, they need to understand the feelings which influence decision making.

Feelings of Responsibility

"I do not want your guilt. I want your responsibility." So speaks a character in the Arthur Miller play, *Incident at Vichy*.

A veteran principal says to a new principal, "The mantle of Elijah has fallen on your shoulders."

It is 8:20 in the morning and an emergency call comes to the office. A child has been hit by a car. I run down to the street in back of the school. The child is being attended by the police. They await an ambulance.

I ask myself, "Could I have done more to have prevented the accident?" The letter to the Department of Traffic requesting a play street wasn't enough. Maybe I should have mobilized the parents, formed picket lines at the crossing, stressed safety more with the children, seen to it that a wooden barrier was placed at the corner to block traffic.

Can I help to avoid every mishap, every street accident, every bump on the head?

A student teacher is sent to get a school aide. She sees a black teacher and mistakes her for an aide. The teacher angrily interrupts her, "I am not an aide. I am a teacher."

The problem of the student teacher's expression of prejudice reaches me. I am asked to deal with the situation. I point out to the student teacher that to peg a black automatically as a nonprofessional is to prejudge. I indicate to the teacher that to be taken as a school aide is not necessarily a slur. My efforts to bring them together to discuss the problem are unsuccessful. I ponder the scope of my responsibility.

The parents' association holds its monthly meeting. Only 20 parents appear. Maybe I should have worked harder to encourage teachers to stimulate parent participation in the school by doing more home visiting, by inviting parents to school events, by sending personal invitations to parent meetings. Perhaps, *I* have to find more time to visit homes, to attend community meetings, to walk the streets, to break down the barriers that exist between school and home.

A child reports that his money was taken as he walked home from school. Workmen renovating a building report that boys have been throwing rocks at the windows of the vacant building. A neighbor calls to inform me that there are children climbing all over an abandoned car in the street. Can I deal with all the problems in the community that involve children? How do I succeed in getting children to remain aloof from attractive nuisances where they may get hurt? How do I help children develop the emotional controls that will prevent harm to themselves and others? I attempt to discover who took the youngster's money. I ask the teachers to discuss with the children the safety hazards in the neighborhood. I call the police department to get the abandoned car removed.

A child in the second grade screams at other children, runs around the room, and generally disrupts his class. His teacher tries to make contact with him. She talks to him privately; she has lunch with him. He develops positive relationships with the guidance counselor and with me. His adjustment improves but he still disrupts the class periodically. Then his family moves out of the school district and the initial reaction is one of guilty relief: "Oh, we won't have to worry about James anymore. He won't be taking up so much of our time." Then second thoughts arise. He'll never make it in another school. He'll be completely lost. The cerebral battle begins. What about the other children in his class who lose time because of the attention he demands? What about the children in the school to which he is transferred? Won't they lose time too? He can make it here even though it's a real struggle. But, legally, he should be transferred. Can I assume responsibility for everyone?

I have come to realize that the principal needs to define for himself the extent of his responsibility. In addition to working in the area of instruction, I necessarily and voluntarily become concerned with such community problems as deteriorating housing, poor sanitation, narcotics addiction, and inadequate police protection. I do feel a sense of responsibility for every child reading below grade level, for drug addicts nodding on street corners, for every pupil with an untreated physical defect, for every unswept street, for every student at odds with himself and the world, for every home without heat and hot water. However, I need to come to terms with the limitations of time and physical and psychic energy, to do all that I can without continually carrying around the nagging sense of tasks unfulfilled.

Feelings of Prejudice

To grow up in a racist society is to be nurtured on prejudice. Prejudice is transmitted by a society which places blacks in inferior roles, by communication media which ignore or distort the position of Negroes. It is absorbed with the tightening grasp of a mother's hand as a black approaches. It seeps in as a child overhears deprecating remarks about minority groups.

A parent comes to make arrangements for her child to have the school lunch. Automatically I hand her a free lunch application. "I want to pay for my child's lunch," she replies. Why do I assume that all ghetto parents can't afford to pay, that all are on the welfare rolls?

A child is pushed, walking down a stairway, and he chips his tooth. I hear a thought whispered that the ghetto is a rough-and-tumble place. Minor accidents are normal and nothing to get upset about. I focus on the thought for a moment. I try to put myself in the parent's place. I begin to feel her distress.

218

An irate mother starts shouting at me. Do I
quietly accept her behavior, figuring that ghetto
parents must be humored, or do I insist on the same
standards of social discourse that I would of a
middle-class parent? Do I always respond with
forced courtesy or do I at times react with feelings
of my own?

A black teacher arrives at school consistently
late. I need to approach her in the same way I
approach other teachers, calmly and reasonably
helping her to see that her professional role calls for
her to be in school punctually. I need to talk to her
but I wonder if my words will be delivered from a
background of anxiety which, if verbalized, might
say, "Blacks are dangerous. They'll whip back. They
must be handled carefully."

At a principals' conference a ghetto school
administrator mutters, "These ignorant people! We
ought to let them run their own schools and let
them fall flat on their faces. They gripe and they
scream. Why don't they just stay out of our way
and support education and their children? Then
they'd make it just the way we did with our parents'
help." If I respond with silence I give tacit approval
to the remark. I need to say, "Sure, parents get in
our way sometimes. They can make things uncomfortable. But isn't it better that the community has
finally found its voice, instead of staying miles from
the school? Now they're getting angry to our faces
instead of on street corners."

The chairman of a local community agency
speaks to a group of principals regarding the hiring
of paraprofessionals. "Don't try to kid us. We know
our rights. If you pull anything, I'm warning you,
we'll get hysterical. To use the words of the ghetto,
'Man, you will die.'" How do I deal with that
portion of the ghetto community which sees each
individual employee of the Board of Education as
an agent of a white power structure that promised
integration and reneged, that staffed their schools
with the most inexperienced of teachers, that
conducted education by fiat rather than involvement? How do I handle the obsessive need of some
blacks to humble whites? Do I accept all such
attacks mutely, or do I seek to maintain my own
sense of self-respect and insist that my own in-
dividuality and integrity be recognized?

I feel fear as I walk the evening streets to a

219

meeting in a Harlem church. I have a sense of being in a foreign country as I notice that mine is one of the few white faces among the many blacks present. As I greet black people I ask myself if I'm being too polite. I struggle to distinguish between what are feelings of prejudice and feelings that are appropriate to the situation.

A group of teen-agers sits in back of the school auditorium during an evening glee club performance. They laugh, they make loud remarks, they disrupt. I tell them they can stay only if they sit quietly. As I say this I am aware of the distance between us, the total lack of understanding, as though we are people from different planets equipped with different languages, with different psyches. I am angered by their failure to have any consideration for the children performing, for their parents watching. Do I then generalize to all black teen-agers?

I don't believe my feelings of prejudice will ever completely disappear. I am certain, however, that almost always now I am attuned to them. My awareness helps me to be more honest with myself and, as a result, more likely to communicate effectively with others.

Feelings of Pressure

Picket lines surround a neighboring school, chanting that the principal must go. The charges against him seem vague, but a community faction pressures that he be relieved. A meeting of the local school board follows; a community meeting takes place. Three days later the principal is transferred to another school.

When I am asked, "How are things going in your school?," the question might better be phrased, "Are you having trouble with the community?" I reply, "Everything seems all right for the moment." The last words are the key words, for if pressure topples one principal, why not another? The atmosphere becomes tainted with threat as stories appear in newspapers of a principal being reviled, another being removed from his position, others transferring to less hostile environments. I try to push anxiety aside. What happens is that feelings retreat behind the door of the unconscious.

I read an article in the local newspaper about a

220

prep school that reports amazing success with dropouts. The ingredient for success, said the headmaster of the school, is teachers who care about students. I feel the pressure of simplistic demands: Just get teachers who care and all academic problems will be solved. Can I reply to the frustrated pleas of the community that the answers to educational problems are complex? Can I say that, in addition to caring, it takes knowledge of how to teach, knowledge of oneself, the development of creativity, the chance to try and fail, time for professional growth?

A parent complains about a beginning teacher. I ponder the problem of the new teacher. Certainly the children do not generally learn as much as they would in the class of an experienced teacher. Can I tell a parent this? Can I repeat the words of the new teacher who said to me, "I go home each night feeling guilty. I feel I'm a fraud. I've had seven weeks of summer training and I'm supposed to be a teacher. A parent says to me, 'You know best. You're the teacher,' and I squirm." Her next words carry hope. "I know I'll do a better job next year. I'm learning all the time." How do I describe the agony of growth, the time needed for a teacher's development, the difference in teacher ability that a child going through school inevitably faces?

Each year metropolitan newspapers throughout the country publish the reading test scores of every school. School administrators are thus measured for their effectiveness. To such pressure bureaucratic leadership responds defensively by proclaiming, "Our principals have been instructed to direct teachers to teach reading in all subject areas, to concentrate on fundamentals, and to spend less time on frills." The directive both angers and saddens me. Of course, reading is taught in all subject areas. As one teacher put it, "This is like saying all schools should be open five days a week." However, a beautiful piece of literature is not interrupted to list new words. The excitement of discovery in science is not disturbed by an artificial introduction of phonics. The joy of exploration in art is not tainted by a listing of art vocabulary.

How do I respond to the pressure which, if portrayed by a cartoonist, might depict a school's test scores on one side of a scale and the principal's head on the other? Do I react, as some principals

221

have, by dividing the school day into two parts, the teaching of reading and the teaching of mathematics? Do I communicate to every teacher that education's primary aim is to produce high scores on standardized tests? Do classes then spend time memorizing the meaning of words found on tests? Does test-taking practice supercede all other aspects of reading instruction? Do I spend sleepless nights worrying whether the children will score well on the tests? Or do I resist the pressure to focus solely on tests and instead continue to work with the idea that helping teachers to develop exciting, imaginative, meaningful class programs will lead to pupil growth in all areas?

Recently, in discussing the need for educational change, words and phrases like "innovation," "experimentation," and "don't live by the book" have enjoyed much use. Is nonconformity really being encouraged? Is the school being urged to stimulate real freedom for its teachers to act? Or are there both bureaucratic and community drives for a return to traditional curricula and rigid patterns of behavior?

What would my response be upon entering a classroom where children are chewing gum and wearing hats? Would shock be my reaction or would I calmly ask the reason for such behavior? Would I allow the teacher to proceed as he had after he explained, "I find that gum chewing relaxes the kids. As for the hats – I try to initiate rules that make sense. I see no point in continually fighting the kids on hats. It doesn't strike me as terribly important." Would this break from conformity be accepted? Would I recognize the teacher's right to establish what he perceives to be the right classroom atmosphere for success?

A parent tells me, "The elementary school is no place for monitors. Children need tight controls. Only teachers can give them that." I can respond to such a demand by clamping down tighter, by seeking new ways to enforce controls, or I can continue to search for means to help children handle more freedom and responsibility.

Perhaps the most burdensome pressure of all arises from questions about the ultimate value of the function I fill. Does the school I lead really make a difference in the lives of the children, or do I serve as the cog in the machine whose job it is

222

simply to maintain the status quo? Am I the chewing gum and scotch tape helping to hold together the wobbly unit that is the large urban elementary school? Wouldn't my efforts be better utilized in pushing for the radical changes that (it becomes more clear daily) are desperately needed? Why not schools of 250 children or less so that children are treated as individuals rather than as statistics? Why not adequate social services so that children in need of help can get intensive assistance? Why not administrative role redefinition so that the principal can devote his full energies to working with the community in the forthcoming era of decentralization and community control? Why not professionally led weekly group sessions for administrators, teachers, and parents so that feelings can be aired and understood? Why not choices of such varied educational patterns as storefront classes, schools-within-schools, schools without walls, widespread day-care centers? What can I do so that things will change, not alone in my school, but in schools everywhere?

I know I need to try to be clear regarding the pressures around me, so that what I do can come from awareness rather than from helpless reaction to shifting forces.

Feelings of varying intensity and shades underlie many of my school decisions. To be in touch with these feelings is to make for more perceptive, more intelligent action, and, perhaps, most importantly, more human response. I need constantly to define myself to myself, both as an individual and as a person within a professional role.

CHAPTER VI: REFORM OF URBAN EDUCATION

This chapter deals with the alternatives to urban school reform. The types of reform mentioned are both of the program and human types. Even though schools have taken upon themselves the role of being people-changing institutions they have not devised ways in which to change the people who make up their faculties. The question or riddle always exists when talking about urban school reform of whether changing the institution will also change the people. Or, if you can change the people, will the institution change accordingly? Robert Havighurst and Daniel Levine feel that if the structure of the urban school bureaucracy is changed, then the people inside it will change to meet the new structure that is developed. Also, Amitai Etizoni has said in several of his works that schools as people-changing institutions have been ineffective and that he feels institutions change people when environments are altered. Nonetheless, despite a great deal of empirical research showing the ineffectiveness of people-changing programs, the educational institution goes on in its self-appointed role as a people-changer, much like Don Quixote.

All of the authors in this chapter agree that sweeping, drastic, and total reform is about the only thing that will save the urban school systems in this country from a greater degree of dysfunctionality than presently exists. The majority of the authors also discuss the urban school system as a social system within the greater society with responsibilities toward that society which are not currently being met. Fortunately, none of the authors feel that reform is out of the grasp of the society in regards to urban school systems. In other words, the point of no return has apparently not yet been reached. However, the task of reform is going to be a long and arduous one laced with many confrontations with established practices, procedures and educators desiring to retain the present status quo. An educational revolution in urban school systems is actually called for in this chapter. Although the organizational type of change called for in the articles might make a beginning teacher feel that he or she is a small, insignificant personage in the total urban school structure, each classroom teacher nonetheless has a definite role. That role is as a change agent within a school and a classroom and more importantly, in a defined community. It is a well-known fact that educational reforms and even new instructional programs never succeed unless they receive the cooperation and dedication of the individual class-

room teacher. Thus, the beginning of urban school
reform much involves all of the elements or actors in
the urban school; the community, the administrators, the
teachers, and the children.

Without doubt, the urban school system is one of
the most rigidly bureaucraticized institutions in our
society and radical change in structure and procedure
will be difficult to establish. Also, it must be remembered by those willing and able to make changes
leading toward reform that something viable must be
present to replace what is destroyed or done away with.

Urban school systems in many cities have become
systems of incest as teachers enter the system, teach,
then become administrators at the building level, and
eventually move up into city-wide positions. Rarely,
if ever, in many urban school systems, does new blood
come into the administrative ranks from outside the
system. It is necessary to pass through the ranks from
outside the system. It is necessary to pass through the
ranks and in essence become fully indoctrinated in order
to become an administrator in many systems. This too,
must be remembered by reformers. New structures and
programs can be designed and put into the demonstration
level but when city-wide implementation of the innovation

is ready to take place, the old guard or incestuous
group is going to be called upon to implement the reform.
When taking this into consideration it can easily be
seen how difficult truly meaningful reform is.

Reform might be established in a system comprised
of many young and even experienced teachers who are
open to new ideas and are willing at the same time to
open the doors of the schools and let out the current
educational hypocrisy and let in the community. What
must not be retained in the future is the procedure where
the young teacher comes into the urban school full of
enthusiasm and vigor only to be knocked down and sup-
pressed until he conforms to the system's ethos.

INTERVENTION ALTERNATIVES FOR URBAN EDUCATION

MARIO D. FANTINI

A vision that arouses both fears and hope is emerging from the crisis in public education, especially in our cities. That prospect is that public education will return to the direct control of the public—but not just a traditionally "prepared" public; not simply the civic leaders who serve on city-wide school boards, or parent-association leaders who are endowed with verbal and organizational skills and college degrees; not just the enlightened business leaders who recognize good schools as a drawing card to local economic development (or a dampener on racial unrest). The murmurs now being heard in two or three large cities are coming from the "garden variety" of parent and community resident—including ghetto parents with little formal education—calling for a say in the operation of public schools.

The prospect is frightening to many because it rises from the soil of civil strife and growing racial hostility, assertiveness, and even hatred. But even without these factors, the prospect would alarm the majority of professional educators (and many sympathetic laymen) who fear the dismemberment of complex systems of education by the hand of people said to be incompetent. For, after all, we are not talking about a plaything. We are discussing a vaunted American institution, which is credited with advancing democratic practices and with opening the doors

HARVARD EDUCATIONAL REVIEW, Winter 1968, pp. 160-175.

of opportunity to millions of immigrants for more than a century. Moreover, it is an institution with an enormous and growing capital plant and annual operating budget.

The positive aspects of this kind of public control are more difficult to perceive. One possibility is that under the right conditions, real public control of public education could provide more effective education. It could also foster the revitalization of one of the most revered canons of American society, citizen participation in democratic processes. And, on the most profound level, perhaps intimate public engagement in public education could lead to realization of one of the most fundamental goals of education: to make better citizens, all along the age spectrum. Merely to suggest these prospects is to invite accusations of romanticism or naïve idealism. But an examination of more hard-headed approaches to modern public education suggests that this idealistic path may turn out to be the most practical and efficient.

Some Premises

Before examining past and future approaches to the solution of the educational crisis, it would be well to make explicit the premises of my argument:

(1) That public education is failing generally. The most visible failure is in the urban, low-income, racial-minority ghettoes. But if one holds education responsible in part for shortcomings throughout American society, education has failed more widely. The shortcomings include such features of contemporary life as the alienation and withdrawal of many economically and culturally advantaged college-age youth and the impotence of social consciousness in mobilizing an adequate response to the nation's domestic crises. Public education's precise share of the blame for these shortcomings need not be calculated in order to assert that it bears *some* share, even a substantial one.

(2) That public education is a governmental function. It is supported by the public at large, not simply by the immediate users, and it is subject at least to review, if not to close accountability, by elected public representatives somewhere along the line.

(3) That while the goals of American public education are not confined to skill development, the present operational definition of quality education is performance in basic skills at or above grade-level as measured by standardized tests.

(4) That the growing complexity of the education process is no cause for attrition of the concept of public control of public education.

(5) That public education is a universal right. Therefore it cannot, even *de facto*, be limited to those who are responsive and congenial to whatever the prevailing mode of public education happens to be. Public education has an affirmative obligation to meet the needs not only of the "normal" but also of the physically and otherwise handicapped, and of those who are unresponsive or hostile to the prevailing process.

(6) That the public has a right to determine educational policy and to hold professionals accountable for implementing policy. Thus, when 70 per cent of ghetto children are not reading at grade-level their parents have a right to question professional performance since the schools are supposed to educate everyone.

(7) That urban education is synonymous with the education of low-income racial minorities whose growing despair is both a threat and a challenge to America's great cities. The general urban crisis is inextricably linked to the crisis of urban education.

The Nature of the Crisis

In the last twenty years, the nation has overcome with reasonable success what were regarded as "crises" in public education. The first was a deficit in facilities and personnel, due mainly to deferred spending during World War II and to a rise in the birth rate. We still have not caught up, but the capital investment has been truly impressive, and progress on the number and salaries of personnel has been almost as significant.

The second "crisis," escalated to a national emergency by Sputnik, was the inadequacy of training in science and mathematics. Sputnik led to additional offerings in these fields, and large-scale curriculum experimentation has resulted in more and better-prepared students in these fields.

But all these improvements in public education have left the basic system unchanged. They have strengthened the status quo, enabling the system to serve better those it has always served best. The heart of the present crisis in public education is the realization that the system has failed a major segment of the population. This failure was the most intractable crisis all along, but it did not come to full public awareness until the nation took official cognizance of poverty amidst affluence and until the nonwhite fourth of society's economic underclass began to assert its civil rights and demand a full share in political and economic opportunity.

Our present preoccupation with the disadvantaged, however, has not diverted critics from concluding that the total system of education is incapable of addressing the challenge of providing excellent education for a diverse student population. Consequently, the mission of fundamental educational reform is not for the poor alone, but for all.

There is little agreement regarding the locus of the problem of school failure. At one extreme is the assumption that the failure of any child to learn lies primarily with the learner—in his physical, economic, cultural, or environmental deficits. At the other pole is the notion that if pupils are failing the school system itself needs basic rehabilitation. Under this assumption, the school's obligation is to diagnose the learner's needs, concerns, and cognitive and affective style, and adjust its program accordingly. In the early stages of concern about the learning problems of the disadvantaged, the searchlight played almost entirely on the shortcomings of the learners. A salutory shift toward a more comprehensive diagnosis of the teaching and learning system as well as the problems of the learner himself seems now to be developing. Emerging with the shift is a set of prescriptions— alternatives for intervention designed to reform the process and practice of public education.

Intervention Alternatives

A continuum of five basic approaches to intervention may be identified: compensatory education, desegregation, model subsystems, parallel systems, and total system reform. With the exception of compensatory education, these are largely untried concepts, but in some cases—model subsystems, for example—the few existing examples are sufficient to provide a basis for examining the likelihood of success or failure.

Compensatory Intervention

Compensatory education—attempts to overcome shortcomings in the learner—is the most prevalent form of intervention designed to raise pupils' academic achievement. It characterizes such efforts as the Ford Foundation-supported Great Cities School Improvement Programs, Title I of the Elementary and Secondary Education Act and New York City's early Higher Horizons Program and recent More Effective Schools Program. Compensatory education seeks to attack a spectrum of defects in the learner—verbal retardation, lack of motivation, and experiential and sensory deprivation—that presumably prevent his participation in the learning process. In addition to grafting extra education onto the regular school experience, proponents of compensation have attempted to nip deficiencies in the bud through preschool programs like Project Headstart.

For the most part, however, compensatory education is a prescription that deals with *symptoms*, with strengthened doses that have been ineffective before—more trips, more remedial reading, etc.—without real differences in kind. It is essentially an additive, or "band aid" approach that works by augmenting and strengthening existing programs. It builds layers onto the standard educational process in order to bring the strays into the fold and to fit them into the existing school mold. The assumption is that the schools need to do somewhat more for disadvantaged pupils, but it does not presume that the school itself is in need of wholesale re-examination.

Enormous effort, ingenuity, and funds have been invested in compensatory education, but the evidence gathered from even the best efforts indicates that they are having little significant impact on the problem of low achievement among disadvantaged children. The proponents of continued compensatory intervention argue either that not enough effort and resources have yet been applied or that greater attacks must be made on factors external to the schools (typically, family stability, housing, and income), or both.

But the compensatory approach is viewed with increasing distrust by the parents of academic failures both because the techniques are not achieving their goals, and because these parents are rejecting the premise that the fault lies in their children. Doubts are also beginning to arise among educational strategists disappointed by the failure of incremental inputs to the existing system to make a substantial difference.

Desegregation

Since the 1954 Supreme Court decision, a principal motivating factor in efforts toward integration has been the assumption that Negro pupils' achievement improves in an integrated school environment. The Coleman Report tends to support this view, and the U.S. Commission on Civil Rights is unequivocal in stating: "Negro children suffer serious harm when their education takes place in public schools which are racially segregated, whatever the source of such segregation may be. Negro children who attend predominantly Negro schools do not achieve as well as other children, Negro and white."[1]

In most urban settings, integration has proved elusive, if not impossible. The

---

[1] U.S. Commission on Civil Rights, *Racial Isolation in the Public Schools* (Washington: U.S. Government Printing Office, 1967), I.

failure to achieve integration to any significant extent was due first to massive white resistance. Now it is even less likely to occur in our lifetime because of the growing concentration in the inner city of Negro and other nonwhite minorities. The only possible plan for achieving integration in many large cities, metropolitan integration across present school district boundaries, seems politically unfeasible.

Moreover, minority group members themselves show a growing shift away from integration at the option of the white majority. The new focus of Negro and other racial-minority parents is on power and control over the schools their children attend. The changing mood springs not only from the poor record of integration efforts, but also from a revolt against the condescension perceived by minority group members in the school desegregation efforts of the post-1954 decade. First, many of them resent the fact that integration is, under current power arrangements, an option of the white community. Second, they believe that the dependent status of the Negro in American society is perpetuated by the notion that the only way to help the black child is to seat him alongside white children. Beneath this mood is a quest for stronger racial identity and pride, and a desire to gain more control of their own destiny. The initial desire for integration was based, say many Negro spokesmen, on the belief that parents in predominantly white schools exercised enough power to insure that the school offered quality education, in which Negro pupils should share. The converse is powerlessness, further destruction of identity, and increasing disconnection from the larger society.

The implication for public education is greater participation by Negroes in control over predominantly Negro schools. This is rather different from the "separate but equal" doctrine, since some "black power" philosophers reason that when Negroes achieve quality education under their own aegis, they will then be prepared to connect (integrate) with the white society on a groundwork of parity instead of deficiency. A good school then would be defined not by the kind of children who attend it, but by the quality of the education offered by the school. In short, they seek connection as equals.

The goals of integration, therefore, must be broadened to restore a quality that has been sidetracked in the emphasis on the educational-achievement goal of desegregation. That is, we must reaffirm our commitment to connect with one another as human beings. We must recognize that viewing diversity and differences as assets rather than unfortunate barriers to homogeneity has as positive an effect on human growth and development as the teaching of academic skills. All of which is to suggest that militant Negro demands for participation in control of public education is actually a means of greater *connection* to society, precisely opposite from the connotations of separatism usually associated with "black power."

Model Subsystems

In an effort to explore new and improved learning strategies and techniques, experimental units are being created in which educators hope to develop improved training, retraining, curriculum, and methodology patterns—and, lately, greater community participation—that may be demonstrated and disseminated throughout entire school systems. Within a school system, a subunit may consist of one or a cluster of schools. Projects under Titles III and IV of the Elementary and Secondary Education Act are seeking to create subsystems on a regional basis, through consortia of institutions.

Although some colleges and universities have for many years maintained experimental undergraduate subsystems (honors colleges, for example), the trend toward this mode of intervention in public schools may have started with a progress report (by a panel headed by Jerrold Zacharias) to the U. S. Commissioner of Education in March, 1964. The report led to the creation of a model subdivision in the Washington, D.C. Public Schools. At about the same time, the Syracuse, N.Y. Public Schools (in the Madison Area Project), and later the Boston Public Schools, created subsystems in a deliberate attempt to provide the total system with a development and training conduit for successful innovative practices. The most recent, and most visible, instances of model subsystems in a large urban establishment are three experimental school clusters in Manhattan and Brooklyn, including the Intermediate School 201 complex. These differ from earlier subsystems in that they are governed by community-based boards, although they must still seek ultimate approval on any number of basic decisions from the central Board of Education.

Many see the subsystem as a means for involving new institutions and persons outside the educational establishment with the urban schools. In New York City, for example, New York University, Teachers College, and Yeshiva University have "adopted" single schools or clusters of schools. Antioch College has assisted an experimental subsystem school in Washington, the Adams-Morgan School, and is seeking to adopt schools in Philadelphia and Dayton, Ohio. In addition to colleges and universities, community agencies, research and development centers, the Peace Corps and Vista veterans, private industry, and the professions are seen as possible sources of new talent and ideas introduced through model subsystems.

234

Intervention through model subsystems represents substantial progress toward a realization that "more-of-the-same" approaches have limited utility. It represents a refreshing intellectual concession that the educational process and system may share responsibility with the learner for his failure to achieve. It also borrows a leaf from scientific, technological, and industrial enterprises in its commitment to research and development.

The vogue for subsystems is developing rapidly despite scant experience with them and even scantier evidence of success. There are intrinsic constraints in the organizational framework within which dependent subsystems seek to explore the avenues of change. First, experience suggests that the model subsystem may lack the autonomy and freedom it needs to follow findings through to their ultimate conclusion. More likely than not, explorations into new school patterns call for breaking the rules, and the mother system is frequently unwilling to give her precocious, adventurous children much latitude. Furthermore, subunits too often depend for their new energies and resources on imported consultants who do not become integral members of the existing structure. And, as a practical matter, the educators selected to head subunits are often irreversibly captive to bureaucratic rigidity; their underlying identification is likely to be with the large system that sanctioned the experiment (that is, with the status quo) rather than with the new territory the experimental subunit seeks to explore. The experimental systems also are under pressure to produce results quickly. The mother system, which itself may be in disarray due to years or decades of decline, nonetheless is impatient to evaluate the subsystem, and perhaps vested interests are only too ready to label it a failure if it does not turn out a shining record of extraordinary achievement in a year or two. Whether the subsystem is dependent or largely autonomous, it is not likely to affect an entire system that is governed by an adept and hierarchy-hardened bureaucracy and conditioned by fixed patterns of behavior. Moreover, the educational substance of subsystems has, up to this point, been fragmented. The experiments tend to concentrate on one or another piece of improved instructional practice—team teaching, new careers for the poor, role playing, teacher training, or reading, for example—but seldom with the form and structure of the total system.

Parallel Systems

One set of approaches to quality education does not take the form of intervention in public education; rather, it calls for opportunities for students to escape into a parallel system. Such approaches assume that if the poor (or others) cannot reform public education, they should be afforded options to it.

A few privately managed schools have been established in urban ghettoes, and several others are in the planning stage. Precedents for such schools exist in southern Freedom Schools (notably Neil Sullivan's school for Negro pupils deprived of educational opportunity when the Prince Edward County, Virginia, public schools closed to avoid integration). Some northern counterparts include Harlem's Academies of Transition and the New School for Children in Boston's Roxbury section. The Urban League-sponsored street academies are sending more than 75 per cent of their students—hard-core rejects from the public school system —to college.

Of considerable potential significance to urban education is an act approved by the Massachusetts Legislature late in 1967 which enables the State Department of Education to assist and sponsor experimental school systems operated by private nonprofit corporations. Assuming a greater role in education and urban problems, states could establish yardsticks, "educational TVA's," by which to measure the effectiveness of different forms of educational innovation.

Project Headstart schools are also "private" in the sense that they exist apart from the public school system and are not subject to its rules and regulations governing personnel, curriculum, and other matters. Some of these schools are financed under Federal tuition grants and foundation funds, and efforts are being made to obtain support for others from business and industry. A special hybrid, a publicly-financed but totally independent school system (an enclave apart from the regular New York City system) with a per-capita budget received directly from the state, was proposed in 1967 by the Harlem chapter of CORE, though it failed in the New York State Legislature.

Nonpublic schools have advantages; they do not have to deal with distant and entrenched bureaucracies, with school boards unfamiliar with their particular needs, or with teachers' unions. They are free to hire teachers from a variety of personnel pools and to sidestep rigid credential-granting procedures. They may even abandon such practices as tenure and retain, promote, or discharge teachers purely on the grounds of merit and performance. If the schools are governed by boards with a substantial representation from the pupils' parents, they are likely to be more responsive to the children's needs and thereby encourage better rapport and partnership between the home and the school. In the most general sense, they afford the poor the choice that is open to many middle-class parents: to educate their children elsewhere if they are dissatisfied with the performance of the public schools. And if enough private schools are available, the pattern ushers in an entrepreneurial system in which parents can choose, cafeteria-style, from a range of styles of education—Montessori, prep school, Summerhill, and others.

Carried to its logical conclusion, however, the parallel-school approach would reduce the scope of public education, if not dispense with it altogether. The establishment of private schools sufficient to handle significant numbers of poor children would require public support and, in effect, establish a private system of publicly-supported schools. Middle-income parents would demand similar privileges. For financial reasons alone, the parallel-school approach is hardly likely to become widespread in the foreseeable future; moreover, the scheme would founder on political, if not constitutional grounds. Finally, since private schools are not subject to public control, there would be no guarantee against the organization of programs by special interest groups for ends inimical to a free and open society. Support of such enterprises at public expense would be intolerable.

These arguments are, of course, no reason to discourage programs that enable more low-income pupils to attend private schools. Private schools could serve a valuable yardstick function if they were run under conditions that simulated the resources and inputs of public education—particularly comparable per-capita expenditures, and admission policies that would embrace a range of low-income pupils, including the "disruptive." But that is the limit of their usefulness as an alternative to improved public education, for they could never serve the majority of the children of the poor.

Total System Reform

Since the compensatory approach has apparently failed, since desegregation is not a realistic short-range prospect, since model subsystems do not give much evidence yet of realizing their promise, and since parallel systems are basically an avoidance of the challenge to reform the schools where most children will continue to be educated, the latest—and, in my view, most promising—approach to intervention is reform of total school systems, structurally and otherwise. There are several approaches to total system intervention.

One approach is to provide new leadership for the system as a whole, while leaving the system's form and structure basically intact. This approach is exemplified by trends in Philadelphia, where a reform-minded central school board, including former Mayor Richardson Dilworth and a new superintendent of schools with a record of innovation are attempting to strengthen the effectiveness of the old system with the infusion of new staff and new styles. Pittsburgh, too, is improving the efficiency of the existing system, within the operational definition of quality education as achievement according to norms.

Another approach consists of reorganization of the system into quasi-autonomous districts—i.e., decentralization. Washington, D.C. has begun moving in this direction, beginning with single model schools. The Passow Report on the District's schools recommends a total system reform by decentralizing the system into eight subsystems of approximately equal size.[2]

Still another form is the proposed merger of the school systems of two entire political jurisdictions—the city of Louisville and Jefferson County. The Louisville-Jefferson County merger differs markedly from the piecemeal metropolitan experiments noted earlier. In this case, the new metropolitan system is to consist of a number of subdistricts, each with considerable autonomy yet federated into a single system to preserve the best of the worlds of bigness and smallness.

In the subsystems, models of excellence must swim against the tide of the status quo system. The total approach has no such constraint; there is no boring from within, for everyone starts at the reform gate at the same time. In a federation of autonomous subsystems, each with an equitable share of resources, instructional practices would operate in an open, competitive market. The most successful models would be on display as a challenge to other school systems to adopt their approaches or surpass them in performance.

New Energy Sources

The intervention proposed in November, 1967 by the Mayor's Advisory Panel on Decentralization of the New York City Schools—the Bundy Report—adds a crucial new energy source to the total system pattern.[3] Administrative decentralization of large school systems had been in the wind. (New York City itself had for the last six years begun loosening the reins of a highly centralized system.) But the Bundy Report's proposals go well beyond administrative arrangements into a form of public engagement in the process of education that is without precedent in large urban systems; and, in a sense, without much real precedent even in many suburbs and small cities.

The Bundy Report was significantly titled *Reconnection for Learning.* The

[2] A. H. Passow, *Summary of a Report on the Washington, D.C. Public Schools* (New York: Teachers College, Columbia University, 1967). (Mimeographed.)
[3] *Reconnection for Learning: A Community School System for New York City* (New York: The Mayor's Advisory Panel on Decentralization, 1967).

plan calls for more than a redistribution of power; it also provides new means of energizing school reform. Reform requires fuel. Sustained school reform needs not only ideas, but human resources and dynamic support from the public and the profession. All too often, the energy for educational reform consists only of a few professionals, practitioners or veterans who have shifted their struggle from the front lines to universities or the author's desk. The Bundy plan expands the base of energy to include the most numerous, and possibly the most powerful, energy source: parents and the community-at-large.

It offers the professional who is working for improvement within the system a powerful ally who is also highly motivated to reform the system. Ghetto parents especially have come to the same verdict as the most astute students and practitioners of education: that urban education is failing and desperately in need of reform.

But professional recognition of this energy concept is slow to come, for it assumes an altogether different professional-lay relationship from what now prevails. In the last several decades, education—in self-defense and for other reasons —has rapidly become professionalized. There has been an inverse correlation between professionalization and parents' involvement. Two other forces have tended to keep parents from participating in the education process. One, earlier in the cycle, though persisting in the urban ghetto, was the low level of the parents' own education relative to the teachers'. The immigrant, regardless of his desire for education for his children, was hardly likely to challenge the assigned authority represented by a native-speaking, better-educated teacher. The other factor, of course, is the growing size and impersonality of public school systems in large cities.

Even well-educated, middle-class parents who seek to engage in *meaningful* school decisions are deterred short of effectiveness by the inertial mass of the system or by the aura of professional exclusivity. Even the atmosphere in school buildings discourages parental presence (parent visiting days two or three times a year are prime evidence) and most parents visit school only in response to trouble. Thus, we have carefully-drawn boundaries for how far parents, singly or in parent-teacher associations, may go, even in asking questions of professionals. A sophisticated PTA member may nag at a school board that does not offer French in elementary school, but she will rarely ask for research results (or for research to be initiated) on the effectiveness of the school's language instruction. Still less is she apt to ask for such information as the school system's criteria for teacher selection or for evidence of its aggressiveness and imagination in recruiting teachers. Even when probing questions are asked, information is often safe-guarded as being in the professional domain alone. Only now are some school systems beginning to accumulate and release performance data on a school-by-school basis.

But perhaps the role of the parent should go far beyond asking pointed questions. Should parents have a voice—preferential if not determinative—regarding school curriculum? Should parents have a say in the kind of teacher they feel is best suited to the needs of their children? These are questions to which most professionals—and, indeed, many parents—would offer a reflex negative. Yet, within the framework of basic standards and goals, there are many options. Mathematics may be taught in any number of ways, and there are a variety of approaches to foreign languages. If the school is dedicated to instilling learning *skills,* content is as much a means as an end, and one choice will often serve as well as another. Why then should not the choice represent what is most meaningful to a particular community? Very often the professional choice is only one of several objectively reasonable choices; his word is final because he has a monopoly on the authority. If community involvement is to be real, if parent-teacher parnership is to have any meaning beyond lip-service, the proper role for the professional would be to outline the educationally-sound alternatives, and to afford the parents and the community a choice among them. Parallels may also be found in such other aspects as selection of materials, personnel policies, and allocation of resources.

Although, as suggested, the parent has never been a true partner in the education process, at least the concept of lay and local control of public education has a long historical tradition. But the tradition has been diluted and is largely impotent against the force of a professional monopoly.

Professional educators have not ignored parents or the community. Elaborate structures and devices have been fashioned—parent-teacher associations, visiting days, American Education Week, parent education programs, dissemination of information—ostensibly to "inform" the parent. The administrator who seeks a "happy" school (or "tight ship," as the case may be) will see that his parents are paid some attention or even a degree of deference. He will be patient in explaining homework policies. Schools of education include community relations in their curricula; and in many systems, advancement through the administrative ranks requires a certain number of credits in community relations.

The chief motivation of most professionals in community relations is to make *their* system work more smoothly. One defect of this goal is that it is one-sided, for if a prevailing system is dysfunctional, anything that maintains it is a deterrent to reform. Perhaps a more serious defect is the assumption that parent participation is so special that it requires special attention and designated periods—similar to the well-intentioned but fundamentally insensitive Brotherhood Weeks. In short, the existing concept of parent and community participation in education is basically misdirected toward supporting the schools' status quo.

The analogue of this interpretation with respect to pupils is adjustment to the culture and environment of the school, even if the school environment has no relation to the pupils' needs or interests. Pupils are judged on how well they fit in —whether the mode of the school be folded hands, quiet in the halls, short haircuts, or an irrelevant curriculum with teaching methods that fail to diagnose the learning style of individual pupils.

Such school systems are essentially one-way avenues. The school and its staff lay out their wares and the "consumer" either accepts them or goes hungry. The schools are acting *upon* raw material; if the material resists shaping and molding, it is discarded and labeled defective. In such a system, conscious or unconscious consumer preferences do not count. There is no feedback loop from parents or pupils; and lacking feedback, the system is not likely to respond to changing conditions and needs. It is to such inflexible, tuned-out systems, as well as to the environment or psyche of the learner, that one must look for the causes of pupil failure, dropout, or tuneout.

The Goals of Effective Participation

What would be the purpose of real parent and community participation? We begin from the position that when people have a part in their institutions, they share responsibility for them and are more likely to pay close attention to the stated mission and actual performance of the institution.

Thus participation has a positive effect on the participants as well as the system. For example, as parents in East Harlem became more engaged in the education process, "quality education" replaced "black power" as the slogan. Responsibility comes with the power of an effective voice. In the train of responsibility, judgment, stability, and dedication to constructive purpose are likely to follow. The pattern of the revolutionary is that upon assumption of power, he shifts from destroying institutions to building order and new institutions (of his own kind, to be sure).

Participatory democracy in education should also give parents and community a tangible respect for the intricacy and complexity of the professional problems in urban education. It is not likely that parents who have gained admission as true partners in the process will oversimplify and lay the blame for educational failures solely on the professional. As things stand now, low-income communities *outside* the system understandably lay the blame squarely on the assigned professionals: "You are paid to teach, to deliver a certain product. When overwhelming numbers of our children fail to learn, you are not delivering. You are not meeting your professional obligation." The syllogism is simplistic: it ignores the fact that professional talent can be thwarted by a system, and it does not take into account extra-school factors in teaching and learning. But it is an altogether natural response from parents to whom the system provides no access and offers but two alternatives: total resignation and apathy; or anger, protest, and, sooner or later, some form of retaliation.

Skeptics who concede the right of parents to participate in the education process nevertheless question their technical qualifications to engage in educational decisions; the question is raised particularly (though not exclusively) in relation to low income, poorly educated parents. But the question should be not what parents know now, but what they can come to know about the technicalities of education. That they want to know is suggested by the few instances in which they have become more or less equal partners in the process. Their concerns soon broaden; they begin to ask, for example, who are the most talented reading specialists in the country, because we want them to help us. In qualifying for school board membership, too, they seek training for themselves—something rare among would-be school board members even in wealthier communities.

Admitting the public to the education process, therefore, should result in the addition of many new hands and minds to the tasks. These would be true partners, who participate in the enterprise and know it from their own experience, who do not simply take the established goals and procedures of the enterprise as virtues because its professional managers say so.

The school, after all, is only one site of the total curriculum to which children are exposed. Considerable learning takes place at home and in all manner of community institutions including the street corner, the church, the press and other mass media, and neighborhood organizations. As parents are admitted to participation in the schools' education process, they will become better equipped "teachers" of that part of the "curriculum" in which they are the prime agents —rearing in the home. Studies under Basil Bernstein of the University of London's Sociological Research Unit have illuminated discontinuities of socialization among the home, the child's peer group, and the schools.[4] Continuity could be restored if parents participated in the formal education process.

Greater public engagement in the public education process should also add political strength to pressures for increased financial support for education; a "parents' lobby" with unprecedented motivation and commitment might arise. Nor should the possible effects on parents in their own right be overlooked. Few people can engage in a social cause and not themselves be transformed. Relevant education in an institutional setting that is willing to experiment in the art—and yes, the mysteries—of learning and teaching is such a cause. It could bring into the lives of men and women working at tedious jobs, or leading lives of boredom (factors by no means peculiar to low-income groups), a new *spirit* in an activity with immediate relevance to their own families. This is to say nothing of the possible chain-reaction that meaningful engagement in the education process could have in stimulating parents to enlarge their own education.

Thus the realignment of the participants in public education could produce rich yields for all the main participants:

—for the parents, a tangible grasp on the destiny of their children and opening to richer meaning for their own lives.

—for professionals, surcease from an increasingly negative community climate and, more positively, new allies in their task.

—for the children, a school system responsive to their needs, resonant with their personal style, and affirmative in its expectations of them.

And finally there is the goal of participation for its own sake, an intrinsic concomitant—and test—of democracy. Education could no doubt be conducted efficiently if it were contracted out as a technical service, without the furniture of lay boards, community relations, and so on, especially if quality is defined strictly in terms of grade-level achievement. But in an open society, the process of participation itself is a social and educational value, despite the inefficiencies it may entail.

This is more than an alternative approach to halting the spiral of public education's failure. It is a design for social reconstruction.

[4] See, for example, Basil Bernstein, "A Socio-linguistic Approach to Social Learning" in J. Gould (ed.), *Social Science Survey* (New York: Pelican, 1965).

Concepts of Bureaucracy In Urban School Reform

By Daniel U. Levine

The public school is a social system established to deliver good education to the students who attend it. Without quibbling about the definition of "good" education, let us assume that one major component is a minimal level of academic skills needed to compete successfully for rewarding employment. By this measure, many urban schools are unequivocally failing.

At another level of generality, most people would agree that a major goal of the public school is to teach students skills and attitudes needed for learning outside the school and for living satisfying lives as adults. Without implying that the schools in and of themselves can be held solely responsible for solving all the critical problems of urban society, it would be ludicrous to argue that most urban schools are succeeding in preparing students to live wisely and well in the bright new world (or, if you prefer, the new dark ages) of metropolitan complexity; to wit:, dropouts, copouts, throwouts, flunkouts, tuneouts, and freakouts littered all over the metropolitan landscape.

Thus, whatever else one may say about them, urban schools today generally are not functioning as outstandingly effective delivery systems in terms of some of their major purposes.

Roots of the Problems

To understand why urban schools frequently are not delivering adequate education, it is best to begin by recognizing that they are bureaucratic institutions in the classic meaning of the term as defined by Max Weber and other nineteenth century sociologists. That is, both within the school and within the larger educational system of which it is a part, roles are defined impersonally, numerous rules and expectations are codified to fit each role within a hierarchy of other roles, and fitness to fill a role is defined with reference to technical training and previous experience thought to be necessary to carry it out properly.

So far so good: The urban school is conceived in an effort to use rational planning and technical competence in the task of educating masses of citizens in an urban society. Where did it all go wrong?

Basically, the urban school as it is now organized and operated is a victim of the same forces and problems which are generating failure in other rational bureaucracies such as hospitals, social welfare agencies, industrial corporations, the military, and municipal service departments; it is not just in education that reformers are concerned with improving the structure

PHI DELTA KAPPAN, February 1971, pp. 329-333.

and performance of urban delivery systems. Among the most important of these problems are *institutional complexity and overload, goal displacement, deficiencies in communications and decision-making processes,* and *social and psychological distance between client and institution.*

This listing is not offered as an exhaustive catalogue of all the logically exclusive dysfunctions which rational bureaucracy is heir to, but it does call attention to some of the critical issues which reformers must specifically take into account in endeavoring to rebuild and revitalize urban schools.

Institutional complexity and overload refers to the tendency for institutions to be ineffective when their internal structures are too complicated to allow for adequate communications, or when the external frameworks in which they function are rendered inoperable by having too large a burden placed on them. In other words, the growing complexity of industrial society tends to make existing organizational structures and networks obsolete. Part of the problem is that a message retranslated 10 times is likely to be considerably more garbled than one transmitted directly to its recipient. Or, as was illustrated in the recent telephone crisis in New York City, the volume of messages may simply overwhelm available communications channels, making it necessary to tear out much of the existing system and replace it with new subsystems more adequate for the load.

Similar difficulties arise because multiplying the layers of complexity which exist in an organization tends to increase the number of points at which vested interests can counter organizational goals. In part, a complex institution becomes more vulnerable to dysfunctions merely because there are more places where things can go wrong — just as one comma out of place in a complicated computer program was responsible for the failure of a multi-million-dollar space probe.

In addition, adding layer upon layer to the organizational structure of modern society leads the individual to perceive the structure and his experience in it as artificial and unreal. Whether exemplified in the curriculum of the school, which becomes further and further removed from daily life, or in the impersonal humming of the Corporate State's computers, the byproducts of complexity become too abstract to be believed. The result, as Ortega y Gasset prophetically foresaw in *Man and Crisis,* is an exploding rejection of institutions and the philosophic presuppositions which undergird them. The whole complex structure begins to totter and topple under its own weight.

Associated with the problems of institutional complexity and overload are those of *goal displacement* in the operation of large-scale rational bureaucracies. Since bureaucratic organizations have been established to impose a degree of order on an otherwise unplanned and chaotic environment, there is a certain drive toward permanency and self-perpetuation at the heart of rational bureaucracy. When the goal of self-perpetuation begins to outweigh other purposes, we have one type of goal displacement. A second type occurs when staff members become more concerned with or adept at retaining their positions than with furthering the organization's stated goals. An example of the first type of goal displacement is the museum or art gallery which evaluates itself in terms of the number of people who pass through its turnstiles. The administrator who devotes much of his time to making his unit look good to his superordinates is an example of the second. It must be emphasized that goal displacement is not so much a result of the dishonorable intentions of human beings as of institutional tendencies toward regularizing the organization's resources and services. Donald J. Willower has illustrated some of these tendencies in education as follows:

> The age-grade placement of students, the division of the curriculum into subjects in company with the all-important schedule that parallels this division, and the classroom arrangement itself, are forms of routinization that speak to the massive logistics of educational organization. They make the enterprise more manageable, that is, they function to channel, order, and regularize the manner in which the organization attends and processes its clients.
>
> At the same time, such routinization reduces the likelihood of instruction geared to variations in client characteristics since procedures that accommodate unusual or unique client requirements are apt to be disruptive.
>
> A quite tangible routinized structure is found in the report card, perhaps the most common formal communication of the school to its patrons. An important feature of this document is that it calls attention to student defects, not to those of the school. No one is ever informed that a student is not up to par because he had the misfortune to draw a poor teacher, or because the curriculum is indifferent or unsuitable. In consequence, the organization is protected and the responsibility for barren performance is placed squarely on the client.[1]

Since an organization is most likely to be deflected from its reasons for existing when pertinent information on what is really happening is not available to decision makers and clients at the right time, *deficiencies in communications and decision-making processes* are closely related to the phenomenon of goal displacement. Many interrelations between inadequate communications, uninformed decision making, and organizational dysfunctioning are vividly illustrated in a series of essays by the British writer C. Northcote Parkinson, as well as in anecdotal records of urban schools such as Bel Kaufman's *Up the Down Staircase.*

One major impediment to communications and decision making which already has been mentioned is the simple multiplication of hierarchical levels without corresponding adjustments to ensure that the right information flows up and down the hierarchy to the right people at the right time. The most obvious immediate response to this problem is to reduce the number of hierarchical levels at which communications can be slowed or distorted and to allow for more fluidity in locating decision-making authority at differing levels in accordance with types of decisions to be made. When adequate adjustments are not made, institutions often continue to function largely as they did in the past, even though the environment has changed drastically and has outdated many of their operational rules and regulations.

Social and psychological distance between client and organization not only contributes to poor communications within an organization but also increases the likelihood that the organization will serve goals other than that of providing services to its clients. When the people who staff an organization and the people it serves have divergent values and personal histories, staff members and clients may not view the claims and expectations they press upon one another as legitimate and acceptable. Without a modicum of shared social experience and common psychological space between staff and clients, role incumbents may tend to

246

place personal interests such as tenure in the job over the interests of clients, and clients may be unwilling or even unable to utilize the institution's resources as they were intended to be used. Thus reduction of social and psychological distance between school personnel on the one hand and students and parents on the other is imperative if urban schools are to become more effective institutions. This problem seems to be growing as critical in predominantly middle-income schools as it already has become in low-income schools in the inner city.

Perhaps the most logical way to reduce social and psychological distance between organizations and their clients is to increase the clients' participation in decision-making processes within an organization. Although the term "participatory democracy" recently has become something of a slogan, it is a concept that can do much to help rebuild and reinvigorate urban schools. Participation of clients as well as wider participation of employees in decision-making processes can help to make an organization seem less complex and can contribute to the beneficial flow of information and feedback; in both these ways participation can enhance an institution's legitimacy and minimize tendencies toward goal displacement.

The difficulties involved in overcoming bureaucratic dysfunctioning should not be minimized. For example, reducing the number of hierarchical levels and providing for more client and staff participation in decision making easily generate new forms of goal displacement and additional communications distortion. The introduction of technologically advanced communications processes and equipment may increase the psychological distance between clients and staff or between staff members at different levels of the organization. Thus gains

in one direction frequently seem to entail losses in other directions, and reform-minded administrators end up confronting what may turn out to be almost insoluble dilemmas. The problems of rebuilding urban schools are not about to be solved through the application of a few glib generalizations.

Much more could be said about any or all of these themes and their implications for urban schools. A recent issue of this volume of the *Kappan*, for example, was devoted to the specific topic of accountability, which is intimately tied to the larger topic of organizational dysfunctioning in the schools. Many variations on these themes can and should be explored in redesigning educational programs as well as in theory and research on urban education. Decentralization, community control, performance contracting, voucher plans, and other topics could be fruitfully examined at length in terms of the concept of bureaucracy. The focus in this issue, however, is on the rebuilding of the urban school as an institution, and these related topics are introduced only incidentally as they bear on the focus. It is apparent that new ways of looking at and organizing bureaucracies are needed if urban schools are to grapple successfully with the myriad problems that beset them on all fronts. Several such perspectives selected from among the many that might be included in a longer paper are reviewed in the next section.[2]

New Perspectives on Bureaucracy

One useful way to highlight differences between newer and more traditional approaches to bureaucratic organization is to distinguish, as Berton H. Kaplan does, between rational, efficiency-oriented bureaucracy and "development" bureaucracy.[3] The latter, according to Kaplan, is an organization whose major concern is with development, as contrasted with an overbearing emphasis on efficiency. This does not mean, of course, that development bureaucracies are unconcerned with efficiency; obviously the question of utilizing resources economically cannot simply be ignored. What the term does suggest is that some organizations have as their predominant goal the "management of change, that is, the direction of efforts to alter the basic pattern(s) of a way of life," rather than a more direct focus on the attainment of predetermined output goals.[4]

Organizations which must put emphasis on development before it is possible to make much progress in satisfying efficiency criteria include those in which paramount importance is attached to socialization of clients into new roles. Socialization goals are overriding when the organization is not in a position to achieve its output goals because it is not able to work effectively with its clients. Examples cited by Kaplan include organizations functioning in environments in which social disorganization and disintegration are widespread and organizations heavily constrained by "enduring child-rearing frustrations, motivational problems, learning problems, problem-solving inadequacies, etc."[5] Urban schools, it should be evident, are (or should be) particularly good examples of development bureaucracies inasmuch as their first imperatives are to socialize students in productive learning roles and to reduce incongruence between client and institutional expectations. It is easy to conclude that this in turn requires a more "client-centered" approach, but to leave the matter at that is harmful, because doing so allows the naive to conclude that problems can be solved simply by being humane to clients (e.g., love and respect the child and give him something called "freedom"). The thesis of

this paper and indeed of this issue of the *Kappan*, however, is that the real challenge is to reorganize and reform existing organizations so that institutional structures and processes achieve the goal without relying solely on the good intentions of professionals or other staff personnel.

Orion F. White has spelled out some of the implications of this position for administrative structures within bureaucratic organizations. He argues cogently that a client-centered orientation is most likely to be achieved and maintained by allocating authority to roles in accordance with "functional necessity." Authority relations, in this type of organization, are "lateral instead of vertical," and staff relations are specifically organized in accordance with the principle of "nondominance." Structurally, such an organization "operates with overlapping administrative roles, in that one person may be over another in one functional area but under him in another area."[6] The primary purpose of these adjustments is to make it less likely that traditional efficiency criteria and rigid hierarchies will obscure the "helping relation" and lead to segmental treatment of the client.[7]

Eugene Litwak and Henry J. Meyer have carried this type of analysis still further in an important theoretical paper titled "A Balance Theory of Coordination Between Bureaucratic Organizations and Community Primary Groups."[8] Litwak and Meyer begin by rejecting the notion that bureaucracies (such as the school) and primary groups (such as the family) should be viewed as "alternative means for the achievement of most goals." They admit that bureaucracies and primary groups have "unique social functions" and characteristics which make them "incompatible" and even "antithetical" in some respects, but they also believe that the two kinds of social units must perform complementary functions if there is to be "optimal" social control and goal achievement. Hence they conclude that there should be "close communication between these two forms of organizations and that one of the major tasks of organization theory is to select the most suitable "coordinating mechanisms" to achieve proper balance.[9]

Although the argument in Litwak and Meyer's paper is subtly developed at much greater length, for the purposes of this essay it is sufficient to emphasize implications pertinent to the topic of rebuilding urban schools. Of special interest are their conclusions concerning 1) organizations "confronted with deviant families or neighborhood groups" and hence in need of "some mechanism of coordination that permits communication over social distance"; and 2) organizations "confronted by both distant and supporting primary groups" and hence in need "of a range of coordinating mechanisms."[10] The inner-city elementary school with a particularly alienated constituency probably comes closest in education to fitting the first situation; the comprehensive urban high school is a good example of the second.

In the first situation, Litwak and Meyer conclude, emphasis should be placed on 1) working with local opinion leaders in the client community; 2) delegating functions as much as possible to associated groups with presumably better access to primary units among clients; 3) a "settlement-house" approach which locates physical facilities and services in the client community and makes change agents available to work there; and 4) a "detached-expert" approach which gives professionals in the organization "relative autonomy" to participate directly in the affairs of external primary groups.[11]

In the second situation, emphasis should be placed on selecting a situa-tionally appropriate mixture of the coordinating mechanisms described above plus traditional rational-bureaucratic coordinating mechanisms such as 1) sponsorship of voluntary associations bringing organization personnel and clients together in a formal setting (e.g., PTA's); 2) utilization as a "common messenger" of an individual who is regularly a member of both the organization and the primary group (e.g., the child); 3) utilization of formal authority as a "basis for communicating with external primary groups"; and 4) employment of mass communications media as a means to influence primary groups.[12]

The final point in Litwak and Meyer's paper is one it would pay us well to particularly keep in mind in education. After noting that some organizations have a better base than others for linking to the community, the authors point out that *"if an organization is not self-conscious about its coordinating mechanisms"* (italics added), then it will tend to communicate with primary groups using the common messenger and the opinion leader mechanisms, because these mechanisms develop informally and require little or no initiative from the organization.[13] This is precisely, of course, what has happened in education: Most public schools have relied on the child and on a few visible, presumably influential persons in the community for communications with constituent primary groups. That abdicating responsibility in this way has led to the bankruptcy of many urban schools is hardly open to question.

Comments and Conclusions

The material in the first section of this paper suggests that efforts to reform urban schools should: 1) aim to rebuild them as less complex institutions and/or equip clients and staff with better ways to handle institutional complexity; 2) reduce social and psychological distance between clients and the institution, particularly by increasing student and parent participation in decision making; and 3) provide specifically for additional information feedback in every aspect of the operation of the school.

The material on concepts of bureaucracy suggests that 1) urban schools should place major emphasis on gaining the cooperation of their clients rather than first using traditional efficiency criteria to allocate institutional roles and assess institutional processes; 2) this type of client-centered, service orientation is most likely to be achieved and maintained when authority is allocated laterally rather than hierarchically and organizational structures are experimental and fluid rather than fixed and permanent; and 3) urban educators should self-consciously select a situation-specific mixture of outreach-type as well as traditional communications mechanisms to coordinate the work of the school and the external primary groups whose cooperation is required to achieve the goals of education.

Some related points which should be made concerning the rebuilding of urban schools in general and inner-city schools in particular are that:

1. Making authority relations in a school or school district less "vertical" in order to place certain necessary decision-making powers and responsibilities in the hands of staff members who work directly with clients has little to do explicitly with "democratic" administration (whatever that is). As Fiedler has shown in an important but frequently ignored study on leadership, situations which are highly problematic for an organization create a need for administrators who supply relatively "structured" leadership.[14] To put it mildly, urban schools today are highly problematic institutions.

2. For this reason, outstanding ad- ministrative leadership is by far the most important variable necessary for successful reform in urban schools. Successful inner-city schools invariably have particularly outstanding building administrators who absolutely refuse to engage in bureaucratic games of any sort.[15]

3. The critical importance of the **building principal** is closely linked to the cherished dream of individualization of instruction. On the one hand it is an obvious truth that instruction for disadvantaged students cannot possibly be successful without individualized diagnosis and prescription of students' strengths and weaknesses. On the other hand it is also a truism that individualized instruction has seldom been achieved in schools anywhere in the United States. One thing that outstanding inner-city administrators have in common is that they organize their schools so that methods and materials actually are utilized to individualize instruction and then insist that nothing – but *nothing* – will be allowed to prevent achievement of this goal. Visitors to their schools can expect to hear of such incidents as the following two reports from unusually successful schools:

"My teachers were supposed to be attending a district-wide workshop that summer, but we found they could not achieve anything in these large groups so I pulled them out and brought them back to the school to work in small groups on planning for the next year."

"Our excellent new programmed reading materials were not working very well, mainly because teachers and aides had no space to work together on planning or to meet with students individually or in small groups. So the principal increased class size – the central office never found out — in order to free space for this purpose."

4. Much of the principal's leadership in establishing lateral authority relations can be discussed in terms of what he does to provide each party (i.e., teachers, students, parents) with a firm power base in school decision making. Once each group is in a position to stand up and say, "I know from direct experience that the way we are doing things is not working and I insist it be changed," the orientation in the school becomes one of solving problems rather than keeping the lid on or sweeping them under the rug. In a successful inner-city school, in other words, "End the nonsense" is the operating theme not just of the principal but of every interest group.

5. Urban schools should be built up of (or broken down into) small, relatively autonomous operating units. It is not important whether functional units are referred to as "houses," "grade levels," "families," "mini-branches," or some other term, as long as authority and responsibility are located primarily at the unit level and units are supplied with the resources and supporting services necessary to carry out their tasks.

6. The crucial factor in making use of promising practices from another school is to make sure that the organizational structure of the receiving institution is designed to implement the innovation effectively. For example, the receiving structure must be modified to ensure continuous feedback across hierarchical levels, to minimize psychological distance between staff and clients, and to maintain a client-centered service orientation, or promising practices borrowed either eclectically or as a total package from outside sources are not going to make very much difference.

7. Urban schools are not going to

be rebuilt as effective institutions unless we first sweep the deck of existing organizational structures and practices which constitute fundamental obstacles to the attainment of educational goals. As Morris Janowitz points out in the following paper, specialists and technologists have a vital and indispensable part to play in reforming urban education, but piling more specialists and new technologies on top of an already overloaded institutional structure will compound rather than alleviate our problems. What all this boils down to is the old rule of first things first — and the first priority in urban education is to introduce new concepts of organization and bureaucracy that emphasize the creation of authentic institutional communities, so that specialization and technique are not plugged into essentially dysfunctional vessels.

Emphasis in most of the following papers is placed on the difficult practical problems encountered in building or rebuilding an institution and on the crucial decisions made in solving them. In describing specific problems involved in implementing effective programs in urban schools, the authors show how the concepts reviewed in this paper are being applied in different ways in different schools. It is hoped that this combination of conceptual analysis and practical examples will prove useful for teachers and administrators impatient to rebuild their own schools.

---

[1] Donald J. Willower, "Educational Change and Functional Equivalents," *Education and Urban Society,* August, 1970, p. 392; see also Alan Schick, "The Cybernetic State," *Trans-Action,* February, 1970, pp. 15-26.

[2] Examples of other perspectives which it was not possible to include in this paper include Warren Bennis' writing on post-bureaucratic, temporary organization and Kenneth Parsons' analysis of needs-cycling organizations.

[3] Berton H. Kaplan, "Notes on a Non-Weberian Model of Bureaucracy: The Case

251

of Development Bureaucracy," *Administrative Science Quarterly*, December, 1968, pp. 471-83.

[4]*Ibid.*, p. 472.

[5]*Ibid.*, p. 482.

[6]Orion F. White, Jr., "The Dialectical Organization: An Alternative to Bureaucracy," *Public Administration Review*, January-February, 1969, p. 38.

[7]*Ibid.*, pp. 36-37.

[8]Eugene Litwak and Henry J. Meyer, "A Balance Theory of Coordination Between Bureaucratic Organizations and Community Primary Groups," *Administrative Science Quarterly*, June, 1966, pp. 31-58.

[9]*Ibid.*, pp. 36, 58. In effect, Litwak and Meyer reject the arguments of social analysts such as Everett Riemer and Ivan Illich who suggest that noncognitive goals should have little place in the schools since they are more effectively achieved in primary-group settings (*Alternatives in Education, 1968-69*. Cuernavaca, Mexico: Central Intercultural Documentacion, 1970) and of psychologists like J. M. Stephens (*The Process of Schooling*. New York: Holt, Rinehart and Winston, 1967) who believe that school-

ing in modern educational bureaucracies is too far removed from real life to be effective in interesting more than a minority of the young in abstract academic studies. Although there is no space in this essay to weigh all the arguments for and against these points of view, it at least can be said that unless existing educational bureaucracies are significantly transformed and unless this rebuilding includes new mechanisms for coordination and communication with primary groups in the urban community, observers such as Riemer, Illich, and Stephens probably will be proved right by default.

[10]*Ibid.*, pp. 51-52.

[11]*Ibid.*, pp. 39, 42, 52, 53.

[12]*Ibid.*, pp. 40, 41, 50, 53.

[13]*Ibid.*, p. 57.

[14]Fred A. Fiedler, "A Contingency Model of Leadership Effectiveness," in L. Berkowitz, ed., *Advances in Experimental Social Psychology*. New York: Academic Press, 1964, vol. 1.

[15]Russell C. Doll, *Variations Among Inner City Elementary Schools*. Kansas City, Mo.: Center for the Study of Metropolitan Problems in Education, 1969.

THE URBAN SECONDARY SCHOOL:
TOO LATE FOR MERE CHANGE

Francis S. Moseley

It scarcely needs argument that a great deal of dissatisfaction exists with the current purposes, the present direction, and the recent results of secondary education. The wide acclaim for our high schools that greeted their expansion to the service of older age groups in the late twenties and early thirties has long since abated. For several decades now, the usual public comment about secondary education has been that it has failed. Civil rights promoters tell us that, at best, the high school's form of organization perpetuates segregation and that, at worst, its teachers actively refuse to teach minority-group youngsters. The civil libertarians would have us believe that the secondary school exists partly to trample the legal rights of teen-agers. The romantics inform us that its methods are hidebound and obscurantist. The activists among its students roundly denounce it as irrelevant to their needs. Everywhere, talk is heard of the necessity for "quality education" (the term reminds one of a department store sale), for the upgrading of "inferior" schools, and for the equalization of educational services.

That these criticisms reflect a real and important problem, no one with even a cursory acquaintance with our high schools could deny. That they represent anything like an accurate diagnosis of what is wrong is quite another matter. The mirror of criticism in which we are shown our American high schools is a badly flawed one which distorts more than it reveals, which is pointed in the wrong direction, which highlights the aberrant aspects of the image, and which affords an imperfect and unreliable design upon which to impose a plan for desirable change.

PHI DELTA KAPPAN, May 1972, pp. 559-564.

Let us submit this judgment to the test of the facts by going to the point where the critical storm rages loudest, the large city. It is here, in urban and suburban America, that the vast bulk of our population congregates and where by far the larger portion of our youth goes to school. Let us take one such city, New York, which I know best, as a sample of the urban school scene. Here, against impossible odds, many a high school continues to operate an effective and worthwhile program, but the achievement must be a surreptitious one, without the support of officialdom and without the knowledge of the public. Other, less happy schools have succumbed to the destructive forces around them. On balance, the net result must be assessed as downward. But our New York schools did not decay. They did not slowly lose a sense of purpose. Their ethical sense did not imperceptibly corrode, degree by degree. To the extent that they suffered deterioration, they were the victims, not of gradual dissolution, but of deliberate vandalism. They were destroyed — those that were destroyed — by warfare.

The attacking columns may be enumerated as follows:

1. Political attitudes were substituted for academic attitudes, and the attempt was made to reduce education to a merely governmental function.

2. Lay (and therefore ignorant) administration of the schools resulted in gross mismanagement. Inept cover-up of the mismanagement led farther and farther into still more mismanagement.

3. Propagandistic techniques in public relations led to wholesale misinformation about the schools so that they became impenetrable to intelligent criticism or to clearheaded reform.

4. The normative function of the schools, as giving ethical and moral guidance and contributing to the formation of character, was first abandoned and then denounced.

5. Without governance from within or friendly support from without, the schools, even though still nominally public institutions, became to a considerable extent available to private spoliation and exploitation. This was accomplished through a device sanctimoniously named decentralization and local control.

In the cultural revolution which has been sweeping America (one wonders whether cultural is the right word), the schools were the first target of those who wished to uproot the old order. This was because they were the most vulnerable, because their leadership was least tough-minded, because violence could be done them with greater assurance of impunity than it could any other institution. It is the ghetto school, where such interference with education is most common, which, unhappily, suffers most from the assault. And it is in just such schools, of course, that youngsters stand most in need of peaceful and workmanlike schooling. To march into a public school with a small group of determined militants and to arrogate to oneself the authority to keep it open or to shut it down, to use its students for one's own political purposes, to stand in the schoolhouse door and bar entrance to others, to seize the principal and hold him prisoner, to boycott the institution, to vandalize its property, occasionally even to burn it to the ground — all these are illegal actions. But they have been commonplace, even daily occurrences for years. They go generally unpunished and sometimes unremarked.

This is largely because of fear on the part of school and public officials that they will suffer a loss of popularity, of political acceptability, if they act otherwise than they do. The cultural pluralism of which we were wont to boast is fled. In its place has come a tacit acceptance of the lowest subculture, the point of view and the line of action of the street brawler and the neighborhood terrorist. Those in authority may still permit themselves to deplore such attitudes in private conversation, but in their public stance they cooperate with them and, doing so, they produce a *sub rosa* cultural homogeneity which plunges all of society, and most shamefully our schools, into something several degrees lower than simple mediocrity.

What is happening is the application of political method to the school problem. Accustomed to pursuing the tactics of bargaining and of trading, even of capitulating entirely when a position becomes untenable, the political mind makes an easy translation of the same techniques to the schools. It is a system that works well enough in its own field. It permits legislative bodies to carry out their task.

255

It brought the very Constitution of the United States to birth. It solves dock strikes. It is operative in our electoral processes. But these are purely **practical matters and their management yields to purely pragmatic procedures. The business of schools, on the other hand, belongs to a quite different order of human activity. It is full of issues** that cannot be compromised. The particular devices by which senators are elected are not derivable from any eternal verities. But what, and how, and, above all, whether a child is taught in school are questions more deeply plunged into the essences of things. The stars remain in their courses when we change our political forms; not so when we teach our children shiftlessness, or violence, or contempt for reason.

The political bureaucracy (political in the sense just described) installed in the offices of the Board of Education – in New York where its personnel numbers in the tens of thousands, or in other places where hopefully it is smaller – should not be merely an object of amused contempt. It should be regarded as a positive evil, as a malignant influence on the lives of young people, as essentially inimical to education. It is the spiritual heir of the Athenian cabal which brought about the death of Socrates. If education is a public service, it is so only by sufferance and by financial necessity. There is nothing about its nature, its purposes, its methods, or its characteristic atmosphere which brackets it with the police function, with street cleaning, with foreign diplomacy, or with law suits. When politics qua politics invades it, education is destroyed.

For these reasons, the undue intrusion of legislatures and courts, quasi-legislatures and quasi-courts, into the affairs of schools is mischievous. In New York's schools, for example, students in disciplinary difficulties are accorded many of the same rights adult defendants are granted when tried, in peril of their lives or their liberty, in our criminal courts. No longer is the management of pupil behavior a guidance concern. It is invested with all the formalism of a courtroom procedure. Voluminous papers are filed. Lengthy hearings are held. Witnesses are called and cross-examined. Appeals are taken. "Lawyers" are permitted to represent their "clients." Any parent who comes to school to talk about his child's educational progress, or any other matter, may bring a lay attorney with him to advise him at every step of his conversation and, in many cases, to provoke as much controversy and ill feeling as he can. This list of pseudo-legalisms could be extended indefinitely. Indeed, it is hard to think of a conventional rule that might be expected to govern student conduct which the Board of Education or the superintendent (now the chancellor) has not abrogated by a specific interdiction. A recent howler among these was an order (since recalled) to refrain from sending out any recommendation, reference, or any piece of information, good or bad, about any student without the explicit consent, in each instance, of the parent. More recently, it has been enacted that no student may be denied a diploma for any behavior, however reprehensible. "Scholarship" alone is criterion.

In this situation there are days, and even weeks, when every moment of the principal's time is required for hearings on disciplinary matters, hearings on grievances, required meetings and conferences without number, all on the pattern of the legislative committee or the law court. Educational concerns are effectively smothered out.

Another aspect of essentially the same problem of political orientation arises around the selection and appointment of teachers and supervisors, undoubtedly the central question with which education has to deal. Good teachers, everything else apart, make good schools; poor teachers, poor schools. How are we to get good teachers, keep them, and use them to maximum effectiveness? New York City had a unique and absolutely nonpolitical device for accomplishing this, or at least the recruitment and selection phases of the process. It is one that, along with other excellences of our schools, has been systematically pillaged. It was the Board of Examiners, an agency which tested prospective teachers, licensed the successful candidates, and placed them on ranked eligible lists from which appointments were made in order. This function, still exercised in a pro forma way, has been reduced to a pale shadow of its former vigor. The lists, when published, have been ignored. In the high schools the examination system had become so attenuated that it would be difficult indeed to fail many of the examinations given. In the case of elementary and middle schools there have been instances of persons' literally being invited in off the streets by community boards to staff classrooms. These people are without any vestige of official qualification either in the form of a license from the Board of Examiners or a certificate from the State Department of Education.

In the effort to phase out the examiners, an effort well along the way toward completion, part of the damage was done by courts in response to legal actions brought against the examiners. The rest was accomplished by the Board of Education's deliberate forfeiting of such cases, or by their ignoring of published eligible lists, or by other circumventions of the merit system. The use of the courts to write administrative rules for the schools, for the supervision of the most detailed matters of student conduct, and even for local ceremonial, has become a tedious, repetitious nuisance. The thing follows a well-worn rut: Some outrage is committed in a school; a local penalty is assessed upon the culprit by the principal; the youngster goes to court for an injunction against the action; the board abandons the case; the injunction sought is granted by default. A new administrative rule is applied to a million school children.

The indigenous student governments, formerly democratically operated in each school, have been abolished in favor of a new system, imposed by decree and supervised by a central office. Extra-curricular activities, keyed to these student associations, have generally withered and died. Concurrently, it has been determined that students have all but complete freedom in what they say in the school publications that still exist. They have similar freedom in the distribution of handbills and literature in and around the school. They may organize for almost any purpose, however "unpopular," and use public resources to further their ends. They need not salute the flag or sing the national anthem. As a result of endless technicalities, they may usually not be effectively suspended from school even in the direst emergency. In short, student life has been refashioned to suit only the desires of the dissident; other students simply ignore it.

Other communities across the land have had different experiences in this general area. But most have had some similar experience. The issues are local, but the change in national educational philosophy is pandemic. The end result is everywhere the same. You may turn a school into a legislature, or into a law court, or into a political bureau if you wish, but the price is this: Your school ceases to exist as a school.

There seems nothing wrong with lay control of our public schools. This has been a long and respected tradition in the United States and one which has given the voter and taxpayer a feeling of involvement in and concern for the processes by which the young are trained and brought to maturity. This control was traditionally a highly restricted one, affecting mainly financial affairs, the selection and employment of a superintendent, and a very general policy making. The actual administration of schools was always left to a professional staff. This is not so in New York any longer and it is not so in a great many other places. In education, no less than in other fields, the layman has become the expert, and the expert has become his adjutant. For example, in New York, appeals from disciplinary decisions on student conduct are heard by a board member and decisions (often in the form of a reversal) are written over his name.

Unfortunately, the confrontation syndrome which affects so much in urban life, which exacerbates ethnic tensions and intensifies racial polarities, is imported into the schools via the very process by which these lay-politicians-turned-educational-administrators are selected and appointed. Unofficially, qualifications both for the board posts themselves and for the jobs in the schools which it is in the power of boards to confer are blatantly stated in terms of racial affiliation. No educational good can come of this.

The substitution of public image for hard fact has become so complete in certain circles that we lose the reality entirely and work only from the fabricated symbol. It is a human failing, this replacement of *is* with *seems*. After Hamlet warns against it, he too falls victim to the same mental quirk: "Assume a virtue if you have it not." Our school politicians have out-Hamleted Hamlet; they wish to assume a vice if they have it not.

Does some pressure group make some outrageously false charge against school administration? The unalterable rule is that it is not and can never be denied. Yes indeed, the public is told, we have sinned. We have sinned and we will mend our ways. We do indeed, miserable wretches that we are, discriminate ruthlessly against minority children, we do indeed fail to prepare them for college, we do indeed give them poor advice and ill-considered counseling. Our curriculum is antiquated, our methods quaint. Our buildings are in sad disrepair, dangerous to boot, firetraps as well. This line of response, it is fatuously assumed, will disarm anger and pacify aggression. It cannot possibly do either because there is no anger, only feigned anger; and no aggression, only a ferocious mask designed to gain power. But what it can do, this supineness, and do quite well, is convince the general public that the schools are quite as bad as their public guardians admit them to be.

If this ruse does not have effect enough, there is another ready to hand: It is to permit the mixing of the two meanings of the word *school* so that the school building and the institution that goes by the same name become the same thing. (The title "building principal," outside of New York, tends to reinforce the same confusion.) Thereafter, it is a very simple matter to tell a good school from a bad one. A good school is one housed in a handsome building; a poor school, the opposite. Yet those who are sensitive to good classroom practice and who have had the opportunity to observe it in a great variety of localities are often convinced that, in a great many cases, this test is an absurd one.

It is as absurd as a great number of other attempts to improve the high schools by applying quantitative or mechanical standards to a problem which is, at bottom, qualitative and intangible. The notion that education is a commodity which can be weighed and measured like wheat or coal, priced like potatoes, bought and sold like automobiles, is implicit in such projects as performance contracting with its incentive payments for guaranteed learning. It is implicit in the concept of "accountability," the idea that it is the teacher alone who is responsible for whether or not the learner learns, an idea which turns reason around and stands the whole teaching

260

process on its head. It is an integral component of most teacher union contracts, documents which strive mightily to relate teaching effectiveness inversely to the number of hours a teacher works, to an attenuation of nonclassroom responsibilities, and, of course, to an automatically escalating salary schedule. These may often be desirable economic gains, but they have little to do with the quality of the services teachers render. Still less do the thousands of other quantitative specifics of school administration, down to the tiniest and most preposterously insignificant detail, which are written into such agreements and which make school management a labyrinth of negotiation and bickering and each school day an exercise in polemics. For this unhealthy situation, both signatories to such contracts are to blame and the employer much more than the employee.

It should be noted, in passing, that collective bargaining is an entirely singular process as it applies to teacher unions. In industry the union bargains with management and both operate under the terms of the contract during its life. In school negotiations the daily chore of management is carried out by the principal, but he has no effective voice in the bargaining. Those who do, the members of the board, construct and sign the contract as if they were going to be party to its implementation. But once it is signed, they become arbitrators or middlemen between the principal and the teachers, a role in which their assumed impartiality becomes an anomaly and makes possible continuous renegotiation of what should be a stable set of rules. This situation is doing its part, and a major part it is, to render the city school educationally inoperative. Into the same category, that of inordinately mechanical devices, may often be placed the teaching machine, the language laboratory, and other expensive electronic or computerized teaching programs. One would not wish to argue that these items do not have their utilities, even unique ones, especially in their functions of reinforcement and of individual drill. But we must begin to take issue with the concept that, singly or in combination, they can ever substitute for the human meeting of minds which is the teaching process properly so called.

261

In New York, and I suspect in other metropolitan areas, there has all but fully emerged now, in unembarrassed candor, the doctrine that the behavior of pupils is no concern of the school. The school's function, whatever it is, does not include the inculcation of moral principle, or any monitoring of conduct, or any attempt to develop character. Our friends in the colleges have traveled this road before us, with what justification and what results each must judge for himself. The prognosis for its leading to success with teen-agers must give the boldest pause. While this no-prescription ethic is being preached, and practiced without being preached, crime and violence among the young continue to mount. Incidents of disruption of the school's program by its own students continue to be reported. It has been suggested that the cause of this is to be found in the internal practices of the schools themselves, in their methodology, in their poorly constructed courses of study, in the failure of school people to relate warmly to the young.

There is a simpler and a more persuasive explanation. Pupils are not disruptive because they are not well taught. They are disruptive because superintendents of schools and boards of education have taught them to be disruptive. (The greatest compliment we can pay our young people is to point out how relatively few have accepted the lesson.) They do not absent themselves from school because they are not loved. They stay away because, as in New York, the superintendent of schools appears on television and invites them to play hooky in order to engage in some political activity. They do not beat teachers because they are irritated by the irrelevance of the curriculum; they do not engage in the narcotics traffic only as some symptomatic outgrowth of a deeper psychological urge. Those who do these things do them because those in the highest positions in our school systems often encourage them.

The encouragement takes many forms. By far the most effective is the device of treating the perpetrators of similar crimes with such laxity as to give the assurance of safety to those who would repeat them. Another is the practice of responding to violent confrontation by simply repealing the regulation that is defied. In New York, this places the principal in the unhappy position of attempting, against bitter odds, to enforce one of the board's own rules while, behind his back, the board itself is undermining its own authority and his.

There is a defense for this, as there is for everything. It is the theory that what is wrong with our schools is an excess of regimentation and repression. The cure for the defect is simply to accord even greater freedom to the young. All evils are attributed to the one cause and all remedies are prescribed with the same medicine. The medicine is itself an ethical system and a code of conduct. It is a preachment quite as much as were our more conventional admonitions against cutting classes, tardiness, insolence to one's teacher, dishonesty with examinations, and similar schoolboy infractions. It constitutes a very powerfully motivated list of *do*'s and *don't*'s, those which are approved by what has come to be called the power structure. Moreover, the new ethic represents even more than this; it represents a meeting of minds across the generation gap, not, to be sure, with the young in general, but with their least worthy spokesmen.

We continue to tell one another that the young are merely acting out ancient and predictable reactions to their elders' constraints. It is a lie. We continue, in the face of the terrible degradation many of our children are plunging themselves into, to exculpate them, and thereby ourselves. We have made doing one's own thing the new global religion, theirs and ours. In this way, the gulf across the generations has been bridged indeed. We blind ourselves to the obvious fact that we have accepted a philosophy of anti-intellectualism and anti-culturalism. As we rush headlong into a new dark age, we sing the praises of our coming emancipation while we forge our own mental and spiritual fetters. In this madness, those who have charge of education are active and merry participants. It is they who are, too often, at the entering wedge of anarchy. If the schools and the civilization which depends on the schools are to be saved, this destructiveness must be blunted and arrested.

With the abdication on the part of the New York City board of responsibility for the management of essential educational services, with the cultivation by them, instead, of various partisan and doctrinaire pursuits, with their retreat into the trivia of administrative detail where they have no competence, a whole train of abuses has followed. Aware of this, and bowing to pressure for neighborhood control of the schools, the state legislature has twice revamped the central board, transferring many of its powers to smaller local boards, first turning over all the schools to the new boards, then later returning the high schools to central control, a control from which they are once again to be removed in the near future. We have a good example here of a favorite method of educational "reform," a reform which proceeds by rearranging the line and staff diagram but which leaves essentials unchanged. Leaderless before the change, the schools remain leaderless after it because leadership itself is frustrated by a bureaucracy which contemns it on principle.

Local power brokers, cultists, racially motivated leaders, and pseudo-civil-rights activists have snarled and clawed at each other over issues such as which of them (with no slightest show of legality) can select a new principal or discharge an old one. When they should have been attending classes, youngsters have been pressed into illegal service by these people to mount protests or to engage in demonstrations. Lately, student "representatives," chosen by pressure groups, in a move ultimately approved by the board itself, have been assisting with the selection of new high school principals. The de-academizing of the schools has come full circle. Those who were the clients become the practitioners. The disciple plays the master. The mentor is tutored, the untutored is mentor.

A public facility, supported by general taxation and presumed to serve the body politic in the most disinterested and high-minded way, becomes instead the private stamping ground of demagogues. The high school, in too many cases, has become an institution no one wants to attend. Students have disappeared from its classrooms by the thousands and have become perennial truants whom no attendance official bothers any longer to trace. The turnover of teaching personnel is frighteningly rapid. During the past few years, a sizable percentage, perhaps half, of the hundred-odd high school principals have resigned or retired. It is a fact carefully avoided that the sharp plunge in school attendance was contemporaneous with the most recent teacher strike. When the strike was over, battalions of pupils never returned. One wonders whether any justification for a teacher strike could countervail this appalling circumstance.

The usual suggestions for the cure of the ills of the secondary school come either to 1) more money or, what comes to the same thing, more teachers, a smaller pupil load, more apparatus and gadgetry; or 2) new and better organizations or rearrangements of things: the school day or the school year, the elements of the curriculum, the administrative flow chart, and so on. I suggest that we have tried both remedies for a long time and in massive doses and that they have not accomplished results. What we have not tried is to get reform at the point where education takes place, at the synapse which connects the mature mind of an alert and dedicated teacher with the immature but motivated mind of the learner. To do this, we must alter teacher training and selection on the one hand and pupil conditioning and management on the other. But this will not avail unless we first sweep away a number of secondary obstacles which prevent our dealing with these primary issues. To sweep them away, some such program as this is needed, radical and utopian as it very likely is:

1. Politicians, professional politicians but especially amateur neighborhood politicians, labor politicians, and all others with axes to grind must be **rigorously isolated from the educational pork barrel**.

2. In many places, high schools as they find themselves today, in early 1972, must be discontinued by being phased out. If they are not, they will discontinue themselves, as some of our urban schools have, in effect, already done.

3. New institutions under competent, upright, and, above all, scholarly leadership must be inaugurated to supplant them.

4. A new staff, entirely divorced in administrative control from the old (but not necessarily made up of different personnel) must be chosen to serve in them.

5. State education laws must be radically rewritten to accomplish this.

6. Local government (and other governments as well) must be thoroughly excluded from any *direct*

connection with the operation of schools.

7. The old board-of-education government of schools must give way to a single commissioner solely responsible for operation and powerful enough to be placed above all factional pressure.

8. The principal must be made relatively autonomous in his school, and the teacher, an impregnable authority in his classroom. Both must be willing to accept the responsibility this authority implies.

9. School strikes, school boycotts, and organized school disruptions must be legally prohibited. More important, some way must be found to see to it that public officials are made to enforce such prohibitions.

10. Courts must cease interfering in the daily administration of schools, except, of course, as to the application of the general civil and criminal law where it applies. The notion that the child's relationship to his teacher is a matter to go to law about must be laid to permanent rest — by constitutional change if need be. The status of the school as being *in loco parentis* must be reestablished beyond any possible successful assault.

That it is possible to draw up so long a list of malpractices in urban and other secondary schools should not blind us to the undoubted excellences of which so many of them can still boast. Many continue to be orderly and quiet halls of learning even under the tremendous harassment to which they are being subjected. The great potential they have in numbering among their staffs so many exemplary individuals to whom teaching once seemed a career of service and an opportunity to raise the general level of their fellow-men; the tremendous energy that has been ploughed into reinvestigations of the learning process and into highly innovative programs of instruction; the great reservoir of public support for public education, not yet dissipated after so many assaults; the movement for greater self-direction in learning among young people, a good thing in itself if not allowed to operate in the absence of adult guidance, these and many more elements of the educational patrimony are available to us to assist with a new forward movement. The plea made here is that we dynamite away identifiable roadblocks so that these forces may not continue to be frustrated.

CHAPTER VII: THE COMMUNITY TAKES CONTROL

In urban communities throughout almost all areas of the United States in the past decade there have been movements by poor people to grasp hold of some of the power that controls their lives. The "powerless" have attempted to gain some say about how the welfare programs will be operated and local government agencies will cater to their needs. This grasp for community control by the formerly "powerless" urban people perhaps furnishes us with a view into the future of urban areas. Perhaps the days of frustration and cultural stripping of urban migrants has begun to decline and an emergence of a true urban community is beginning to take place.

This awakening of the urban dwellers to active participation in the institutions that affect their lives has even reached into the schools. In fact, in many cases, the urban dwellers have seen the school as about the only urban institution they can get a real hold on. The reason for their efforts is quite understandable since in the eyes of these people the way out of poverty is through education for their children--an education that will make them competitive in the world of work in urban areas.

Many urban educators actively fight this movement by the community toward valid input into the urban schools because of the supposed lack of educational expertise possessed by the community people. The argument goes that educators who are specially trained in the learning process should be the ones making the decisions about what is going to be taught and how it is going to be taught. Is this true democracy? And, how can the educators claim the right to control the education of urban children when they have failed so miserably in the past? There is little doubt that urban schools and urban educators have not met the needs of urban children in the past. Their efforts toward righting this basic moral wrong has been to administer the same medicine to the children in stronger doses. The rub is, that if the medicine does not work the first time, what assurance is there that it will work upon increasing the dosage?

Educators of culturally different children are going to have to bend to the wishes of the urban community in the future because these people are discovering that a quality education can be obtained for their children if they push hard for it. The age of community control of American education in urban areas is close at hand. Community control has always been a feature of suburban schools which do reflect the wishes and desires of the suburban community.

ACHIEVEMENT AND COMMUNITY CONTROL

by Maurice R. Berube

THE IMPORTANCE OF PUPIL ATTITUDES

There is every reason to believe that community control of city schools will enhance educational quality.[1] *Equality of Educational Opportunity*, the most extensive educational study ever conducted, (commonly referred to as the Coleman Report, after its chief

[1] It is necessary to make a crucial distinction between the terms school decentralization and community control. Unfortunately, the umbrella word *decentralization* has come to mean all things to all people; it has been adopted by opponents of "meaningful" decentralization, much in the same fashion as the term integration was bandied about five years ago by its enemies. Consequently, the most hostile and active opponent to "meaningful" decentralization, the United Federation of Teachers, claims to support decentralization: just as the Parents and Taxpayers, which successfully defeated integration efforts such as busing, Princeton plan school pairings, and developing educational parks, was nominally in favor of school integration.

This ambiguous word, *decentralization*, no longer has value in clarifying concepts, connoting anything from administrative gerrymander to publicly accountable school systems. On the other hand, the term *community control* is clear: placing educational power with the public, by means of elected school boards with final authority over budgets, personnel and curriculum.

INSTITUTE FOR COMMUNITY STUDIES, Queens College, N.Y.C., 1968.

author), emphasized the need for an educational system capable of stimulating a strong sense of self among students. In the U.S. Office of Education's poll of 645,000 pupils throughout the country, Coleman discovered that the secret to learning lay with student attitudes. Attitudes toward self, of power to determine one's future, influence academic achievement far more than factors of class size, teacher qualifications or condition of school plant. "Of all the variables measured in the survey, the attitudes of student interest in school, self-concept, and sense of environmental control show the greatest relation to achievement," Coleman concluded.[2] Furthermore, a pupil's attitude—*the extent to which an individual feels that he has some control over his destiny*"—was not only the most important of the various elements studied, but it "appears to have a stronger relationship to achievement than do all the 'school' factors *together*."[3] (Emphasis added.)

Coleman's findings were revolutionary, cutting against the grain of prevalent myths concerning the nature of learning. Until Coleman, most educators did not consider pupil attitudes to be dominant. Rather, they believed that the teacher, her qualifications and background, her working conditions and small class registers, to have the greatest influence on how children learn. Moreover, these educators predicted various strategies to remedy school ills on that premise, so that one simply added more of the same, "compensatory" programs, to help pupils learn.

That approach has failed. Compensatory programs have not justified the claims of their avid proponents. The More Effective Schools Program in New York City, for example, reduces classes and provides saturation services at nearly double the cost of regular programs, only to produce few noteworthy results. After three years of operation, the MES program has not enabled children to read on grade level.

Neither has any other compensatory education program succeeded where MES has so far failed. The U.S. Civil Rights Commission study, *Racial Isolation in the Schools*, found the innumerable compensatory schemes throughout the country to be wanting; none had raised achievement levels. This is not to say, however, that compensatory efforts should be discontinued. In a different atmosphere these programs could possibly flourish.

[2] James Coleman, et al, *Equality of Educational Opportunity*, U.S. Office of Education (Washington: U.S. Government Printing Office, 1966), p. 319.
[3] *Ibid.*, p. 23

Essentially, then, schools will best help children learn when they strengthen pupils' feelings of control over their destinies. That is at the heart of community control of city schools. Big city school systems, unaccountable and isolated, generate feelings of powerlessness and alienation among parents and pupils. Only when these city schools are operated by their various communities can an educational "system" even begin to dispel this powerlessness. And students, developing a greater sense of self-worth, would correspondingly develop a greater motivation to learn.

This entails wholesale reform of the school system, redistributing power to elected school boards. In this sense, a beneficial climate for learning will result as parents have a voice in the running of the schools. The alternative to powerlessness is power.

THE IMPORTANCE OF TEACHER ATTITUDES

What bearing has the "self-fulfilling prophecy" on city schools? One of the unfortunate aspects of urban education is that middle class teachers too often expect too little from the children of the poor. In the case of the black poor, low expectations are often intermingled with racism.[4] The corroborating testimony to this widespread reaction of middle class teachers is overwhelming. For the past two years, the National Council on the Education for the Disadvantaged has singled out the attitudes of middle class teachers toward the poor as damaging to the Head Start programs. Professor Edmund Gordon and Doxey Wilkerson of Yeshiva University, in their evaluation of 76 compensatory programs in the United States, concluded that teacher attitudes were the crucial element in the failure of those programs.[5]

Moreover, there has accumulated a small literature by former teachers on the widespread self-fulfilling prophecies of teachers. These works have gained national prominence, in one instance winning for the author a National Book Award (e.g., Nat Hentoff's *Our Children are Dying;* Mary Frances Greene and Orletta Ryan's *The Schoolchildren;* Herbert Kohl's *36 Children;* Jonathan Kozol's *Death*

[4] Robert Rosenthal and Lenore Jacobson, *Pygmalion in the Classroom* (New York: Holt, Rinehart and Winston, 1968), p. 181.
[5] Edmund Gordon and Doxey Wilkerson, *Contemporary Education for the Disadvantaged* (New York: College Entrance Examination Board, 1966), pp. 56–57.

At An Early Age). The following exchange between a new teacher and an "experienced" one, who expects little from pupils, in the *Schoolchildren* typifies a tragic and subtle scene recurrent in city schools:

That same week I'd picked up second-hand copies of NATIONAL GEOGRAPHIC, NATURAL HISTORY, and other magazines for our library shelf. "You're not being fair to them," said Mrs. Abernathy. "You must not make these demands. Stick to the books they can read."

"But I often read to the child from them . . . Last week Carlos almost cried because he couldn't read the caption under a picture of a snowy egret."

"That's what I mean. You're not being fair."

"But then he went to work—he took the magazine home. Thursday he could read, 'This is a snowy egret.' "

"And will that help him in the reader? You're arousing a desire in him for something he can't achieve. We try to treat the child as a decent human being," she concluded—as so often.[6]

Common to these reports is a unifying theme of an "educational system" destroying the minds of its youngsters by breeding into its teachers defeat even before education is begun. As long as this system is left to its own devices, this poisonous climate will prevail in urban schools.

The implication for urban school reform is clear. Middle class teachers, who commute from suburbs to fortress schools in the ghetto, are not likely to develop positive attitudes towards their pupils who are poor, unless some bridge between the two worlds is built. That, too, is an aim of the community-controlled school. No harmony between teacher and parent, teacher and pupil, can begin to exist when both are isolated from each other by a bureaucratic system designed as a barrier. When teachers work together with parents, under accountable school boards, then, their attitudes will be shaped more by the realities of the needs of the school's clients.

A FLEXIBLE STRUCTURE TO ADAPT PROGRAMS

There is more to community control of schools, however, than returning educational power to the public. There must be sufficient

[6] Mary Frances Greene and Orletta Ryan, *The Schoolchildren* (New York: Pantheon, 1966), p. 29.

restructuring of the system to permit this beneficial climate to develop. In short, size is important to the enterprise. In an article in the magazine *Educational Leadership*, Philadelphia Superintendent of Schools Mark Shedd sums up the problem:

> The most fundamental crisis in urban education today, as I see it, is a failure to produce organizations capable of adapting the program of a given school to the needs of a given child . . .
>
> The trick, then, is to remake and revitalize through decentralization the quantitatively massive and qualitatively sluggish school systems . . . to create a climate in which beneficial changes can flourish.
>
> The involvement of the community in planning, operating, and evaluating the schools would do much to eliminate the isolation, complacency, and irrelevance of urban education.[7]

Central to reform of the total system is developing units of a size small enough to be "capable of adapting the program of a given school to the needs of a given child." Studies of big city school systems dating back nearly thirty years have recommended such reforms of the system to improve the programmatic possibilities.

Additional studies in the fifties and sixties of the New York City school system reinforced the need to decentralize operations to permit sufficient flexibility in developing programs. The most notable of these, sponsored by the Women's City Club, emphasized local control. A key study that emerged from a Temporary Commission on City Finances, Marilyn Gittell's *Participants and Participation*, observed that the centralized New York City system was incapable of instituting educational change. Gittell described the educational system as inbred and managed by a miniscule number of professionals. She reported that this system was without ability to implement far-reaching policies: "New York City has not witnessed any meaningful change in curriculum, administrative structure, teaching recruitment, appointment and training, or general organization for at least three decades."[8]

The Bundy Report, *Reconnection for Learning*, absorbing the research and recommendations of these forerunners, suggested placing from thirty to sixty autonomous school districts under control of

[7] Mark Shedd, "Decentralization and Urban Schools," *Educational Leadership*, October, 1967, pp. 32–35.

[8] Marilyn Gittell, *Participants and Participation* (New York: Frederick Praeger, 1966), p. 21.

parent dominated school boards. Administratively, Bundy's recommendations blended realistic demographic considerations of ethnic communities in the city with established standards of administrative size.

An ideally flexible and administratively productive school district should account for no more than 20,000 pupils. Using the thirty-three present school districts in New York City, serving 1.1 million students as model autonomous school districts, they would serve approximately 33,000 students—close to the administrative ideal.

It must be emphasized, however, that mere administrative reform is unlikely to result in high academic achievement. Although smaller, flexible school mechanisms can originate and enact educational programs more readily, the essential psychological relation between pupil and school, between teacher and pupil, would still be lacking. Mere administrative decentralization would not create the kinetic atmosphere necessary to improve a pupil's self-esteem and learning motivation, or a teacher's attitude. For that, an intimate involvement of parents and community in the educational structure is required.

WHAT CRITICS SAY

There is one final argument, based on extensive research, that must be made for community control of schools. However, this testimony is best introduced through a back door, through first marshalling the most serious criticism against community controlled schools in the cities. The trouble with local control of the schools, critics maintain, is that such an arrangement closes off the possibility of school integration—what these critics view as the most beneficial educational condition for the black poor—thereby raising the "threatening" spectre of black power separatism.

First, let us consider the case for integration. According to census patterns, most American cities are increasing in racial segregation, and within a generation will have a majority black population. School integration simply is neither feasible nor foreseeable in the near future. The movement of parents for community control was based on this default of the white community. In the fall of 1966, Harlem parents at I.S. 201 demanded that the school be integrated; if integration was not possible, they demanded that those segregated schools be run by the community. In short, recognizing that the integration movement had failed, black school activists sought to make the schools accountable.

Fully aware of this, one critic, Sandra Feldman, a staff member of the United Federation of Teachers, still writes:

"There is a very real danger that decentralization will mean an end to the possibility of school integration in New York City . . .[9]
"The trouble is that local control is regarded as *an alternative* to integration . . .
Yet integrated schools are not impossible—just very difficult."[10]

Furthermore, this same writer advances the opinion that "integration is essential to their (Negro schoolchildren) achievement."[11] For this statement, the writer refers to the Coleman Report's findings that the self-image of poor, black school children (and consequently their academic achievement), improved in a socio-economic integrated setting. Coleman also found poor pupils' self-image and academic achievement were raised also in an all-black setting, with middle class Negro pupils. In a later article, Coleman was careful to point out that his findings did not constitute a case for school integration. The significant fact is that a feeling of control over one's destiny influences achievement. This sense of purpose would more readily be encouraged in an educational atmosphere where power was exerted by school parents.

That does not mean that school integration is not a desirable end for other reasons. But it certainly *does not mean* that "integration is essential to achievement." The writer, voicing prevalent views of those hostile to community control of schools, more accurately reflects fears that are at the heart of the local control controversy; fears that "black power," self-determination for black ghettos, threatens the white paternalistic order of the past. Consider the following statements (emphasis added):

"While (local control) has some validity, it is asserted by different groups with differing goals in mind. It is used by *black power militants who regard decentralization as a step toward self-determination for the Negro community;* it is also used by *milder* proponents . . .[12]

[9] Sandra Feldman, *Decentralization and the City Schools* (New York: League For Industrial Democracy, 1967), p. 3.
[10] *Ibid.*, p. 6.
[11] *Ibid.*, p. 5.
[12] *Ibid.*, p. 2.

"To the extent that an *ascendent separatist point of view prevents groups in the Negro community from coalescing* with white allies to demand increased federal aid to schools, and to the extent that the white community uses *black extremism* as an excuse to turn its back, the children, white and black, will suffer."[13]

To this writer black power, black self-determination, is not only equated with "black extremism," it presents a threat to the old coalition, perhaps, even a threat "of violence." Yet, one can infer from the studies of effects of racial isolation—the Coleman Report, Civil Rights Commission Report, Kenneth Clark's early work—that black school children suffered psychological damage in segregated schools *because the prevalent values in these schools were white.* In such a society, not being in an (white) integrated setting naturally creates a psychology of inferiority. However, the thrust of black power is that there are values in black society as substantial as those in white society—specifically, that "black is beautiful." In this context of a "segregated" school system emphasizing black values, one can conceive of psychological benefit to black children.

That is not to say our society should continue on its present segregated course. It is to say however, that the black ghetto can develop its own values and rationale for success. And it is to say that the black power ideology is "extremist" only to those who are themselves psychologically unable to tolerate black citizens who have the equal opportunity to determine their own fates.

THE SECURITY OF THE GHETTO COMMUNITY

The final argument for local school control, then, rests on the positive values to be found in a ghetto atmosphere. Two sociologists, Andrew M. Greeley and Peter H. Rossi, undertook to evaluate the effect of Catholic parochial education on the life options of its pupils. What they unearthed in their investigations surprised Catholics, educators and themselves. Greeley and Rossi punctured the myth that Catholic schools, financially undernourished, overcrowded and badly staffed, accomplished little for their students. Instead, they learned that Catholics who attended all Catholic schools compared favorably, educationally and in terms of the job market, with the best schools and their graduates in the country. At

[13] *Ibid.*, p. 11.

276

first, they surmised that these students became successful in later life because Catholic school administrators have the power of admitting only those students they desire. But, even Catholics who were expelled from parochial schools and sent to public schools did well. *By a process of elimination, the sociologists inferred that the ghetto atmosphere of parochial schools generated an ambience of security which helped Catholic students to achieve.* Moreover, Catholics in their ghetto schools were least likely to be intolerant of other ethnic groups since they felt more secure in their ghetto atmosphere than Catholics in public schools.

Greeley and Rossi posed the question:

"Is it possible that the religious community plays the role of a sort of super ethnic group which provides the emotional support a young person needs in order to develop motivation for achievement in his early years?"[14]

They answered their question in the following fashion:

"It ought to be clear that (our findings) . . . call into serious question the assumption that it is necessary, for the health of society, that the religious and religio-ethnic ghettoes be eliminated. Such subcultures do not apparently impede achievement; on the contrary, they may even promote it. In the long run, they may even promote greater tolerance, because they give a person a relatively secure social location and a fairly clear answer to the difficult question 'Who am I.' "

"(There are) . . . two paths to achievement—the way of the ghetto and the way of assimilation—and that . . . the former had clear-cut advantages . . . In the matter of attitudes toward civil liberties, the way of the ghetto seems to have advantages for the larger society as well."[15]

Following the reasoning of Greeley and Rossi, one can conceive of community control of schools in black urban ghettos to promote exactly those qualities of security, identity and purpose. It is just such reasoning that is behind the efforts of black parents to get more black school administrators as identity models for school-children.

SUMMARY

The most recent and pertinent educational research, then, has a common denominator: the importance of the psychological to the

[14] Andrew M. Greeley and Peter H. Rossi, *The Education of Catholic Americans* (Chicago: Aldine Publishing Co., 1966), p. 155.
[15] *Ibid.*, pp. 161–163.

learning process. Whether a pupil feels his efforts can influence and control his future—feelings of identity and self-worth—emerges as the prime learning factor. What a teacher expects of her pupils has great bearing on how much a child learns. And the sense of security of the ghetto community helps students to achieve.

Considered in conjunction with the long list of studies condemning the destructive climate produced by large centralized school systems, these psychological factors constitute a strong case for local control of public schools. Community control is by no means a panacea. There will still be the task of obtaining large amounts of government aid to finance the schools; there still needs to be devised more and better educational programs. But, without the necessary structure to respond to the many particular needs of pupils, more money and more imaginative programs will have little effect.

The first step to better education in city schools is to transfer educational power to a series of autonomous, community controlled local school districts. The rest will follow.

THE COMMUNITY SCHOOL IN A GREAT METROPOLIS

Leonard Covello
Simon Beagle
Leon Bock

Benjamin Franklin High School is located on the upper east end of Manhattan Island in New York City. It forms an integral part of the Harlem area (community) known as East Harlem. The school building is located in the heart of what was, until recently, the largest concentration of Italo-Americans in New York City (approximately 90,000). Adjoining the Italo-American community is a rapidly expanding Puerto Rican community known as Spanish Harlem, identifying this community as the largest grouping of Puerto Rican Americans in New York City (approximately 60,000). To the West of these communities is the great Negro metropolis of the western world with approximately 300,000 Negroes. Intermingled with these three predominant ethnic groups are small ethnic islands, the vestiges of older stocks, who lived in the East Harlem community even before the arrival of Italian immigrants at the beginning of the century and, more recently, of other immigrants from Europe and elsewhere. A recent census of our student body indicates more than 30 different racial and national origins. This fact has been characteristic of Franklin during the 22 years of its existence.

In recent years the Harlem community has experienced tremendous population shifts. A Jewish population of 178,000 in 1920 has practically vanished. The pioneer Italian community is rapidly disappearing as the second- and third-generation Italians seek homes in other parts of New York City or in the suburbs, or move to other parts of the United States. The low-rent housing development in East Harlem, which began in 1938, has intensified the mobility of the population to the point where by 1958 approximately 54,795 people will occupy these new homes. It is a community constantly on the move, substantially a migrant community. Like other Americans, these new people are constantly seeking avenues to improve their economic and social status. Once that is achieved, the urge to find better quarters results in an outward movement—rapid concentration followed by equally rapid dispersion.

The East Harlem Community has been and still is afflicted with many critical social problems characteristic of blighted or slum areas:

1. Totally inadequate housing: old-law tenements, shortage, congestion, unhealthy living conditions.

2. Lack of normal recreational outlets for children, young adults, and older people.

EDUCATION FOR BETTER LIVING: THE ROLE OF THE SCHOOL IN COMMUNITY IMPROVEMENT, U.S. Dept. HEW, 1957, pp. 193-212.

3. Low economic levels: "the last to be hired and the first to be fired"; in addition to job discrimination, seasonal work, and working mothers.

4. Bilingualism: Language problems characteristic of immigrant communities, requiring many difficult adjustments in the home and the school.

5. Second generation problems involving parent-child conflicts.

6. Juvenile delinquency caused basically by cultural differences and conflicts in the home with the consequent gradual elimination of family social controls.

7. A stigma of inferiority fastened upon this whole community by unwise and exaggerated publicity, affecting adversely the prestige of the community and engendering the feeling that social, economic, and racial equality are high-sounding words with little substance.

The impact of these adverse social factors and confusing social situations is heavy, particularly upon the young people. There is no doubt that the situation is extremely difficult, but it is far from hopeless. There are latent capacities, undiscovered, undeveloped, and unrecognized sources of strength in our community, which can and should be utilized. The gradual rehabilitation of communities like East Harlem can be realized when the school—the one American institution which cuts across political, religious, national, racial, and cultural lines—realizes its real and necessary function as a social institution and assumes its responsibility for social education. The American public school occupies a strategic position in the life of our community. We, who have lived and worked in it for many years could, with the necessary financial support and with increased and adequately trained teachers, grapple with some measure of success, with the many unsolved problems that press so heavily and so insistently upon all our people—particularly our children and our youth. Such magnificent educational (life) goals as "education for social competence" have never been fully realized. These goals could gradually become realities once the necessary resources in personnel and materials are made available.

THE ROLE OF THE SCHOOL IN CONTEMPORARY AMERICA

Throughout the United States there is an increasing concern regarding the kind of education our children are receiving in our schools. We are concerned about their acquisition of the basic tools of learning—the fundamentals—reading, writing, and arithmetic. We are concerned about their knowledge and understanding of American history and the basic elements of our American culture, as well as their awareness of what is transpiring in other parts of the world. We are concerned about their moral and spiritual development. We are concerned about their civic education—about their ability to function as citizens in our American democracy.

There is not the least doubt that we should be deeply concerned about all these aspects of the education of our children.

Education, in its broadest scope, is a social enterprise which demands for its achievement a general mobilization of the energy, intelligence, idealism, and courage of the entire community. The school can play a major role in this enterprise. It can become and should become the center of the educational, civic and social activities of the community. It is a unique social agency because it occupies a strategic position in the life of the community.

Education can and must become a social process through which our children will understand the problems and perils that face our American democracy and, concurrently, learn how to grapple with them intelligently, effectively, and without fear or cynicism.

BASIC PRINCIPLES FOR THE ROLE OF THE AMERICAN SECONDARY SCHOOL IN THE LIFE OF THE COMMUNITY

1 The School as Explorer of Community Social Background

Before the Benjamin Franklin High School was organized in the spring of 1934, a complete sociological survey had been made of the East Harlem community through the Boy's Club Study sponsored by New York University and conducted under the direction of Prof. F. M. Thrasher of that institution. We have tried, in the intervening years, to add significant data, adhering to the cardinal rule of the community-center school: "Know Thy Community." In these surveys the school received valuable aid from other local and city agencies. The type of inquiry undertaken may be understood from the following list of special studies:

a. Racial and Nationality Origins of Benjamin Franklin High School Students.

b. Housing conditions in East Harlem.

c. Land Values in East Harlem—to secure sites for new housing, our new school, and a city hospital on the East River Drive along the East River front.

d. Home Background of the Benjamin Franklin High School Student.

e. Delinquency Records.

f. Student Attitudes:
   1. Reaction to marks.
   2. Teacher appraisals by students.
   3. Music preferences.

g. Racial attitudes in the student body.

h. Population studies.

281

i. Economic Levels in the Community; Economic Conditions in the Families of Benjamin Franklin High School Students.

j. Distribution of Benjamin Franklin High School Students in East Harlem and Other City Areas.

k. "Dropouts"

The "Dropouts" are the boys who have had to leave school for one reason or another. We decided to find out why they had dropped out of school. Contacts were made with the "Dropouts" through separate interviews with each boy and with his parents. To secure the information from the parents, a home visit was made. The questionnaires were then analyzed and the answers studied. Each boy was asked to write out a statement on what he had liked most about the school and what he had disliked most. We were, in other words, studying ourselves to see wherein we might have, in some way, failed our boys.

Valuable data were also secure in the following manner:

a. Interviews with students

b. Interviews with parents

c. Interviews with community leaders

d. Interviews with the rank and file of the people in our community

e. Questionnaires of various kinds on racial attitudes, housing and health conditions, leisure-time activities, etc.

2. The School as the Guardian of the Prestige of the Community

An example of how the school intervened when a whole segment of our people was attacked in the press will suffice to illustrate this point:

Some years ago, a pamphlet was published branding Puerto Rican children as mentally inferior to other children. An article in a national magazine made a scurrilous attack against the same people, implying their cultural and moral inferiority. "Welcome Paupers and Crime— Puerto Rico's Shocking Gift to the United States."

There naturally was great indignation in the Puerto Rican community and throughout the Spanish press of the City. Our Puerto Rican students, as well as members of the Puerto Rican community, brought the matter to our attention. Was it the school's business to do something about it? Emphatically it was, for a situation which brought one of our cultural groups into ill repute touched upon the very foundation of our education for wholesome intercultural relationships, which is part and parcel of our program of encouraging our boys, especially our Puerto Rican boys, to grow into desirable American citizens. Therefore, not only as a gesture of friendship toward this particular group of our community, but also for the sake of the educational experience for our people, the

282

school launched a campaign to counteract the attack brought against the Puerto Rican group and consequently against our Puerto Rican boys in the school. For our school it was a "must" because we knew that these people had limited resources for their defense and that they had a feeling of being abandoned and left to fight their battle in isolation. The school, therefore, helped them to organize mass meetings, devise methods of defense, and otherwise counteract these destructive attacks. In the school assemblies and in the classrooms, these unfortunate incidents were discussed and stress was laid upon the fact that such incidents are contrary to the traditions of America.

Results of this Project

What was achieved? It was questionable whether attitudes toward Puerto Ricans were very widely affected. But the school had reason to view the undertaking as a success since it had become part of a vital educational process for the community. In the first place, the "standing by" of the school increased its prestige in the community and thus assured for the future a greater measure of confidence in school-community relationships. In the second place, the Puerto Rican group was given recognition and its social standing was to some extent improved, at least within the community of East Harlem and within the school walls. The result was undoubtedly beneficial leading as it did to a more wholesome adjustment and, we may say, integration, of this particular cultural group. Moreover, the whole process of stimulating the community, the entire procedure of organizing a project, the participation in a common cause of students and adults—Puerto Ricans and other groups—was a noteworthy experience for our people. When the people were given the responsibility for managing their own affairs and an opportunity to show their capacity for initiative and leadership in carrying out a social enterprise, they went through a process which could lead to only one result—experience in democratic living.

3. The School as:

a. Coordinator of Community Activities

b. a Social Center

c. a Socializing Agency; and—

d. Community Leader

In order to bring about effective cooperation between the various social agencies and the Benjamin Franklin High School, a Community Advisory Council was created in 1935—1 year after the school was organized. Representatives on this Council included teachers and qualified students from the school, parents, social agencies, religious groups, civic groups, educational institutions, foreign language press and foreign language societies, business and professional groups, prominent citizens of the community, and municipal departments of the city.

Basic committees were created and new committees were formed as the need arose. The Community Advisory Council of the Benjamin Franklin High School met once a month, starting with a general meeting in the auditorium of the school, followed by committee meetings, and ending with reports of committees and a general evaluation of the work of the Council. A printed circular, indicating the committees in existence, their particular function, and the specific problem needing community action, was sent out before each meeting.

Listed below are the committees and their functions:

1. ADULT EDUCATION PARENTS' ASSOCIATION COMMITTEE

This Committee functioned for the purpose of providing adequate educational facilities for adults in the community. It also assisted the parents of our boys in determining the educational and social needs of their sons.

2. ALUMNI COMMITTEE

This group was interested in the boys who had left school. It provided recreational and educational programs for them, and advised them about their problems. It sought to maintain constant contact with them and drew them into the school-community program of the school.

3. CITIZENSHIP-NATURALIZATION COMMITTEE

This group contacted those people—parents and others who were not citizens—who wished to secure naturalization papers. It endeavored to help them to become interested in the nation of which they were a part. The committee also worked for the welfare of the foreign-born and aliens in our community, cooperating with other agencies in this field.

4. CURRICULUM RECONSTRUCTION AND SCHOLARSHIP COMMITTEE

This committee studied the problems of curriculum reconstruction as they affected the boys of our school and our community. It also determined the bases for recognizing scholarship and developed plans leading to improved scholarship.

5. EAST HARLEM NEWS COMMITTEE

This committee was entrusted with the important job of publishing a monthly local community newspaper in English, Italian, and Spanish. Its purposes were to disseminate information in East Harlem; to organize and direct public opinion for community betterment and the activity to attain it; to focus attention at specific times on specific problems and needs in the community; and to assist in conducting specific campaigns to work out solutions. The work of our community committees was given particular attention.

284

6. FILM-RADIO COMMITTEE

This committee discovered what films and radio programs were available in the educational field for use in the school. It concerned itself with the following:

a. Discrimination and critical view of films
b. Interrelation of subjects through films
c. Discovery of films and radio programs available for use in schools
d. Making students aware of current affairs, with particular reference to the United States

7. GOOD FORM COMMITTEE

The work of this committee was directed toward improving the appearance of the boys with regard to their clothing, cleanliness, neatness and courtesy.

8. HEALTH COMMITTEE

This committee was charged with the responsibility for making our boys and the community at large intelligently conscious of the problems that affect their physical welfare. The committee cooperated closely with the health agencies of the community in connection with campaigns for the eradication of tuberculosis, venereal diseases, cancer, and infant mortality.

9. HOUSING COMMITTEE

The members of this group tried to improve the housing conditions within the community. They worked for the establishment of slum clearance and housing projects which would benefit members of the community. The committee cooperated with the East River Houses, a low-rent housing unit for 1,200 families on East River Drive.

10. JUVENILE AID COMMITTEE

The purpose of this committee was to develop pupil participation, responsibility, and leaders to cope with difficult problems. It tried to solve some of our vexing behavior problems through its interest in juvenile delinquency prevention.

11. LUNCHROOM COMMITTEE

This committee made recommendations concerning prices and food stuffs in our lunchroom and on the general management of the business. It worked to make the lunchroom more attractive.

12. RACIAL COOPERATION AND PEACE EDUCATION COMMITTEE

The members of this committee worked together to help create understanding and tolerance within our community. The committee sponsored the intercultural education program of the school.

13. REFUGEE-FOREIGN-BORN STUDENTS COMMITTEE

The members of this committee helped refugees and foreign-born students to adjust themselves to their new environment.

14. SOCIAL AFFAIRS COMMITTEE

This committee planned social functions for both the school and the community.

15. SOCIAL WELFARE AND STUDENT AID COMMITTEE

This committee helped boys and their families who were in need of aid, such as clothing, food, and other welfare exigencies. The performance of the duties of this committee required the cooperation of men and women who were sympathetic to the needs of the underprivileged.

16. SPEAKERS' COMMITTEE

This committee provided speakers for meetings of clubs, foreign language societies, young peoples' groups, and other civic, social, and religious organizations at whose meetings the work of our school and the needs of the community were discussed.

4. The Role of the Principal:

The pioneer in introducing the community approach—The key figure in the development of the community school is the principal. He carries a variety of responsibilities for the long-range enactment of the community program. He must define the meaning of the community school theme. In a discussion of the role of the community school issued in 1938 the principal of Benjamin Franklin High School, Dr. Leonard Covello, gave this definition of the function of the Community School:

...[T]he school must necessarily become the center of community life in its own neighborhood, a clearinghouse, if you will, for all neighborhood ideas, programs, and enthusiasms. It must aid in correlating these according to an effective plan through which the well-being of the community as a whole may be forwarded and insured. It must establish intimate contacts with the children, the adults, the homes, the welfare organizations, and even the business interest of the community. The range of such activities comprises the background of the educational processes within the school itself. The really successful school, therefore, cannot function as a detached organization concerned only with the imparting of a certain amount of book knowledge to a fluctuating number of pupils during a specified number of hours daily through a limited period each year.... Rather the school must make a break with the formalism and pattern of the past, sacrificing nothing of the essential integrity of an intelligently planned educational program along intellectual lines, but amplifying its program to meet the larger demands of community and Nation.

The primary impetus for the original planning of a community program must come from the school principal. If a break with a traditional pattern is to be made, the principal is the person with the power and influence to make it; and if a faculty or community needs an education in the philosophy of the community school, the principal is the figure with the abilities and prestige to give it.

Some of the principal's leadership functions may be detailed as follows:

a. Role as organizer of school-community activity program.

The Principal and his Executive Cabinet must develop an organization plan for the liberation of faculty and student energies for an effective community activity program. Arrangements must be made for the allotment of time for activity both during and after school hours and for the division of interests and efforts among various school and community agencies. An administrative arrangement must be devised to give the teacher-adviser of the community program sufficient time to develop the program. In a practical sense, this involves the teacher's removal from a full teaching program and the allotment of a block of time to this teacher in the day's program that will enable him to carry on the community work. In the experience of the schools engaged in a full community program, success has been achieved where the teacher-leader has been assigned to one period of teaching and a four-period community activity program.

b. Role as selector of key personnel

The principal will recognize the social and community interests expressed by the different faculty members and will be alert to select capable teachers to implement the community program. The teacher-leader of the program will turn constantly to the principal for guidance in overcoming problems and for support in meeting the financial and administrative demands of the program.

c. Role as community coordinator

Through a continuity of professional and personal contacts established over the years of service in the community, the principal is uniquely equipped to act as the community coordinator. In this capacity he is able to draw together into common effort the leaders of social agencies, governmental bodies, church organizations, and other groups who share a common interest in attacking major community problems. Furthermore, his continuity of leadership enables him to draw upon the resources of people in the community who are unaware of their own abilities and uncertain of the proper means of expression but who, through encouragement and direction, will rise to an acceptance of responsibility.

d. Role as historian of the community program

The principal possesses a system of recordkeeping and can direct his secretarial staff in the important mechanical task of keeping files and records of the materials gathered in surveys and studies so that a history of past efforts can be used to guide the activity of the present. Movements of the population, trends in housing, school population, and other community changes can be measured and evaluated through the examination of the fund of past and present materials organized by the office of the principal. Of even greater importance than the collection of significant data is the accumulated experience whereby the principal can apply the lessons of past successes and failures of project activity to the difficulties of the present.

5. The School as a Stimulus to Community Action

An extremely important basic and cardinal principle of the community school is to "learn by doing." It is, of course, important to understand social facts and to discuss and analyze community problems. Under the guidance of well-informed and skillful teachers, a high-school student can acquire much information and valuable insights into the many social problems that beset us. But this savors too much of the armchair approach. Real effective education, training in assuming the responsibilities of American citizenship, and the acquisition of social competence occur when the attempt is made to seek possible solutions to community problems through school-community action. The student becomes an active and willing participant in each enterprise. The high-school student craves recognition, enjoys responsibility, and, working with adults, can carry out assignments effectively. Through this process, he develops leadership qualities which will be of inestimable value when he takes his place as an adult in his community. These qualities do not emerge suddenly—full blown. They are a matter of gradual growth. Under present conditions the idealism and enthusiasm of youth, the urge to give of himself in worthy enterprises, is given little opportunity for expression, if not altogether stifled. We think and speak of youth as "high-school children"—a term that is hardly appropriate or descriptive to those of us who saw them in action during the First and Second World Wars and in Korea.

The school-community projects that were undertaken during the 22 years of the school's existence had fundamentally a double purpose. The first of these was to have the community face the problems which confronted it; to realize that through cooperation and continuing effort community living could be improved; to understand that the basic social unit of American democracy was the community; and that our East Harlem not only had to rely mainly upon its own resources to achieve a better life, but that it had many resources and strengths that we could call upon to achieve worthy social goals.

In the second place, that the social experience gained by our students in working on real problems with local and city agencies, with community leaders, with people of different racial and national origins and diverse languages and cultures was, to us as educators of youth, more important than the success of the social project undertaken.

The ideas for these projects came from various sources. The establishment of "street units"—utilizing vacant stores in the immediate vicinity of the school as a library center, as an alumni club, as a community sociological research center, as a Friends and Neighbors Club—came about as the result of a discussion in the Parent-Teacher Association of our school.

The school became involved in the opening of a Library Lounge in the local public library at the request of the head librarian.

The need for the social orientation of our rapidly growing Puerto Rican community induced the principal of the school to call together representatives of the Puerto Rican press and other Puerto Rican leaders for a series of 18 conferences in his office. At each conference, the chief of a City or State department explained the functions of his department. The Spanish press and radio reported the results of these conferences, urging the Spanish communities to utilize the services of these departments.

For 6 years a Latin American Festival was held in the school auditorium to which the leading Spanish artists in radio, television, the theater, and night clubs offered their talents without charge. The proceeds of these festivals went to the establishment of a school-community fund to be used for needy Puerto Rican students. The idea came from a Spanish columnist who had participated in our conferences.

Spanish-speaking students were requested by the local Health Center to interpret at the center, particularly during the annual tuberculosis campaign.

The school-community newspaper The East Harlem News was sponsored originally by the editorial staff of the Franklin Almanac, our student newspaper.

These are but a few samples of projects which the school undertook because an individual, a group, or an organization in our community believed they represented needs which could be met by school-community effort. The school encouraged and welcomed all ideas and suggestions. We felt that this was part of our responsibility.

6. Introduction to Two Projects

An analysis of two community projects conducted by Benjamin Franklin High School are offered in the following section of the article. These projects are significant because they illustrate the application of the principle of the community-school program to concrete social problems that have arisen in the neighborhood. A theoretical discussion of the ways and means of conducting a community school program would fail to give the interested teacher the practical demonstrations necessary for the implementation of the program. The two projects detailed in the article present a step-by-step story of the realistic problems encountered in the development of a program and the methods utilized

289

to carry the program to a successful and meaningful completion. The whole story of each project cannot be told in full detail because of space limitations but it is felt that sufficient material has been included to illustrate how the school acts upon the principles of community education.

The projects are: 1) The Sanitation Campaign, and 2) the Carmine Luongo Playlot in East Harlem.

PROJECT NO. 1: SANITATION CAMPAIGN

Early in September at the beginning of the new school year, there appeared in the New York City newspapers a story, illustrated by photographs of dirty streets and lots in East Harlem. Following the release of these pictures, at a meeting of the Civic Club of the school, the members, after a long and serious discussion, decided to accept the challenge to their community and to try to do something about the sanitation situation in East Harlem. The majority feeling expressed at this meeting was that the press was again "picking on us." The boys decided to go through the streets in their immediate neighborhood to see if conditions were as bad as they had been described in the newspapers.

At the next meeting of the Civic Club the majority opinion became what had been the minority viewpoint—most members agreed with the newspapers. After each boy described what he had seen on his tour, and told of conditions on his own block, one member said, "The truth is the truth, and instead of complaining about the press, we should see if we can do something to clean up our neighborhood." This was the problem that the Civic Club set out to solve.

The boys first discussed the problem of responsibility for the poor sanitary conditions. The duties of the tenants, the landlords, the janitors, the storekeepers, the Department of Sanitation, and the children were explored. To obtain information from the Department of Sanitation and to get the benefit of schoolwide opinion, a forum was planned for the weekly school assembly. The Educational Director of the Department of Sanitation and the Secretary of the East Harlem District Health Committee were invited to act as forum consultants. The topic for discussion at this school assembly was, "How Can We Keep East Harlem Clean?" A lively discussion took place and the Civic Club used this forum as an opportunity to interest the entire student body in its project.

One of the results of the discussion was that 20 boys joined the Cafeteria Squad as a Sanitation Division to get student cooperation in keeping the cafeteria clean.

A few days later the Secretary of the East Harlem Health Committee invited the Civic Club to attend a special evening meeting of the East Harlem District Health Committee to discuss the Civic Club's project to plan cooperative action. In preparation for the meeting, the Civic Club drew up a program of action which they formally presented to the meeting of the adult group for discussion and adoption.

The program included:

1. A conference of all concerned in this campaign: students, parents, tenants, landlords, Police Department, Sanitation Department, Fire Department, Health Department, interested merchants.

2. The use of a sound truck to tour the neighborhood with live speakers and printed material; also a recording of a transcribed speech by the Mayor of New York City.

3. A trailer in the local movie houses.

4. A cleanup of one or two lots and the distribution of a specially written appeal to tenants living in the immediate area to keep the lot clean.

5. A leaflet issued by the Committee for distribution in the immediate neighborhood of the school.

6. An original play by the Civic Club to be presented to the school and to parent groups.

7. Special school assemblies and class discussions.

8. A parade through the neighborhood.

9. A mass meeting in the school auditorium with speeches, entertainment, movies, etc.

Shortly after this meeting the President of the Sanitation Sub-committee and the Executive Secretary met with the Executive Board of the Civic Club and the Principal of the school to plan the implementation of the program suggested by the Civic Club. Plans were specifically made for a fact-finding conference of tenants, janitors, landlords, storekeepers, parents, and students to get a complete picture as seen by all the groups intimately concerned with the problem of improving the sanitary conditions in East Harlem.

As the boys began to carry out their plans, the Educational Director of the Department of Sanitation provided materials and guidance. She supplied 5,000 leaflets and posters which the students distributed to the people of East Harlem. The president of the Civic Club kept her informed of the progress of the campaign.

All these activities had stirred up such interest that the Daily News, a leading New York City newspaper, agreed to award prizes to the winners of a cleanup contest in a six-block area. The Outdoor Cleanliness Association of the city and leading Sanitary Engineers from Columbia and New York Universities would be the judges. The boys again readily agreed to sponsor the cleanup contest. They met to discuss their ideas and plans and presented such plans at a meeting with representatives of the Department of Sanitation and a staff writer for the Daily News.

The school-community student groups held their planned schoolwide parade as a prelude to the contest which was to start in a few days. In preparation for the parade, the Civic Club, together with the special leadership classes in Franklin and Otis Junior High School, the General Organization and the School Community Committees, carried out the following activities:

1. They contacted the East Harlem District Health Committee for co-operation. The Committee decided that it would devote its energies to a Fact-Finding Conference.

2. They contacted the Department of Sanitation and the Police Department. The Department of Sanitation promised a 50-piece band and pieces of new equipment. The Police Department promised protection and guidance along the line of march.

3. The Department of Sanitation printed 5,000 copies of a leaflet written by the Civic Club for distribution along the line of march.

4. The Civic Club distributed 5,000 special leaflets announcing the parade and its efforts to help the schools and the community to improve sanitation in East Harlem.

5. Announcements were made over the public address system to all classes each morning of the week of the parade.

6. Announcements were made in all school assemblies.

7. The Art Department and the Shop Department cooperated with the Civic Club and prepared 70 placards.

8. The Science and the Social Science Departments prepared a special lesson plan on "Sanitation in East Harlem," containing specific material on our neighborhood. This lesson was taught by all teachers to all classes the day of the parade. Each teacher emphasized the magnitude of the problem, the need for the clean-up campaign being conducted through the initiative of the Civic Club and the cooperation of the school, and the necessity for cooperation on a community-wide basis.

9. The Photographic Department of the school made plans to take a movie of the parade and to take interesting "stills" for use with school, parent and community groups.

10. Leading civic, political, and educational leaders of the community were asked to act as marshals of the parade. The Deputy Mayor, the Commissioner of Sanitation, and the local State Senator, among others, marched at the head of the parade.

In preparation for and during the cleanup contest, the abovementioned groups planned and carried through the following activities:

292

1. They chose adult and youth block-captains in the six-block area of the contest.

2. They distributed about 20,000 pieces of literature, some in Spanish, Italian, and English, to the inhabitants. This material was distributed with the aid of the students of the local public and parochial schools.

3. They placed 400 specially printed posters in the stores and hallways. These posters were printed free of charge by the owner of the Empire State Poster Co. He offered these posters as his contribution to the campaign.

4. Five meetings of the boys living in the six-block area for the project were held to plan, execute, and evaluate every step in the campaign.

5. A meeting of the parents in the area led to plans to urge an amendment of the City Sanitary Code and to petition the Department of Sanitation for daily, scheduled garbage pickups, including Sundays and holidays.

6. A Community-School Conference was held to plan all-inclusive cooperation and to involve the leaders of the community in the cleanup campaign, of which the contest was only one phase. At this conference, the following, among others, were present: The local Congressman, the local State Senator, representatives of the Health Department, representatives of the Department of Sanitation, the local citizens Sanitation Committee, religious leaders of four denominations, representatives of the community division of the Board of Education, principals of local public schools, Civic Club members.

This conference decided to support a campaign to amend the City Sanitary Code; to make a survey regarding the needs as seen by janitors, storekeepers, landlords, and tenants; and to request of the Department of Sanitation daily scheduled garbage pickups, including Sundays and holidays.

The Civic Club drew up a simple questionnaire, 3,000 of which were distributed. Again the local parochial and public schools helped.

The leader of the Civic Club made a transcription of an appeal to the people in the community and the New York City sound truck broadcast this appeal throughout the neighborhood. Similar appeals by the Mayor and the Sanitation Commissioner were broadcast on other days.

Trailers, made by the Department of Sanitation, were shown in local movies.

The Civic Club sent letters to each of the religious leaders in the community and urged them to talk to their parishioners on sanitation, suggesting as a theme, "Cleanliness is next to Godliness." Many of the religious leaders did so, as reported by the students who attended the various churches.

Civic Club members participated in the Fact-Finding Conference and found that what was stated at this conference was in essential agreement with their own findings.

Another conference was called of community leaders and students to evaluate the contest and to plan further action. This conference voted to call another meeting to which representatives of the city departments most concerned with the problem of sanitation would be invited.

The school and community groups called another meeting of civic community-school leaders to which the following departmental heads were invited: The Police Department, Fire Department, Health Department, Sanitation Department, and the Housing and Buildings Department. All sent official representatives. This conference organized a subcommittee to prepare amendments to the city sanitary code and selected from its ranks a Continuation Committee to meet with the subcommittee and make such recommendations as it might see fit.

A meeting of the subcommittee was held and a report was made at the meeting of the Continuation Committee. It was decided to write to the Health Commissioner asking him to consider the need for the amendment to the city sanitary code. It was also voted to write to the Mayor asking him to support a campaign to get more funds for the Department of Sanitation so that it could give improved service to the people.

During the campaign, members of the Otis Civic Club appeared before school groups. They also participated in radio forums (WMCA, Du Mont Television, WNEW). They participated in discussions held in the Board of Education Civic Club Headquarters and attended interviews with prominent people, arranged by central Civic Headquarters. They also, in order to get firsthand information, visited the city's disposal plant on Welfare Island. At its last meeting, before it began to plan its end-term party, the Otis Civic Club evaluated its campaign and voted to continue the project for at least another term. The play was finished and presented to the student assembly and the Parent-Teachers Association. All groups who participated were invited to the event. The various City Commissioners and the representatives of the Daily News were the invited guests. The Sanitation trailer and the movie of the parade were included on this program.

The problem of sanitation and particularly of garbage disposal in a congested and blighted area of a great metropolis has challenged the wisest of our city administrators. It is an unsolved problem; but an important step in the right direction was taken through this Sanitation Campaign. The Commissioner of the Department of Health effected a change in the City Sanitary Code making it mandatory upon landlords to provide a specified number of garbage cans per tenant for a specified period of time. The Sanitation Commissioner arranged for a definite time for the collection of garbage by the Sanitation trucks. This Sanitation campaign, by being featured and dramatized in the Daily News, attracted citywide attention to the problem.

Other major New York Dailies, such as the New York Herald Tribune and The New York Times, considered the project important enough to give it adequate space. The result was that other communities attempted to grapple with similar problems.

In our opinion, however, the most important result was the experience gained by our boys in the planning and execution of a community project which daily affected their lives and the lives of their families and neighbors. They learned that changes in laws cannot be wrought overnight; that the heads of the city departments are limited in action by the amount of money that is available; and that their principal and teachers, their parents and religious leaders, together with community agencies, are anxious to plan and work with them in and out of school; that all concerned are willing and ready to have them assume responsibility. Thus, they discovered that within proper and reasonable limitations they have an important role to play as junior citizens; that they, too, have a job to do in making democracy work.

PROJECT NO. 2: CARMINE LUONGO PLAYLOT IN EAST HARLEM

Another vexing problem that faces underprivileged communities like East Harlem is the lack of sufficient play areas for children of elementary school age. It is true that recreational opportunities are available in afternoon play centers in some of the schools and in several community houses, but these are not enough to take care of about 30,000 children in this age group. Moreover, the distances that children have to go to reach these centers and the hazard of crossing heavily congested city streets often prove to be a deterrent to the children as well as to the mothers. During the play period the mothers want the children on the block where they and their neighbors can exercise some measure of control. Often in our surveys we discovered many empty lots created by the demolition of unsanitary and unsafe tenement houses. The debris left during demolition and the accumulation of garbage intensify the ugliness and drabness of our congested city streets. The teen-ager and the young adult find a haven in the numerous candy stores that dot the East Harlem neighborhood. In a survey made some years ago in our community we spotted on an outline map of East Harlem, 504 of these "social centers" in 160 of our city blocks.

The boys in our Civic Club were keenly aware of this situation. They wanted to do something about it—not merely for themselves but particularly for their younger brothers and sisters. Within a stone's throw of the school was one nice lot. In the course of discussing the problem of recreational space, the idea emerged that the Club, as an experiment and a demonstration, should undertake the task of cleaning up the lot and making it available to the children in the immediate vicinity. Further discussion brought out the fact that the creation of a play area from a dirty, abandoned lot was not a simple matter. The owner had to be discovered and consulted regarding his willingness to have it used for this purpose. The resources available to the students were insufficient for cleaning up and carting away the debris. The lot had to be properly paved. Equipment had to be procured and receational leaders had to be found who would direct and control the play activities. It was agreed that the total job would require assistance from local interested citizens and community leaders, and City Departments—Sanitation, Police, and the Borough President's office.

The first meeting of the Playlot Committee, held in the Principal's office, brought an immediate and enthusiastic response from community leaders and civic and social organizations. The plan was fully discussed, the necessary steps were outlined, and the various committees were created to carry out the project. It was agreed that the students were to carry the major burden of the project. The adult members were to act mainly in an advisory capacity, to make the necessary contacts, and to pave the way. The owner of the lot was contacted and readily gave his consent. The Department of Sanitation, with whom the school had established friendly relations, agreed to move the garbage and debris which had accumulated there. The students worked enthusiastically with the sanitation men in removing the unsightly mess. The Deputy Commissioner of Public Works for Manhattan, an East Harlem leader, had the lot paved. The Sixth Deputy Commissioner of Police in charge of the Juvenile Aid Bureau (J.A.B.) and the Police Athletic League (P. A. L.) entrusted the job of manning the playlot to a Franklin graduate who was in charge of personnel for the P. A. L. The P. A. L. assigned another Franklin graduate as director of the playlot. The Police Department donated an outdoor shower. The athletic and play equipment came as a donation from "We, the People" as a result of the appearance on their television program of the executive committee of the Civic Club, Mr. and Mrs. Luongo and their entire family of 16 children.

The Dedication ceremony was held in mid-July and attended by local and city notables, members of the local community, and the children who had already become familiar with the playlot. It was a notable community event.

Several days before the dedication of the playlot the following mimeographed invitation was distributed throughout the neighborhood:

Dear Friends and Neighbors:

Good News! A new play yard is opening in our neighborhood on Monday, July 18, at 2 p.m. We invite you to be with us at the opening.

The dirty, rubbish-filled lot at 411 East 115th Street has been cleaned up and paved. It has been equipped with showers and drains. It is now a safe place for children to play and cool off on hot summer days. All because we got together and cooperated like good friends and neighbors—the landlord, the businessman, the plumber, the carpenter, the city departments, the schools, the churches.

On Monday, July 18, at 2 p.m. we will celebrate. There will be songs, music, and folk dancing. Prominent speakers representing the city government and civic organizations will attend. Come and celebrate with us.

Cordially yours,

The Boys of Benjamin Franklin High School and Otis Jr. High School, Civic Club

Simon Beagle, Teacher-Leader
Leonard Covello, Principal

Cooperators

Carmine Luongo
Nicholas Siviglia
Board of Education, Borough President's Office
Fire Department
Health Department

Housing and Buildings Dept.
P. A. L.
Sanitation Department
Sachs Quality Stores
WNYC
Courtesy of Sachs Quality Stores

Results? An East Harlem Playlot Committee with local leaders, teachers, and students, was organized. The owner of another available lot was contacted and his consent for its use was obtained. The same procedures that had been used for the first lot were carried out, and another play area was made available to the children of East Harlem. In order to alert the community to what was going on and to get its cooperation in expanding the work of the Playlot Committee, a sound truck was loaned to the committee by Station WNYC. Students, teachers, and community leaders, spotted eight strategic street corners in the Italian and Spanish neighborhoods and brought the message to their East Harlem neighbors. We were well satisfied with the results for we had achieved what we felt should be one of the basic aims of education—improvement of community life, not merely through discussion but through a demonstration of school-community action. Other communities in other parts of the city initiated similar projects.

But this job cannot be done in this piecemeal fashion. It should be a matter of local and national policy to provide sufficient money to create many such play areas, particularly in our congested cities. The president of the General Organization of Franklin brought up the matter of increased budgets for recreational purposes at the budget hearing of the local Board of Education. But the local Board can only suggest and urge that necessary funds be provided for educational and recreational purposes. Final decisions are made by the Mayor, the Board of Estimate, and the City Council.

Recreational space, equipment, and personnel are city problems and the responsibility for their solution rests partially on these city agencies.

The citizens, however, should assume the final responsibility, for that is basic to the democratic way of life.

We pay heavily for our apathy, indifference, and shortsightedness. We pay heavily for erecting and maintaining jails and other custodial institutions. What is more tragic, we pay in the broken lives of thousand of our children, the great majority of whom have the potentialities of becoming good American citizens instead of delinquents, from whom the future criminals in our American society are recruited. Land is valuable in our big cities, there is no doubt about that. But our values are grossly distorted when we deny and curtail our educational budgets to the detriment of our children.